Shine the L
Shame: Da~~i~~y ~~Reflections~~

By

Barb Tonn, MA

Shine the Light of Truth on Shame: Daily Reflections

Acknowledgements

This book would not have reached publication without the help and support of many friends and family members. I am profoundly grateful for the encouragement, editing, and sharing that they provided.

I give special thanks to my dear friend, Chris Snyder. She sat with me for the final, tedious editing. She provided encouragement, was my wordsmith, gave me the compassion that kept me going and got me to completion. Her experience and knowledge were integral to getting this book to publication.

I thank Tia for coaching me on my book for over two years. She inspired me through the tough times and believed in my message. I couldn't have asked for a better coach.

I send love and hugs to my dear husband, Michael. You helped me edit, and gently encouraged me to keep writing. I so appreciate your constant support and love.

Additional thanks to: Christina MacLeod, Barbara Thomas, Gloria Hearten, Angela Gainer, Sandy Miller, Carrie Martinek, Michele Morton, Mary Deaguero, Jane Westbrook, Jackie Robb, Brenda Tonn, Cheryl Baker, Cher Hager, Joanna Clark, Alicia Robb, Peggy Jackson and Pati Nagle

I thank all of my clients. Your trust and sharing were instrumental in the creation of this book. I cannot name names, but your help has been immense. Thank you.

Writing this book on the dense topic of shame was a challenge. It was difficult to sit in the presence of shame for months on end and hundreds of hours. The support and patience of my family and friends made it possible.

This book represents a career of work and a lifetime of healing. I am grateful for all of the experiences that brought me to the awareness of the destructive force of shame and the absolute necessity of bringing it into healing. I offer thanks to my colleague, Kathy Anderson. She shared her shame knowledge with me early in my career. It greatly influenced my work with shame.

The title, Shine the Light of Truth on Shame, came to me early on in my work with shame. I have presented workshops on healing shame around the country for over 30 years. I needed a title for the workshops I was offering. This title continues to capture the healing of shame. I acknowledge the light that inspired me in picking the book title and that guided me as I wrote this book.

I thank all of you from the bottom of my heart. I am eternally grateful to all who supported me, trusted me, and loved me through this process.

Table of Contents

Introduction

Shine the Light of Truth on Shame is a book on healing shame. It is a book of solutions for those who have lived their lives believing they are not good enough, not worthy, not lovable, frauds, etc. It can benefit people actively working on healing their shame, people in therapy or on a "self-help" journey, therapists who work with shame based clients, people healing from addictions and those who are just learning about shame. This book focuses on practical interventions that can be easily integrated into the structure of our daily life.

I chose a daily format because of the dense nature of shame. I wanted examples of shame and healing exercises that would not overwhelm. This book is meant to start on day one and continue to day 365. As we move through a year of information and interventions on shame we take the healing concepts to a deeper level. We begin to move out of an identity of shame and move into identifying with love as our essence.

This is a book of practical examples of when shame is engaged and how to intervene on it. I was convinced that addressing core shame issues was critical in the healing of most people who have been diagnosed with mental health issues and addictions. I have become convinced it is enmeshed throughout the Western culture and is in the very fabric of most every aspect of our lives. I see it as active in those who do not have an addiction, or mental health issue as well as those who do.

Daily Themes

Each day has a theme. The theme is written at the top of the page. It is meant to help the reader focus on what they can gain from the information on that page.

- Tools
- Red-Flag
- Rule
- Healing Actions
- Shame Indicator
- Shame in our world
- Voice of shame
- Rights
- Shame originator
- Shame defined
- One thing different
- Forgiveness
- Shame loop
- Model for a shame free world
- Multidimensional
- Specific shame-based issue

By working with the information in this book we will finish the year with:

- Clarity about what shame is.

- The ability to identify when we are receiving a shameful message, both internally in our thoughts, and externally from our environment.
- A list of useful tools to intervene on our shame.
- A list of our own "red-flags" indicating when we are in a shame loop.
- Knowledge of the "shame loop" and clarity on how to intervene on the loop.
- Information on how to live differently in our world, with kindness and compassion leading the way, instead of shame.
- The awareness and motivation to live in a more loving and non-judgmental way with all of life.
- The information to put our lives on a solid path of healing our shame.

I have put some of my own poetry in this book, and shared many of my own healing stories. Shame of our shame has kept our stories and creativity hidden. My sharing provides a model for healing.

Lastly, I work with a muse named Maude. She represents my inner wisdom, and the inner wisdom I believe we all have in our core. She and I will have conversations on some of the pages. When she and I wrote, I accessed a deep wisdom that I experienced as beyond my conscious self.

My heart has gone into this book. Healing shame is a demanding, and powerfully transformative process. In my opinion, it is as simple and as complicated as changing our entire paradigm for living, from that of shame, to one of **LOVE**.

Days 1-30

Day 1
Shame Defined

We can't heal shame if we don't know what the problem is. Many of us are haunted by shame. It may not always be there in our consciousness, but it is always right below the surface, and it defines us.

Examples of shame-based core beliefs are:

- I am not enough
- I am inadequate
- I am unworthy
- I am unlovable
- I am flawed
- I am stupid
- I am inferior
- I am less than
- I am bad
- I am a fraud

When the core belief gets triggered, we cannot be talked out of it. We go into a predictable shame loop, and our thoughts and behavior become self–defeating.

This book is about learning to identify when we are living in our shame, how to get out of it, and how to utilize these new skills to create a life free of shame.

Reflection: We get to start from the beginning. If we have ever used any of these phrases to describe ourselves, then shame is lurking in our core. We start our healing process by naming the shame and bringing it into the light of healing.

Day 2

Shame Defined

Shame is driven by perfectionism. It demands that we be perfect at whatever we do. It does not allow mistakes, a learning curve, forgiveness of self, forgiveness of another, change, or kindness. Because of the dynamic of perfectionism we have "shame of our shame." We are not even comfortable saying we have shame It signals a fault of some kind and shame will not allow that. So, we hide it. We pretend we don't have it. We compensate for the feelings of inferiority hidden below our surface. We are fearful that others will discover the shame at our core. Then, whatever good things they thought about us will go away, and they will no longer want to have us around.

Shame of our shame is a voice inside of us that lies. It convinces us that we not only are something to be ashamed of, but that we will be worse off if we acknowledge it and bring it out into the open to heal. Yet, we have to bring shame into the open in order to heal. We will talk about how to do that safely.

Shame of our shame leads the way in our relationships. It is the voice inside of us that keeps us isolated and fearful of being found lacking in some critical, unchangeable way.

Reflection: First, we become aware of our shame. Then, we notice the shame of our shame, and then, we find safe ways to bring it into healing.

Day 3
Tool

We begin to become conscious of the nasty voice inside our head. We begin to notice a voice that has been there for a very long time. We give it a name. That name is: Shame. Although we may not believe this for a very long time, shame is NEVER true. However, we are convinced it is true, and that it will always be true. We feel like it is hopeless to even think we can change. Shame wants us to believe we can't change, and that we don't deserve to change.

- We begin by noticing the voice and naming it: Shame.
- We can write it out. We can say: "My shame is telling me..." and see what follows.
- We can voice it out loud to someone else if we feel safe to talk about our shame.
- Although shame is never true, we don't argue with it.
- We become aware of how often shame shows up and how nasty it is.

- We might become aware of what triggers shame, or sets it off.

Reflection: Noticing shame begins to move us in a different direction. We are now the observer. We get to decide if this is the voice we really want to listen to.

Day 4

Red Flag

There are many indicators we can become aware of that indicate we are in our shame. I call each of them a Red Flag. As we go deeper in our healing we will find many signals telling us we are in shame.

One strong indicator we are in our shame is: We start feeling very cut off from others. We may have been going through our day feeling okay, and then we begin to withdraw. We don't feel like we belong. We want to leave where we are, or don't want to go where we were going. We want to isolate ourselves.

When shame is engaged, we begin to feel very self-conscious. Maybe we never called it shame before, but shame is what drives the self-consciousness.

We will be looking at what happens when shame causes us to withdraw like this, and we need to name it. It is shame. "Withdrawing" is the red flag that signals we have gone into shame.

We notice when we withdraw. We become curious about what triggered the withdrawal. Did we have an internal thought that caused us to pull back? Did something happen outside of ourselves that caused us to pull back?

Reflection: When we isolate because we don't want to be seen, our shame is engaged.

Day 5
Shame Defined

Our healing can get delayed and derailed if we focus on "why" we have shame instead of on "how" to heal. In truth, we live in a shame-based world. All our lives, we cook in a "shame stew." Not everyone has all the ingredients of the stew, but we can't avoid having some. When we cook in this stew, we end up with shame at our core.

Ingredients for Shame Stew

- We don't know we have rights, or what they are.
- We don't learn we have choices.
- We don't learn that we get to have boundaries.
- We live in a hierarchy, which determines our importance.
- We are taught that we are damaged in some way and that we have to work hard to prove we are good enough or worthy.
- "Things" are valued above "relationships."
- We don't learn how to forgive.
- We are driven by "perfection."
- We live in an internal war with ourselves.

- We don't know how to talk about the important things.
- We don't learn the language of feelings.
- We don't know how to trust and be trustworthy.
- We learn to blame instead of taking appropriate responsibility.
- We learn how to be "nice" instead of honest.
- We live in an addictive culture.
- We don't value people unless we get something from them.
- We are dishonest about who we really are and learn to "impression manage."
- We keep our real truths secret.
- We judge instead of accept.
- We learn to value how we "look" more than "who" we are.

All of these ingredients set the stage for shame. We cook in it. We become shame-based.

On top of this, some of us get fried in the oil of abuse. It thickens the broth that our culturally inherited shame has anchored us in.

This is what creates shame. None of us entirely escape it.

> *Reflection: We don't need to get lost before we start. We don't have to stall our healing by having to figure out why we have shame. We*

just get to notice the shame and begin our healing.

Day 6
Shame Defined

One of my wise friends calls shame, "the biggest interference on the planet at this time."

That sentence speaks volumes.

What does it interfere with?

- Knowing that the essence of self is love and peace
- Forgiving ourselves for our mistakes
- Forgiving others for their mistakes
- Extending love
- Living in a peaceful space with self and others
- Knowing our rights and other peoples' rights
- Being in the now
- Taking responsibility for our choices and being able to change our minds and choose again
- Basic trust
- Compassion toward self and other
- Accepting self as we are
- Valuing our relationships above all else
- Kindness
- Honesty

Shame interferes with what is good and what moves our world in the direction of healing.

Reflection: If we experience what feels like interference in our lives, we might want to be curious which inner voice we are listening to. Is it the voice of shame or of love?

Day 7

Tool

This book is about learning what shame is, identifying when shame is triggered, recognizing messages of shame, seeing when shame is part of whatever system (family, school, work,) we are in, and then learning a new thought system which supports a more peaceful and functional world.

In order to learn a new thought system, we need to be able to identify the old one and be clear about the consequences of staying in that thought system. If we identify negative and painful consequences, we become open to a new thought system. Thus, we are willing to learn this new system. We will give ourselves time to process and release from the old system and step into the new.

What many of us will discover as we move deeper and deeper into the process of healing, is that the healing may take the rest of our lives. We get to learn this new shame free way of being and living, get frustrated that it seems to take so long to learn and change and that the world often does not support the new. Having a good and clear reason for doing this work will hold us up during the discouraging times.

We get to know that there "must be a better and more peaceful way to live our lives." Then we get to learn this new way. I say this early in our year together so that we know that getting overwhelmed and discouraged is an integral part of the process of healing, and certainly a part of healing something as insidious as shame.

> *Reflection: We get to learn a new thought system and it is a process.*

Day 8
Maude

This book is co-authored by Maude. She is my inner wisdom. I take the hard questions to her. I know that I have connected with her when I get answers I know I would never have come up with on my own. She will

appear from time to time in this book and write some of the "hard truths." Those pages will be conversations between her and me.

The picture on this page is Maude. I began to get an image of her while writing a play on shame. Then when I turned 50, my sister-in-law gave me a doll. The picture is of Maude, the doll; she looks wise and compassionate. She is a character and she is herself. When I need to access my internal wisdom, I turn to Maude and ask what she would say. Sometimes I just connect and have a dialogue with her. Sometimes I grab paper and pen, and have a dialogue in writing. Our dialogue always helps me.

We all have inner wisdom. We may not know it and we may not be able to access it when we first attempt to, and our inner wisdom is there. There are many ways to connect with this inner wisdom. One thing we can do is look for an object, like Maude, which represents wisdom to us. It may be a pottery statue, a picture, a doll, a stuffed something, a token of some kind, or a spiritual figure. It may also be an internal place we go to mentally access wisdom or a wise figure.

We can consciously develop our inner wisdom by listening for it. We can ask, "What would my inner wisdom say about this?" We know that we have connected with our inner wisdom when we have a compassionate answer that comes from love.

Reflection: Accessing our inner wisdom is helpful in healing shame.

Day 9
Tool

Most of us have an inner voice that puts us down. It is hurtful and critical. I call that voice an "Inner Gremlin." That Gremlin is good at hooking us into our shame. If we can know the gremlin as a voice that never speaks the truth and most likely will show up the rest of our life when we are the most vulnerable, then we can be more prepared for it. We see the Gremlin as a shame-based thought in our minds. We can then shine the light of truth on the gremlin and see it for the lie it is.

Observing our Gremlin(s) also helps us distance our self from the dishonest voice. This can help us get a different perspective. As we learn more about shame, we can hear the voice of the "Gremlin" as the shame in us that always lies.

At times, it can be helpful to visualize the Gremlin. We can draw it or see it in our mind's eye. Then we can dress it up in silly ways that can help take some of the power from it. An example would be to draw the Gremlin and put a diaper on it.

We are most likely more familiar with the voice of the critic or Gremlin, than we are with our inner wisdom. The Gremlin is the voice that usually speaks first, speaks the loudest, and always speaks in lies. The wisdom speaks quietly, calmly, and brings peace. It tells the truth.

> *Reflection: To name the Gremlin and observe it as a constant liar is helpful in taking power away from shame.*

Day 10
Red Flag

The more "out of control" we feel, the more likely we are to use shame. This is what makes it such a hurtful weapon. If our partners, children, co-workers, etc. are doing something we don't like, and we don't know how to change it or stop them, we may try to make them feel guilty for what they are doing and who they are. We may use shame to stop what they are doing. In a way, it is like saying, "shame on you."

Often the immediate effect of our shaming is that we get what we want. However, there is a very negative boomerang effect from the shaming. The person may stop or change what they are doing, but they will resent us manipulating them. At some point, they are likely to use shame on us in a hurtful way in return.

Shame is a profoundly hurtful way of gaining control. It damages relationships and trust. It tears down and does not build up again. Shame is NEVER the way to attend to problematic situations. If we want a more peaceful world and more loving relationships, we get to find non-shaming ways to communicate and deal with conflict.

Example:

Instead of saying, "shame on you," we can say,

"I am very uncomfortable and would very much like for you to change that behavior and do _____ instead."

In the example, we can identify our discomfort and ask directly for what we want or need.

Reflection: We have the right to ask for what we want. It does not mean we will get it.

Day 11

Shame Loop

There is a very predictable loop of shame that happens whenever our shame gets triggered. (See Appendix.)

To learn this shame loop and how it impacts our lives is one of the most empowering tools we can have to intervene on shame. In the Appendix, is a drawing of the Shame/Rage Loop. Let's look at the first 4 steps.

1. Something triggers our shame. It can be something external, or an internal thought.
2. We immediately become defensive.
3. We shut down our real feelings. Although we may look like we are having all sorts of feelings, what we are expressing are the defensive feelings, which push people away, instead of exposing the vulnerable feelings that are going on internally. (Fear, sadness, hurt, etc.)
4. At this point we move into self-defeating behaviors or thoughts. We feel powerless to stop the thoughts or behavior.

Example:

1. We make a mistake on an important project and start feeling like we are real failures and frauds at what we do.
2. We become defensive and rationalize the mistake and project it onto another person.
3. We shut down our fear for our job and get angry that our working conditions are so bad.

What others observe is a defensive, angry person.

4. We move into a self-defeating mode of thinking. Our inner critic takes off and won't stop. We lay awake all night obsessing about what happened, unable to stop. If we have an addiction, we start that addictive behavior and can't seem to stop.

Unless we can intervene on the shame loop, it can go on and on and turn into other shame, which we feel powerless to intervene on.

We can begin to see the shame loop and name it.

As we continue in this book we will get many tools directly related to the shame loop and how to interrupt it.

Reflection: Seeing when we are in a shame loop is an important step in healing our shame.

Day 12

Healing Action

Years ago, I was typing a list of skills we can learn to move us out of shame. I inadvertently typed- "learn to receive" two times. It brought my attention to the importance of receiving help and support in healing shame. And, it isn't easy. Receiving requires a level of trust and vulnerability, which can be difficult when we carry shame.

The keyword in "learn to receive" is learn. Learning is a process. We have had our trust betrayed and it requires "setting intention" to heal. We take baby steps in the direction of trust.

We get to start small by just being around people we think we can trust. We get to watch people in relationships and observe how they trust. We get to ask people how they built trust. We get to start with small requests, like, "could you hold this door open for me?" or "could I call you sometime?" There is no hurry in learning to receive and it is important to develop the ability to receive.

Grab a few pieces of paper and a pencil. Do some stream of conscious writing (writing without stopping) around the question: If I trusted enough to receive, what would I want to receive? It may be interesting to learn what our inner self really would like to receive.

> *Reflection: We get to receive. Often, our shame has interfered with that process.*

Day 13
Rule

There is the "rule of perfection" which supports shame and there is the "rule of being human" which supports compassion. We choose each moment which rule we want to live by. We decide that for ourselves.

Perfection says we can't make mistakes and everything we do needs to be perfect. It doesn't allow for learning something new. We don't get to be mediocre. It doesn't let us be human and mess up or have a bad day. It doesn't allow for others in our lives to be less than perfect.

The "rule of being human" is "compassionate." It lets us do things just because we want to, whether we are good at them or not. We get to make mistakes, mess up, be mediocre, and just enjoy something without being good at it. It lets us forgive others and ourselves. Compassion lets us "be" and enjoy being human.

Which rule do we want to live by?

Once again, we get to decide. If we choose the "rule of being human," we may meet with resistance from others who want to demand perfection of us. However, if we are clear about which rule we choose and why, we will be able to claim our "right to live the way we choose." Claiming our rights is part of the healing process. Knowing and claiming our rights is empowering.

> *Reflection: We get to be human, unless we don't allow it.*

Day 14
Tool

Years ago I was fortunate enough to have learned a distinction between anger and rage that helped me intervene on shame in a powerful way.

Anger is an emotion that gives us useful information. It tells us that a boundary has been violated or that we need to set a boundary. When we notice and see what we need to do to reestablish our boundaries, and act on that information, the anger is released.

Rage is what we feel when our shame has been triggered. It can be destructive to self, property, or others. It can be external in our actions or internal in our thoughts. It can seem never-ending. If I gave you a bat to do anger work, and it was really rage, you could do anger work forever and it wouldn't shift the rage. That is because rage is really shame. If we ignore the triggered shame, the rage stays in place.

Anger helps us. Rage is destructive. To begin to notice which emotion we are feeling is a very important step in the direction of healing. Under our rage are the feelings we talked about in Day 11. We need to be able to get to identify and feel those feelings in the healing process.

We need to distinguish between our anger and our rage. If it is rage, we can absolutely know we are in shame. Then we can begin to apply the tools in this book for healing shame.

Reflection: For now, we can begin to name our anger and name our rage. We will do more with that as we move further into the healing process.

Day 15
Maude

I am including a conversation with Maude on shame. As I said, she is quite the wise woman.

Barb (B)—Maude, I wonder if you could give me a good explanation of what shame is?

> Maude (M)—It is all the things we believe about self except the truth.

B—What is the Truth?

> M—The Truth is that we are Love and ONLY Love.

B—I always thought I wasn't quite enough, not quite pretty enough, or smart enough, or good enough. I felt I was okay, but nothing special. I always tried hard to do better. I usually fell short. I tried to prove myself most of the time. Is that shame?

> M—The part of you that tries to prove herself, who feels she doesn't quite measure up, and isn't quite enough, is shame.

B—Most of my life I have felt that way, most of the time.

> M—I know.

B—How do I change that? Knowing I am enough and am lovable sounds a lot nicer.

> M—You have to begin to hear the voice that tells you that you are not enough, you are a fraud, and not lovable. It tells you that you are just a big loser. You have to know that voice is never telling the truth.

B—Never?

> M—Never.

B—It must be true sometimes. I mean I can be a loser, mean, crabby, and not thinking well. You get the picture.

M—Yes, and that is about the things you do and think. But under the things, that you do and think is the never changing truth—that you are lovable!!

B—I have to sit with this. When I am a mean and crabby loser, I feel like I am bad and unworthy.

M—Barb, the essence of you is lovable. Your behavior is sometimes not so stellar. You have to learn that you are not your behavior. You are not how you look or what you do. You can always change your behavior, but you are love and that never changes.

B—Wow!

M—Let's go watch some baseball and relax. ☺

Day 16

Voice of Shame

There is a voice in our head most of the time. This voice usually goes unnoticed. That is because we are used to it, like a fan that is just background noise. However, as we consciously move into healing shame, it becomes important to notice this voice and notice what it is saying.

Often this voice is the voice of shame. It is critical, unkind, and very mean. It tears down. It hurts. The voice may be saying unkind things about self, or others. There is another voice that is there, but it is much softer. It is the voice of compassion and kindness. It is a voice that has not been noticed because the shame overrides it. The voice of compassion is the voice of love. It speaks the truth about us.

To heal from shame it is important for us to listen and hear. If we hear the voice of shame, we notice what side it enters on (left or right). Then we turn in the other direction to begin to hear the voice of love. As we start on the healing journey we may not be able to hear the voice of kindness, love, and compassion. We get to learn to hear it.

The first step, again, is noticing. We listen. We take note. If the voice is shame, we name it. We may have always believed this voice. It may have been the dominant voice we have heard most of our lives. It is NEVER true. The voice of truth, of love, of compassion, never tears down. It is the voice that tells the truth.

We get to become willing to hear the voice of compassion. We get to learn to turn in the direction of love.

Reflection: The voice of love is there. We learn to listen to it.

Day 17
Shame Indicator

Unless we can sit in the presence of self and love ourselves as we are, we will act out in some way. We won't be able to love ourselves because we will be spinning in a constant loop of shame.

Shame is a breeding ground for addiction. Having worked with my own addictions and also in the addiction field for years, I have seen the consistency of this truth. The core work in having a peaceful recovery is to heal the shame that feeds the addiction. Many of us spin in and out of our favored addictions, switching from one to another. Others of us deny we have an addiction. We live in a world of addicts. Anne Wilson Schaef wrote, *When Society Becomes an Addict.* It is an exceptional book that points to the myriads of ways we can become addicted. Nothing is as scary as not looking at the truth. But, we can't heal if we don't look.

The biggest defense in addiction is denial. The second step in the shame loop (see Appendix) is moving into a defensive posture. We can get stuck in denial and this feeds self-defeating behavior. We can live in this behavior, and many of us do. These addictions can be anything from substances, to food, gambling, busyness, sex, worrying, amongst many others.

If we have been stuck in a behavior and cannot seem to stop, we are very likely stuck in shame. As we deal with the shame and changing the addictive behavior at the same time, we are more likely to have success recovering from our addictions, than if we never dealt with the shame.

Reflection: Let us ask for the courage to be brave enough to be honest about ourselves, our addictions, and to know that we have the opportunity to bring our shame into the light of healing.

Day 18
Shame Indicator

If we have a belief that deep down there is something wrong with ourselves or we are unlovable, inadequate, unworthy, frauds, etc., we may spend our lives trying to compensate for that feeling. We will try to prove we are not those things. We will look to the outer to make up for those feelings of shame. The term "little big man" is how this dynamic works. We feel little, so we act big to compensate.

We can spend our entire lives trying to prove ourselves and never feel like we have gotten there. We can attempt to prove ourselves in our relationships, our work, to our self, to our friends, and families. We can work ourselves to the bone and always feel like we fall short.

To change this, we get to address the shame directly. We address the shame that feeds the behavior.

A question that begins to get under the shame is: "What does it feel like to spend my life seeming so inadequate, or not enough?"

The feelings that are driving the shame can then begin to surface. We can address those feelings and the underlying needs that have gone unmet.

When we work so hard to "prove ourselves," we become exhausted. Often we give up, because we are in a "no win" situation. Our exhaustion and constant vigilance can take the form of depression.

Reflection: If we are trying to prove ourselves "good enough" we are most likely covering up unhealed shame.

Day 19
Tool

There is a process we experience as we actively bring our shame into healing. This process will continue throughout our lives. We may become faster at catching when we are in shame and be able to utilize our tools more quickly in intervention. However, healing is still an ongoing process.

- We go from not knowing our rights and choices to learning and living by our rights and making conscious choices in all areas of our lives.

- We go from not knowing our personal limits to learning what they are and being able to set appropriate boundaries according to those limits.

- We go from our lives being defined by an external judge (they say) to the internal judge (what is our truth according to our internal value system?).

- We learn that people and relationships are more important than "things."

- We learn that instead of receiving no recognition for "self" or only being defined by what we "do," we begin to feel "part of" the world and count self as equal to others.

- We learn to just "be" instead of constantly "doing."

- We learn to take appropriate responsibility for ourselves, and our actions, instead of blaming.

- We replace the word "should" with the word "could."

- We learn to discern shame that feels dishonest and trust our own perceptions. Our perceptions feel honest and help us define who we are.

- We learn to navigate our way out of problems we cannot reconcile or people we can't forgive by learning to forgive.

- We step into peace, freedom, and love, as we release shame as the definition of self and move into love as the definition of self.

It is a journey well worth taking and it is a lifelong process.

Reflection: Part of healing our shame is learning that we get to live in process.

Day 20
Tool

One of the tools we can utilize in our healing is noticing what triggers our shame. If we identify the triggers, we can see the loop that ensues, and more effectively and efficiently intervene on the behalf of the self.

Some shame triggers are external. These are often easier to identify than internal triggers. Something happens outside of us. It may be the way someone looks at us, or something that was said, or insinuated. We can begin to see that we were feeling fine until something happened and then we started feeling crummy. That does not make someone else responsible for our feeling shame, but it helps us see where we have unresolved issues, which keep triggering our shame. It is like wearing our zipper on the outside where anyone can inadvertently unzip us.

Other shame triggers are internal. These come in through our thoughts. We may be doing fine and then begin to feel horrible. We can ask self what thought came right before we began to feel horrible. For instance, I may have made a mistake. I start feeling bad. Then I begin to notice my inner critic is calling me a loser for making the mistake. This is an example of an internal trigger.

If we can identify the trigger we can say to ourselves, "If I had not gone into shame when that happened," or "I had this particular thought, what might I have felt and what might that part of me need?" Then we can begin to address those needs.

Reflection: Triggers are the first identifier of shame. They allow us to see what we need to heal. Knowing our triggers can help us intervene on the shame loop.

Day 21

Shame Indicator

One aspect of shame I want to address is, "loneliness." When shame is at our core, we can be surrounded by people (even those who love us) and feel a deep sense of being alone. We wall ourselves off. This is driven by a sense of transparency that tells us that if someone gets too close they will see us and reject us. We feel like damaged goods that can't be repaired.

The sense of being alone and feeling lonely is a universal aspect of shame. Bill W, the founder of Alcoholics Anonymous, reported feeling like he was looking at the world going by as if he was viewing it through a window. He felt perpetually cut off from everything.

Part of the loneliness is not being able to trust when we are told we are loved. We are sure that either:

a. The person who says they love us is lying.

b. If they really knew us they would not say they loved us.

We begin to take baby steps into relationships as we heal. We learn to create safety and directly address the loneliness. We create safety with ourselves by learning how to set healthy boundaries and care for our inner selves in productive ways. We begin to listen to our feelings and needs, and we learn how to advocate for our needs. This helps us break the spell of loneliness surrounding us.

> *Reflection: Perpetual loneliness is a hallmark of shame. The loneliness speaks lies that we have*

believed. We learn the truth, that we are loveable and loved.

Day 22

Shame Indicator

When we live in shame we feel "different" from others. We feel like we "aren't normal" and "don't belong." It makes it hard for us to feel comfortable in our skin and in the presence of others.

Shame originally got locked into our system when we perceived ourselves as different from others. Often, as a therapist, I had people ask me if what they perceived about themselves was "normal." The quest to feel and be normal is the quest of the person feeling shame at their core, trying to fit in.

As we heal our shame, we begin to look inside for our truth, instead of outside. When we were looking outside, we tried to "fit into" others' truths. One of the lovely gifts of bringing our shame into healing is claiming our true essence and living in a way that "fits" for us. We stop fixating on what others think of us and focus on what we think of ourselves. It ceases to matter if we are different from others.

We may feel very uncomfortable when we show up in the world as "ourselves," instead of how we think "normal" people would be. In truth, there is no "normal." "Normal" is an illusion. We can chase after it, and we won't be able to catch it.

Reflection: It is truly a gift to ourselves when we look inside to see what fits for us in our life, and can love ourselves, no matter what.

Day 23
Right

An extremely empowering tool to help us move out of "shame" is to learn our "rights" and to live from them. In our shame-based culture, we often don't know our rights. In some situations, our rights have been withheld from us.

There are "rights" that are important to learn as we grow up. We can learn these rights at any age. Often, we feel shame that we don't know them and have to learn them as an adult. Dr. Charles Whitfield in his book, *Healing the Child Within*, has put together an excellent list of rights to teach our children and to heal ourselves.

Rights empower us. In conflict-filled situations it is critical to learn our rights. Sometimes we need help in asserting our rights, but learning them is an important first step.

In this book, I will feature some rights that are very beneficial to learn as we navigate our way out of shame. This is by no means an all-inclusive list. My hope is that we will all learn and respect our own rights and the rights of others. This sets the groundwork for shifting our shame-based world to a love-based world.

*Reflection: Learning our "rights" is an
important step out of shame. Filling in the
sentence, I have the right to _____,
helps us move out of shaming ourselves and
others. It sets the groundwork for love.*

Day 24

Shame in Our World

Shame is everywhere. It has woven itself into the very
fabric of our world. We accept it as the way things are.
We become it and don't even realize it. We shame
people constantly and think shaming thoughts each
moment. We must be aware of shaming and be honest
about it to change our world to a more loving and
kind place.

The other day, I was pulling out of the post office. A
person in a car driving by gave me a really nasty look.
I guess I was not driving the way she thought I
"should" be driving. At first, I wanted to be defensive,
but then I decided to be honest with myself. I often
give dirty looks to others when they aren't behaving in
the way I think they "should." I may not say it, but I
think it. I think I know what is the best way to drive,
to act, and to think. I think I know what everyone
"should" do. I communicate this non-verbally and
verbally. It is the way I send shaming messages, often
with a smile on my face.

What would it be like in our world if we just let each
other be? What would the environment be like if I
noticed when I wanted to shame people, caught

myself, and replaced my thoughts with, "You have the right to be the way you are"?

That woman didn't like my driving. So what? I can let her be and let myself be and know we both have the right to be ourselves. I don't have to accept shame from another (internal boundary) and I don't have to shame someone for being different from me.

> *Reflection: We all get to become more aware of how we send shaming messages and how we accept shame from others. We get to change. Isn't that lovely?*

Day 25
Shame Originator

One of the ways our shame gets locked into place is when a relationship we had every right to believe would support us, is ruptured. This can happen in powerful ways like abuse and addiction, but also when someone consistently is unable to be present to us and denies our needs. This rupture begins to define us as "defective" in some way.

When we are young, we cannot see relationships clearly, so when something goes wrong, we think it is our fault. We define ourselves as "bad" in some way or the relationship would have been there for us.

Because of the original rupture happening in the primary relationship, we have ruptured other relationships. Our biggest healing happens when we find safe ways to share our shame in relationships.

Praying, journaling, reading, meditating, etc., are all important ways to bring healing to our soul.

To bring healing into our relationships, we risk exposure in safe places. This is why a safe group can bring such profound healing. When I share my shame with someone else, and they not only hear me, but they understand, I no longer feel so alone with my shame. I begin to feel a bit more connected with the world. I am no longer isolated in my shame.

Reflection: The original "rupture" that happened in an important relationship was the foundation of our shame. The foundation of our healing shame is in bringing our shame out in a safe relationship and learning that what we originally believed about our worth is a lie.

Day 26
Shame Indicator

As we start becoming familiar with our shame, we begin to see that often we look outside of ourselves for truths. This is called: External Referencing. What others think or what we perceive others will think is what generates our opinions, behavior, truths, politics, etc. It is a way of living that doesn't allow us to truly define and know who we are, and doesn't allow ourselves to risk living in our personal truth. We can certainly get by this way, but it promotes fear. If allowed, we all have our own personal dreams and goals. If our shame keeps us from knowing our personal truths, we will not feel fulfilled.

The truth of who we are is traded for approval. We are moving in the direction of healing as we start to let ourselves know our own opinions, dreams, goals, feelings, and needs. As we allow ourselves to get to know ourselves, we begin to take steps to living our own truths, instead of looking to others to define us. We intervene on shame and replace it with our true selves.

At this point, we get to begin the process of moving from "external referencing" to "internal referencing." First, we just get to look at what our truth is. Then, as we develop our internal strength and trust, we learn how to live by the truths about ourselves that we are discovering.

> *Reflection: We get to take a moment to learn what our own truth is in a given situation. We don't need to share the truth to know it. It is the first step toward stepping into our own true selves.*

Daily 27
Voice of Shame

Shame would have us believe that making a mistake defines us as mistakes. It would teach us that we never deserve forgiveness and that we need to suffer and pay penance. It does not allow us to learn, grow, make amends, and let go.

Love allows us the grace and dignity and humanness of making mistakes. It does not demand that we be perfect. It lets us have good moments and bad moments and to know that we get to go on with the grace of peace that comes from self-forgiveness. It accepts our amends and does not define us by our mistakes.

Which voice we listen to in our heads makes all the difference. We do have the power and ability to listen to the voice we choose. We get to notice and choose again if the voice of shame is what we hear.

I fervently hope that we all begin to pay attention and choose the voice of love. We may find that for the rest of our days we will need to retune our listening from the internal station that broadcasts shame to the internal station that broadcasts love.

> *Reflection: We have the power and ability to retune our inner listening to the voice we choose to listen to.*

Daily 28
Shame Defined

For many years, I have made it a habit to take note of words people use to describe the essence of their shame. One such statement I heard was: "Shame feels like a flash flood when it hits."

I live in the Southwest where signs on highways will warn you to be aware of flash floods in the area. The floods come out of nowhere and nothing in their path is safe. People are encouraged to climb to a higher elevation immediately. For this person to describe "shame" as a "flash flood" was very telling of the intensity of shame, how it can come out of nowhere, and how we can be flooded with shame in an instant.

What do we do when we notice the shame? We climb to "higher ground." We connect with something greater than ourselves. What that "higher place" is varies with each individual, and it is important in our healing to determine what that is for each of us. The "higher place" allows us to climb out of the insanity and destructiveness of shame and into the peaceful sanity of truth.

Shame is never true. What a hard statement to believe, when the entirety of our life we have believed that shame has defined us. In the middle of the flash flood we may not be able to reach the truth. However, we can immediately climb in the direction of truth. Otherwise we feel like we are drowning.

Reflection: When the flash flood hits, we get to climb to higher ground immediately.

Day 29
Tool

One of my very favorite "tools" for helping me step out of shame is: Flow of Consciousness Writing. Shame thrives in our heads. When we find a way to bring it out of our heads, in safe ways, and expose it, the intensity of the shame can diminish. Flow of Consciousness writing is one way to expose the shame. This form of writing is not a start and stop type of writing. It is a form of writing where we put pen to paper and don't stop until we have given shame a voice.

- We start by writing the sentence: "Right now my shame is telling me..." and keep on writing.
- We write everything that we are hearing in our heads. The work can be shredded immediately if there is a fear of someone finding and reading the words.
- We let the shame voice out on paper. (I find it works best by using paper and pen, but if the choice is between not doing it and using the computer, it is better to use the computer than not write at all.)
- Once it is out on paper it is imperative to end with a non-shaming sentence. This sentence can start: "Whether I believe it or not, the truth is ...."

I am going to give some examples of some truths. They are meant to get us thinking in the direction of the compassionate voice.

- I am a good and loveable person who has done the best I can in a difficult situation.
- I am a worthy person even if I made a mistake.
- I have the right to learn, grow, change, and make mistakes.
- Whether I believe it or not, the truth is: I am loveable and deserving of kindness from myself and others.

This tool can move us far beyond the shame or drop us close to the edge of climbing out of it, but the tool will take us in the direction of healing. Getting the shame out of our heads is extremely important in the healing process

> *Reflection: Utilizing tools helps to move us out of shame as we begin to notice our shame and notice when we are in a shame loop. Flow of Consciousness writing is a powerful tool.*

Day 30
Shame Indicator

So, we have trouble trusting? We don't know how to trust ourselves or others? Sounds like shame is running the show.

A very wise young man who is on a healing path out of shame said, "the T word." I didn't know what he was referencing. We had been talking about trust. He was seeing how shame had impacted him and had interfered deeply with his ability to trust. At this point in his healing he wasn't even saying, "trust." He was saying, "the T word."

His statement captured how difficult it is to begin to trust when we have shame at our core. Most who carry shame, have been betrayed by someone we had every right to believe we could trust. We turn that on ourselves and feel like there must be something wrong with us, or the person would not have betrayed us. So our shame gets locked around a "betrayal bind."

Repairing that betrayal bind requires learning to trust again. It can be terrifying. We take baby steps and we learn to build trust with trustworthy people. We learn how to take care of ourselves so we are not so vulnerable to other people and their bad actions. We learn we are loveable and worthy. We start to trust ourselves and then learn to trust others. It is a process that helps move us out of isolation and self-loathing. It is worth taking the risks, baby step by baby step.

Reflection: We move from "the T word" to trust in ourselves and then to trust in others. We learn to live in the world of people and relations.

Days 31-60

Day 31
Healing Action

We have been working for a month now. We have been learning to identify when we are in shame. It becomes apparent that shame is around more than we ever thought it was. We have gathered some awareness and tools to start intervening on shame.

It can be easy to get discouraged at the intensity of shame and how tenacious it is. We have begun a process of "undoing." Shame has been in place most or all of our lives, and it is reinforced by our culture and our world. The "undoing" process is going to take the rest of our lives. It will not always be this hard, and because we live in the "shame stew" of the world, we will catch it surfacing in us, long after we thought it never would again.

BUT...

If we don't do this work, we won't find the peace we deserve. We won't find the gentle, compassionate voice within ourselves that can open our hearts and let us heal. We won't be able to let people in and we won't be able to let ourselves out. We won't discover the richness of what we really are when shame is not directing our lives. We won't really learn to love and live.

I promise you the healing work is worth every one step forward and two steps back. It is, because after the "undoing" is the "doing." That is, when we learn the truth of who we are, we learn we are so beyond anything we could have imagined. The essence of what we truly are is the innocence of love. After we "undo" the shame, we learn the truth: I am love.

Reflection: Healing is worth the work. We get to hang in there, do this work, and give the gift of healing to ourselves.

Day 32
Maude

Maude has a few words for us as we begin February, the month of "love."

Maude (M)—The work we do in healing our shame is the work necessary in order to fall in love with ourselves and the heart of each person we meet. Without healing the shame that tells us we are not good enough and are not lovable, we cannot truly "join" in this world.

Barb (B)—What do you mean by "join?"

M—Shame isolates us in our bad feelings about ourselves. Whether we feel like a bad parent, or bad person, or just "less than" or "unworthy," we will hold back from reaching out. We will let the shame convince us that we are not good enough to really contribute anything of worth in our worlds. We will stand back and believe others have the answers and what it takes to make a positive difference on our planet.

B—I have noticed that Valentine's Day triggers so many people. Either we feel shame that we do not have a Valentine or we wish that the one we had, loved us more. The whole Valentine idea seems to spotlight the shame that people carry that they are not quite lovable.

M—Yes, it is another construct in our culture that seems to feed the shame loop in which people live. It is a perpetual feeling that gets underlined at certain times of the year. Valentine's day is one of those times. It seasons the "shame stew" mentioned on Day 5.

B—What can we do about it?

M—It can be helpful to identify ahead of time that the Valentine's day phenomena sets up a dynamic that is not about truth. Our culture thrives on "special" people we need in order to feel "special." In healing shame, we learn that the essence of who we are, which is love, is the same essence that is in everyone. We don't need a special person to prove our worth or how lovable we are. We get to be enough and lovable, no matter what the circumstances are in our life.

B—So, we don't need the perfect Valentine to feel okay about ourselves. It seems like that can take a while for us to truly believe. It is such a part of our culture to believe we need to have a partner to feel lovable.

M—It may take a while to truly believe and it puts the balls back in our own courts, where they belong. We have the power and ability to know we are love, no matter what. It helps to see the construct that tries to convince us otherwise. The truth is: We are love, and we don't need a Valentine to prove it.

B—It sounds like February is the month we get to fall in love with ourselves, just as we are. We get to extend that love to every person we meet. I like that much better!

M—When we love ourselves, we mirror love to each person we meet. The best Valentine we can give is the Valentine we give to self. It can be fun to go, buy a Valentine that we like, and mail it to ourselves. Maybe even send some chocolate!!

Day 33
Red Flag

Most of us have at least one area of our lives in which we really struggle, or feel stuck. It may be in body image, finances, sex, meaningful work, self-esteem, etc. We will in all likelihood feel shame that we just cannot seem to "get it together." We may have tried, done affirmations, had therapy, and still struggle. What we often have not done is expose the shame that holds the struggle in place.

In the shame loop in the Appendix, we drop into #4, self-defeating behavior. The shame holds us there until we deal directly with the shame. We cannot brow beat ourselves into change. We need to expose the shame and bring it to compassion and forgiveness. We get to deal with the trauma, and/or underlying feelings and needs that hold the shame in place.

When we bring compassion to the struggle we are having, we can bring up the underlying feelings and needs that have not been addressed. We can then see how to be a friend to self and take care of the unmet needs that are holding the shame in place.

An example of this may be: The struggle with body image may be a lifelong challenge. If we view this as a shame loop, we can look at what feelings and needs are under the shame of our weight or shame of our body. We may discover that we feel angry and alone. We let ourselves feel the feelings and see what that part of us may need. The part of us that is angry may have been made fun of and then not allowed to be angry. That part may need to claim the anger and set boundaries for ourselves, if we are ever made fun of again. The part that feels alone may need a support system. The shame has isolated the self.

Finding other people who understand the shame and the struggle can make a big difference. We let the struggle be a "red flag" that shame is involved and we are caught in a shame loop. We can then begin to use the tools of healing shame to move us out of the stuck position.

Reflection: Being stuck in a struggle is a strong "red flag" that we are in a shame loop. Unless we bring the shame into healing, we stay in the self-defeating behavior.

Day 34
Shame Indicator

I have mentioned how important it is to be able to identify when we have shame in our core. Identifying shame helps us utilize the healing tools for shame. Growing up in our shame-based culture, we end up with certain behavioral indicators of shame. One of these is: feeling shame about certain feelings.

I once knew someone who would have suicidal thoughts quite frequently. This would definitely be #4- self-defeating behavior, in the shame loop (see Appendix). We were very curious as to what was the trigger that set the suicidal thoughts off. We looked for what he was experiencing immediately before having the suicidal thoughts. What became evident was the feeling of anger that came right before the suicidal thoughts.

This person grew up in a home environment where anger was used to shame and feeling anger was shamed. So, every time he felt even the slightest tinge of anger he went into a shame loop. He could not stop the suicidal thoughts.

- The feelings that are consistently shamed as we grow up will trigger shame.

Once we knew what the trigger was we could begin to bring healing to the trauma around anger and anchor different messages around having anger. He continued to be triggered by anger for quite some time, but once he knew what the trigger was he could catch it and intervene on the shame more quickly.

Reflection: As we learn our triggers we can develop our own list of our personal shame triggers. It helps us heal the inner child and we can utilize our tools much more quickly if we know what gets our shame loop going.

Day 35
Voice of Shame

Am I crazy?

When shame hits, we feel crazy, and/or we think others will think we are crazy. We may also think:

Am I normal?

Our shame has a very rigid set of internal rules about what is acceptable or not. It has internalized many "should" statements without really seeing if they make any sense or fit for whom we are. If we entertain ideas that go against "status quo" or if we act out of these ideas, we are often afraid others will think we are crazy. Our shameful self has a big investment in looking and behaving in a certain way. It wants us to look normal, no matter what. What normal looks like varies, depending on the subculture we are part of, but it seems important to fit in and look normal in that group.

If we find that we are thinking we look crazy or not normal, it can be quite useful to look for the shame message that is driving that feeling. Then we have a chance to really see what that message tells us if we vary from the message. We can work at consciously changing a belief that no longer serves us, or does not really reflect who we are or what we want to stand for in our world.

Reflection: Thinking we are crazy or not normal gives us an opportunity to unearth a shame message, or a "should," and change it.

Day 36
Rule

Shame gets internalized in many ways. One way is that we live in an environment where certain rules are in place. The rules are dysfunctional, in that they lock in shame instead of a healthy sense of self.

A rule I will talk about is: Be in control at all times.

Shame is about attempting to control. It is a paradox because when we are in our shame, we are out of control. But shame is used to control. In shame-bound systems, being in control is the primary objective. However, it is rarely a conscious awareness. We will use shame to get the desired results.

Watch a parent whose child is out of control in a public place. Watch what the parent will do or say to attempt to get control. It may not be something that is overtly abusive. We may not be able to put our fingers on what is wrong, but we will feel uncomfortable watching. We will feel embarrassed for the child or parent or both. That is because shame is being used to attempt to get control.

(I want to say to those parents reading this, who are identifying with the parent in this story that I am not intending to shame you.) Every parent can relate in one way or another. That need to control our children's behavior is something that is part and parcel of our culture and gets to be looked at and changed.

Why? Because it is damaging to the child. We, the adults, are out of control and using shame to try to be in control. It creates shame. It is like throwing a boomerang. It can appear to work in the moment, and yet it always comes back to haunt us.

There is another way. It is about respect and dignity, rights, choices, and boundaries. One thing we can say when we realize we are out of control is: "Clearly, in this situation, this person is not reading my script. In truth, there is no reason for them to read my script. They deserve to be treated respectfully and I am not treating them with respect." It brings awareness to what we are doing and helps us step out of control mode.

> *Reflection: We all want what we want when we want it. Our peace of mind depends on what we do when things don't go our way. We do have the ability to change and bring dignity to ourselves and others, instead of shame. The need to be in control, at all times, holds the dysfunction of shame in place. We get to learn how to be comfortable when we are not "in control."*

Day 37

Shame Indicator

There is a strong "victim consciousness" in our culture. Some common thoughts and statements that come from victim consciousness are:

- I can't do anything to make a difference.
- I didn't do anything to cause this.
- I have no choices.
- I am innocent of any responsibility.
- I can't.

We ALL do this. There is no shame that we do this or sound like this. We learned the language of "victim consciousness," and it feeds shame. It is also not true.

We get trapped in either/or, and black/white mentality. We end up feeling powerless and scared and "less than."

This is shame. It is not based in truth.

To step out of victim consciousness we need to take responsibility for our choices and begin to make conscious choices. We don't take responsibility for others' actions and choices, but we take responsibility for learning our choices and making them. We take responsibility for the choices we have made, forgive ourselves for when we messed up and look at what we can do differently in the future. We do this with great compassion for the selves that made bad choices because we did not know how to do it differently at the time.

We regain our sense of power when we look at our choices and choose consciously. Choice is an empowering movement out of shame and out of victim consciousness.

> *Reflection: We always have choices. If we can't come up with them, we get support to help us look at all the choices we have, and support in making the ones we truly want to make.*

Day 38
Tool

On Day 11, I talked about steps 1-4 of the shame loop. The entire loop is printed in the Appendix. Learning the shame loop and seeing when we are in it is one of the most powerful tools we can use in healing our shame.

I want to share steps 5-6 of the shame loop. After we have triggered shame (step 1), have gone into a defensive posture (step 2), have shut down our real, vulnerable feelings (step 3), and have landed in self-defeating behavior (step 4), we continue to spin in shame.

We can have many loops going on at the same time. We can live in step 4 (self-defeating behavior), for extended periods of time. We can continue in the same pattern for our entire life. This is because we have not gotten under the shame, and walked through the healing. We have not confronted the shame (with compassion), so that we can claim our feelings and needs and care for them in a healthy, kind way.

Steps 5-6 are as follows:

Step 5 is where we try to get control back. If we have been out of control with an addiction, we make promises to ourselves or others to change that. If we have raged, we apologize or send flowers, or try to make up for our bad behavior. If our inner critic has been out of control, we try to change what we feel badly about. We may even unconsciously get ourselves in trouble with the law to try to get control over a behavior. We let the courts insert a level of control where we have had none. We may punish ourselves for what we did in step 4 on the loop, as a way to stop the shame. We are attempting to reconnect with the "self" that we lost when we stepped into our shame.

Step 6 is where we feel a level of control again. The promises we made to ourselves or others give us the illusion of having some power back. We feel a tentative sense of being connected to ourselves again. However, because we never addressed the shame that set the whole loop in motion, we are still in the loop. We just have a false sense that we are "okay" again.

One of the biggest gifts we can give ourselves in healing is to identify where we are in the shame loop as soon as we identify we are in shame.

We will look at how to intervene on the shame loop, and we have to see where we are in it to utilize the interventions. Steps we use to intervene are listed on the same page as the "shame/rage" loop in the Appendix.

Reflection: The shame loop is predictable. We all have our favorite self-defeating behaviors, defenses, and forms of self-punishment.

Day 39
One Thing Different

Healing shame can seem overwhelming. I don't want to minimize the overall process and I want to focus us on baby steps that make a difference in our movement out of shame.

Shame focuses us on the things we don't like about ourselves and others. As we focus on the negative, we reinforce the shame we already feel about ourselves.

What if we really put on different glasses and looked only for what we liked or appreciated or what we wanted reinforced? What if, when the shame reared its head and started its nasty criticism, we noticed and looked in an entirely different direction? Personally, I have noticed it makes a huge difference in the quality of my life, and in the hold shame has over me when I take this step.

The image I have is of me carrying a basket, or back-pack. My quest each day is to look for expressions of "loving kindness." I want to collect these expressions and put them in my basket or container. I want to find ways I can become kind to self and others, and to notice ONLY when others are expressing loving kindness. I look for the exact opposite of what my shame would have me look for. At the end of the day, I like to look back at what I have collected and take a moment to reflect on these kindnesses. It feels really good.

One of the things we notice in healing shame is that we have often been so focused on what is wrong with us and others that we have truly forgotten the "felt sense" of the opposite of shame. Or, maybe we never knew it in the first place. To feel kindness reinforces a different way of being in the world. Kindness is the opposite of shame. We can look for it.

> *Reflection: There is something other than shame. That something needs consistent reinforcing. We can start collecting "loving kindness." It helps move us from the conflict of shame to the peace we so deserve.*

Day 40
Poem

As I have written this book I have been inspired from time to time to write poetry. Occasionally, I will include a poem and utilize it as the daily thought.

Silence

My ear curled around the quiet

I listened hard to that silence

I awaited Love's instructions

I yearned and wanted

Then I knew

The lesson, the learning, was there all the time

Silence

The voice of Love is: SILENCE

That silence brings Peace

I'd heard it all along

Peace,

Barb Tonn

Reflection: Shame is a raucous backdrop in our life. To turn to silence opens us to what we really are. We are the peace of love.

Day 41
Right

One of the ways we get stuck in victim-consciousness and our shame is by not knowing and living by our personal rights. Living with shame keeps us from knowing we have "rights", and even understanding what these rights are. It is never too late to learn our rights and live by them. One right we could all benefit from learning is:

I HAVE THE RIGHT TO DETERMINE MY OWN TRUTH

Depending on the people we are with, or the subcultures we are part of, we are often shamed if we do not believe what these people believe. Our truths, be they political, career, religious, what to wear and how to look, etc. are defined for us. We often don't know what our truths would be if we were left to our own devices to determine our own truths. However, without going through this process we really aren't living our own life and certainly will not feel fulfilled in our own personal way.

It is in living from our truth and empowering ourselves with our truth that we are able to turn away from shame. However, that is not often easy to do. We can get trapped into thinking that our truths need to fit for others, or need others approval. It is hard to claim a right when others do not agree.

I love to step into different subcultures and just listen to people share. I begin to hear their belief system. I hear their opinions and biases and what they do and do not support. I have learned there are so many different ways of viewing the world. One is not better or more correct than another.

We have the right to determine what "truths" fit for us. We get to live our lives in the ways that mirror our own truths. We don't need to defend them. We just get to live them. It empowers us in the movement away from shame.

> *Reflection: What is my truth? What fits for me? Can I claim that for myself and let you claim yours for yourself?*

Day 42

Healing Action

A set of powerful actions we can take to move out of our shame is to follow the "Resolving Rage/Shame Steps" in the Appendix. This is a tool that can be used in the here and now when we realize we have been triggered into a shame loop.

- We start by naming: I am in a shame loop. It is very important to name the shame. We can say we are feeling inadequate or unworthy or unlovable, etc.

- We then get curious about what triggered the loop. We may not see an external trigger like how someone looked at us or something said by someone else. It may have been a thought we had that triggered us. Sometimes the trigger is very difficult to note, like a smell or an unconscious thought. We search for the trigger that started the looping.

- Next we say, "If I had not gone into this shame, what might I have been feeling?" We look for feelings like: mad, sad, fear, hurt, or glad. We then feel our feelings. (Note, that feeling may have been what triggered the shame in the first place.)

- Then, we identify what that feeling part of us might need. (Again, this need may trigger shame.)

- We now look at what we can do to take care of that need in a healthy and productive way. We continue to build the skill sets to help us advocate for our feelings and needs.

The following is a story to demonstrate this process:

I may find myself ruminating about a recent encounter with someone. I may find myself turning the encounter over and over in my head and feeling really self-conscious or inadequate about how I handled it. I stop and say, "I must be in a shame loop. I feel inadequate."

I notice that I feel powerless to stop this ruminating. I look for the feelings under the shame. I may feel hurt. I let myself feel the hurt. I look for what the hurt part of me might need. Maybe I need an apology or some reassurance. Then I can take an action to get the need met. I learn how to get the support I need to take care of myself in healthy ways. This series of steps helps me get out of the loop of shame.

Reflection: Learning to incorporate this set of actions empowers me to move from the endless loop of shame to the self-care of compassion.

Day 43
Forgiveness

Shame interferes with forgiveness. We have few working models for truly moving into forgiveness.

Forgiveness is a process, not an event. In our culture we have little, if any, idea of "process." (An excellent book on process is by Anne Wilson Schaef. It is titled, "*Living in Process.*") The following are some steps that can help us move through the process of forgiveness.

1. Identify that we are feeling a lack of forgiveness toward a person or group.

2. Identify the consequence(s) we may be experiencing due to this lack of forgiveness. We may be losing sleep, so to speak, while the person or group we are ruminating over remains oblivious to our distress.

3. Become more willing to forgive than to be right.

4. We declare our intent to become willing to move into forgiveness.

5. We ask our "Inner Wisdom" what we could do that would help us release our distress, forgive, extend love, and move on.

6. Forgiveness is a process of reaching compassionate acceptance of self and others. It allows one to be human. It is a way of extending love.

When we reach a place where we realize what our lack of forgiveness is costing us, we become much more willing to do something different.

Reflection: Forgiveness allows us to accept ourselves and others as we are.

Day 44
Shame Indicator

Having the same "needs" that were shamed in our formative years will often trigger shame in us as adults. In some of us, any need creates a shame bind. We feel "needy," no matter how human the need is. Being perceived as "needy" feels horrible and shameful. Often, this leads to an inability to identify needs. I noticed when I was a therapist that one of the hardest questions for my clients to answer was: "What do you need?" That is because we often have not learned that to have needs is human and it okay to be human.

One group I worked with, as a therapist, made a list of feeling words. The next list they made was what one might need if they were feeling certain feelings. That list was difficult.

However, it helped develop a language of needs. The following is a list of some needs:

- To be comforted
- To be heard
- To be validated
- To be understood
- For quiet
- For a break
- For sleep
- For food

As we learned with claiming feelings, it can be helpful to name a need without having to do anything with it. It helps us begin to identify needs without the stress of doing anything to fulfill them. It is also useful to norm our needs. That may sound like: "I need to 'be heard' and that is okay. The need to "be heard" is a human need and I am human."

Reflection: Learning the language of needs helps us begin to break the shame loop that can come from having needs. It is a process.

Day 45
Model for a Shame-Free World

The need to be loved is a normal, human need. Extending love allows the creative energy of love to manifest. When we have shame in our core we do not know we are love. We don't know how to love and so we struggle with extending love. This isolates us in deep loneliness.

In our shame-based world, we have most things backward. One of the areas we struggle the most in is knowing the truth of what we are. We believe we are bad and need to prove ourselves worthy of love, instead of knowing we are love and extending love. It starts with self-judgment and extends to judging others.

I read a quote I believe can help us begin to move in a different direction that helps us extend love. The quote is:

"From the Heart, May it go to the Heart"

-Beethoven

If we think heart to heart and speak heart to heart we are speaking a different language from shame. If we allow ourselves to even begin to imagine what love would think and speak in different situations, we begin to dance to the voice of love. That voice is the opposite of shame.

If my heart connects with your heart and that leads the way in my life, then I am moving out of shame.

We can imagine how that could make our world a more peaceful and loving place to be.

Reflection: We get to be the love we are and extend it to each other on this Valentine's Day.

Day 46
Red Flag

We need to differentiate rage and anger.

Rage is an immediate response to shame. It is the "red flag" that we are in a shame loop. The perceived threat to ourselves is so strong, the threat so intense, that the individual must immediately go into hiding. We "clear the decks" of the perceived threat. We do this with rage. This blocks the true underlying emotions of hurt, sadness, despair, and anger. Rage is a cognitively based, bottomless, cumulative avoidance of emotion. The intent of rage is to destroy in order to defend from a threat to our self. One cannot work rage out. One must deal with the underlying emotions that are blocked.

Anger is a potential response to guilt or to one's boundaries being invaded. It is qualitatively different than rage. Anger is a physically based, short-term, finite emotion. One can work anger out through physical action. Setting appropriate boundaries can also release the anger.

If we are destructive to self, property, or others, then we are in "overt" rage. If one is thinking destructive thoughts to self, property, or others then we are in "covert rage." Rage is the strongest indicator that one is in shame.

> *Reflection: To rage means we are in shame. We are in the shame loop and we need to work with resolving the rage. The steps to resolving the rage are in the Appendix.*

Day 47
One Thing Different

When shame is either our basic identity or when it hits us, we can feel like we are drowning. One of the most natural things to do when we are drowning is to reach up and out, to grab for something to pull us out. I almost drowned once. I was in the deep end of a pool and was automatically reaching for a hand to pull me out. When shame is pulling us down and we can't seem to get to solid ground on our own, we get to reach out for support and help. That can feel like a hard thing to do. Reaching out may be a prayer, a phone call, a meeting, a group, picking up a book, calling a helpline, calling a therapist, or many different things. The bottom line is: we need to get out of ourselves. Shame will absolutely have its way with us if we stay in isolation. It will beat us up and leave us to die. We need help. We need to reach out.

It can be helpful to make a list of all the different places, people, and things we can reach out to. We can have that list close at hand so that it is easy to find when we most need it. If the list is minimal, we can seek out ways for developing and enhancing our support.

There is a lot of support in the world. At times, we need to risk having the support network to reach out to when we are drowning in shame.

Reflection: Reaching out can save us from drowning in shame.

Day 48
Healing Action

Healing shame requires compassion. Shame is not compassionate. It is judgmental, unkind, harsh, unforgiving, and unloving. Learning how to be compassionate is a big shift in how we look at the world, ourselves, and others. There must be a willingness to shift to compassion. We must have reached the place where we know that there must be another way, because this way is too painful.

It is so easy to look at choices we have made, or others have made, and feel regret about those choices. We can't seem to find compassion for ourselves or others, and often live with profound regret. "If only" or "why did this happen" are phrases that run through our minds, and dominate our thoughts.

In truth, we can only be at the level of consciousness we are at. We can only be where we are in our developmental path. The same is true for others. If we could teleport ourselves back to the time and space we made the choices we are regretting, we would make the exact choices we made, and so would others.

If we can learn to look back with compassion for where we were when we did things we regretted, or where others were when they did things we judged, we will find forgiveness and peace. When we judge ourselves or others we will feel shame and pain.

Reflection: Compassion helps us look at ourselves and others with loving eyes, human eyes, and the love we all deserve.

Day 49
Healing Action

One thing we can know about shame is that we cannot talk ourselves or anyone else out of it. Logic does not budge it. For example: If I believe I am stupid, I could have many degrees and incredible grades, and a high IQ, and I will still believe I am stupid. To truly change a core shame belief, we start with acceptance. I stop fighting the belief and accept that I have the belief. Then, I can move in a different direction. When we resist or arm wrestle with a belief, it just locks the belief in that much harder. What we resist persists.

When we begin to move in a direction away from our shame we can feel very vulnerable. In our shame, we are in our comfort zones and we are heavily defended. When we accept, we drop our defenses and turn in a different direction, the direction of love. We feel different. There is softness when we embrace ourselves in love. It is a softness that is strong.

Shame is a bully that looks and sounds tough. However, it is brittle in its rigidness. To embrace a truth such as, "I am lovable just as I am," feels silly and vulnerable. Our rigid shaming does not allow this vulnerability. As we continue our healing, we begin to step into our truth in a softer, more vulnerable way.

> *Reflection: Shame is our old comfort zone. To move into healing is a vulnerable, yet empowering journey. Out of the old, painful comfort zone we have a chance to find a truth and strength that we never could have imagined.*

Day 50
Right

I HAVE THE RIGHT TO BE MYSELF

As I have mentioned, learning our rights can be very helpful in our healing journeys. One of the reasons we may not have learned our rights, is because schools, and families would experience a loss of control if the children's rights were truly honored. I doubt if this need to control would be conscious. To truly encourage a child to live by their rights could leave the family or school without the resources or skill sets to really support the children in the way they individually need.

We often are left having yearnings or dreams that don't get met. Part of healing shame is noticing where we have developmental holes in our learning and then to begin to consciously fill in the holes. If we notice we are doing something that just does not fit for ourselves and that we truly want something else, we can begin to work with our inner child and give him/her the message, "You have the right to be yourself."

I grew up in a home where my mom was a teacher. I went to college and became a teacher. It was unfortunate I did not get to student teach until just before I graduated, because I would have realized I really did not want to be a teacher. I just had done what my family did and hadn't really looked at what was right for me.

I did switch professions and believe my personal fulfillment has been much deeper because of that. When I began to listen to my inner guidance and worked with the right to be myself, I found what really fit for me. My dad said to me once, "you picked the one profession I know nothing about." If I had waited until he guided me to become a psychotherapist and public speaker, I would never have done it. I did, however, get the message that, "I have the right to be myself."

Reflection: As our shame heals we learn to live our own lives, the lives of our dreams, and live from the knowing that, we have the right to be ourselves.

Day 51

Model for a Shame-Free World

What would a shame-free world look like? How would we experience ourselves and others if we weren't constantly judging? What if we considered being "kind" the most important task we have?

This book helps us identify when we are in a shame loop, and when we are in a shaming environment. I want to look at what the antithesis of that would be.

- True kindness would lead the way.
- We would value everyone as important, even if we disagreed.
- We would know that the heart of everyone is the same. Our behavior may have been horrible, and the heart or essence of ourselves is love.
- We would learn how to forgive and practice forgiveness at all times.
- We would treat ourselves and others with dignity and respect.
- We would turn to "Love" to guide our words and actions.

Obviously, we are far away from this ideal. We may not even really want the "ideal," I just proposed, as a goal. We may find many reasons why we don't deserve such kindness, and we can find countless examples of others whom we don't believe deserve it.

However, I am proposing moving in a direction away from the deep and pervasive myth that "shame" has instilled in our minds. That myth says we are bad and deserving of sacrifice and punishment. To shift such a deep and dark paradigm requires uprooting the entire belief system that supports it and beginning to imagine a completely different paradigm.

Reflection: We get to look and decide if the way things are, are really what we want. If not, we get to start from the ground up and set intention to move in a different direction entirely.

Day 52

Rule

It is helpful to know the rules that shame bound systems live by. It helps us identify when we are reinforcing shame, and when we are in it. These rules are some of the things we will change as we step more deeply into our healing.

One rule of shame-bound systems is: BLAME. Because shame demands we need to be perfect, we demand perfection of ourselves and others. In shame, we tend to either blame ourselves 100% or blame others 100%. With this dynamic in place, it is impossible to make mistakes or allow others to make mistakes. Because of this we cannot reach forgiveness. In relationships and family systems the same mistake is brought up for decades or long after a person is gone. There is blame and no forgiveness.

In "healthy" systems, people are allowed to make mistakes, and learn to take appropriate responsibility for their mistakes, instead of blaming. We can do this because we know we don't have to be perfect and will receive forgiveness for our mistakes. When there are problems we learn to ask the question: "What is my part in this challenge?" We can take responsibility for our part, and give the other person responsibility for their part.

When the dynamic is blame, we are too fearful to take appropriate responsibility. We know that shame is a cruel taskmaster and we will be punished for our human errors. So, we blame.

If we look at our culture, we will see blame as a major dynamic in governments, schools, politics, religions, family systems, relationships, and most places where conflict is involved.

It is so helpful in our healing to learn about being human and that making mistakes is human. When we operate from this framework, we can take appropriate responsibility and move on.

> *Reflection: Where blame is involved, shame is involved. I can learn to ask myself what part of this issue is my responsibility, change my part that is a problem, forgive myself, and release myself from shame.*

Day 53
Voice of Shame

One of the things that can be helpful in healing shame is to learn to discern the different voices in our head. The voice of shame is harsh and unkind. It may sound like truth, but only because we have heard it our whole lives and have identified with our shame. The voice of love is kind and supportive. It builds us up and NEVER tears us down. It is a voice that is always there, but often has not been truly heard or acknowledged.

Usually the voice of Shame enters more dominantly in one ear, and the voice of Love enters in the other. As we begin to listen, the voice of Love may sound softer and be harder to hear. That is because we are not used to listening for it. Shame is louder, raucous, and is familiar, so we hear it first. We begin to deliberately turn in the direction of Love. We get to learn to listen for Love.

We can develop the ears to hear Love by turning in the direction of Love. We will then begin to hear the kindness that was there all along but which had been drowned out by the shame. We can also ask: "What would the voice of love/kindness say in this situation?" Then, we can be still and listen. If it is peaceful and brings peace, it is the voice of love and kindness.

We begin to listen for kindness and love. We become willing to believe the voice of kindness and love instead of the voice of shame.

Reflection: Being willing to listen for the voice of "loving kindness" goes a long way. We can turn toward "loving kindness," whether we believe it or not.

Day 54

One Thing Different

I was reading an article written by Gerald Jampolsky the other day. He was talking about our "hurry up" world. I doubt many of us escape this. In our busyness, we are not in our moments and not truly conscious. Shame loves it when we are unaware. If we are hurrying and not conscious, our shame has a much better chance of raising hell in our psyche. Most of the tools in this book require us to be present to what is going on in our minds, thoughts, and bodies. We have to slow down to become conscious. We have to be conscious to intervene on the destructive path of shame.

There are many ways to start slowing down. The important thing is finding the way that works for ourselves. For many years, I have started the day slowly. I get up hours before I need to show up in the world. I take this relaxed, deliberate time to read, meditate, and write. This has helped me slow down. During the day, I can work up a great head of steam and completely lose sight of my consciousness, and I can catch myself. I can stop, take a breath, sit consciously, slow down, and be still. If I notice and do not pay attention, I will end up tired and crabby and be absolutely vulnerable for a shame attack. Early morning does not work for many people. Some people become more mindful by exercise, or some form of art they work on, or by sharing with others. We can all be curious about the way that helps us slow down and become more conscious.

Reflection: We can slow down and that sets the stage to help us heal our shame.

Day 55
Shame Defined

What does shame feel like?

Shame can definitely be felt on a continuum. It can be experienced as anything from mild embarrassment to deep humiliation where one wants to disappear. I once heard someone say her shame left her feeling like, "being thumbtacked to the wall and flailing around but not being able to do anything or get anywhere."

There is truly a sense of powerlessness when shame floods us. We can know that what our inner voice is saying is not true. However, we can't always act on that knowing or get away from the horrible voice of shame. Shame can strike us in seemingly benign situations as well as in ones that we have placed a lot of importance on.

Normally, when we are hit with shame we get very internal. We disconnect from what is going on or being said in our immediate environment. We become very "self-conscious." We loop around and around the same situation trying to find a way out of the distress, but we are unable to. (This is the experience in the middle of the night when we keep replaying a scene or situation and can't get any sleep. We lament, "what if," and "if only." We try to figure out how to "make up for" or "make amends to" in order to get out of our shame loop and pain.)

Often, we are flooded with a sense of deep rage (destructive feelings or thoughts toward ourselves or others). We want them to hurt like we have hurt or suffer like we have suffered. We go into a self-defeating addiction or behavior and are unable to stop. Our thoughts and behaviors become obsessive and compulsive.

Shame feels untenable. We can't tolerate it, but it also is usually a very familiar voice, feeling, or behavior that we are entrenched in. It is so important to begin to realize that when we are in any of these familiar places, we are in a "shame loop." There are truly ways out of this shame, but we have to stop, and name it "SHAME" before we can begin the movement out of it.

> *Reflection: Once we start having a name for what we have experienced, we often see that shame is with us much of the time.*

Day 56

Shame Indicator

One of the harder things we might have experienced growing up in shame is an "abandonment phobia." Growing up in shame we most likely experienced betrayals from people we had every right to expect would be there for us. This would have been experienced as abandonment. We may feel like we are being abandoned for the rest of our lives, whether it is actually happening or not. We become so fearful that we will be abandoned that we turn ourselves inside out to not be abandoned. We may set ourselves up to be abandoned, or see abandonment where it isn't happening. We get to bring the fear of abandonment into our healing process. That can be hard to do because we may feel deep shame that we have experienced so much abandonment, or fear it so much that we try not to look at it.

Our healing process can involve trauma work from when we were abandoned either emotionally or physically. We may end up doing inner child work and reassuring the inner child that we are there for them now and can care for them now. We notice when our fear of abandonment is up for us and work with the shame/rage loop to identify the underlying feelings and needs that need to be addressed. We do Flow of Consciousness Writing on our fear and what our shame is telling us. We can end feelings of abandonment by claiming the truth that we are loveable. We now have the ability to care for our self.

> *Reflection: If we have a deep fear of being abandoned it is often coming from trauma that entrenched us. Fear of abandonment and the shame that we are not lovable is what remains. Trauma work can be done with a therapist who specializes in trauma.*

Day 57
Voice of Shame

If there was one word I could get us to erase from our vocabulary it would be the word, "SHOULD." Years ago, when I lived in Minnesota, I saw a t-shirt that said, "Don't Should on Me." That pretty much sums up my feelings on the word, "should."

If we examine any sentence in which the word, "should or shouldn't" is used, we see that it involves someone else determining what is right or wrong for us to do or not do. It is an external belief that is being imposed on our internal belief system. Rarely said, but implied, is the message, if we don't believe or act in accordance with this "should," there is something wrong with us or another person. If we look deeper, it is a message of shame, and we will all have a response to this message, whether we realize it or not.

If we change the world "should" to "could," we will be moved into choice, and have an opportunity to determine what fits for us, as opposed to having something imposed from an external source. The "should" will feed our core shame beliefs.

On the surface, using the word "should" may seem like a small thing. However, "should" represents a part of our shame-based culture that is very quick to decide what is right for someone else. We often think poorly of people who do not see or do things our way, or believe as we think they "should."

> *Reflection: Notice how often "should" is used, how it feels, and how it would be to change the word "should" to "could."*

Day 58
Red Flag

Another red flag that may indicate we are in a shame loop is when our inner critic is very active. We cannot effectively intervene on and stop the criticism.

This is often experienced in the middle of the night and we can't sleep because our inner critics won't stop beating us up. Or, we are going about our day but totally distracted because our inner critics won't stop. In the shame loop in the Appendix, we get stuck in #4, (self-defeating behavior). The hallmark of #4 is experiencing the feeling of "powerlessness." We can't seem to stop the inner critics.

For some of us, the inner critics seldom, if ever, stop. It is judgmental, mean, critical, and gives the message that we just can't do something, right. We are never good enough. It attacks and won't let up.

An inner critic that won't let up is not helpful. Some of us are afraid that if we did not have this inner critic we might be out of control and behave badly. In truth, the inner critics are part of our self-defeating behavior. It is part of the problem, not the solution.

> *Reflection: If we have a strong inner critic that we cannot get to let up, we are dealing with shame. If we frame it as shame then we can*

utilize the tools we are learning to intervene on the criticism.

Day 59
Tool

If we are familiar with the 12 steps of AA (Alcoholics Anonymous) and other 12 step programs, we will know the 1st step is: We admitted we were powerless over _____ and our lives have become unmanageable. This 1st step works very well if we insert shame. It would read "we admitted we were powerless over our shame, and our lives have become unmanageable." For those of us already familiar with the 12 step programs, this immediately opens up a way of working with shame.

The 12 steps directly intervene on shame. This will surface in different ways in this book. However, to start with, we can begin to write specific examples of how shame, when triggered, renders us powerless. We look at all the ways we have tried to stop or intervene on our shame and have not been able to stop it. We look at all the ways our lives are unmanageable when shame leads the way.

We can begin to work the 12 steps to intervene on shame. It helps to have tools other than the 12 steps. However, the steps may offer a familiar language to assist in healing our shame. The 12 steps can be a powerful foundation for our shame work.

Reflection: Utilizing the 1st step in the 12 step programs is a way of framing shame in a familiar light for those working 12 step programs.

Day 60

Specific Shame-Based Story

I am going to start March with a story that demonstrates intervening on the shame/rage loop.

This is a story from my own history.

I was on a summer vacation at a lake. I had been blissfully floating on an air mattress, peaceful and content, when a group of late adolescent boys came running into the water. They were making a lot of commotion and I decided to leave the water until they left. As I was exiting the water one of them yelled, "She has cellulite, she should be swimming, not floating." It was one of those stop action moments for me. I felt intense rage. I felt publically shamed, exposed, found lacking, hideous, and less than. I wanted the water to open up and take me down. I wanted to hurt the boy who yelled that. It was horrible.

So, I got myself to shore and sat there for a while. I had been working on my shame for quite some time. Therefore, it was easy for me to know my shame had been triggered. However, I did not want to run the old familiar scenario. That would have been to punish myself for being found lacking, especially by a man. In my past, that would have ended my blissful day off. I would have had to go for a killer run, forgo the marshmallows planned for that night, and my inner critic would have had a hay day.

This is what I did instead:

I utilized the steps found in the Appendix. I went back to the words that triggered me, and said, "What if you didn't go into shame over this and got in touch with the feelings under the shame? What would those feelings be?" What came up was grief. I became profoundly aware of the standards I had absorbed from my culture and how inhuman and harmful they had been. My culture worships slenderness and youth, and would never stand for any sign of normal aging. In their eyes, I was a used up person, ready for the dump heap if I slipped at all in the body image department. I flashed through the years of messages I had absorbed until I totally believed them and turned myself inside out to meet those standards. I felt enraged and tired and so very sad. I had been duped. I had believed that I was less than myself if I got older, heavier, or looked like a woman instead of a girl.

I let myself grieve, mourn, and feel the anger and sadness that grief brought with it. My inner child, my inner self, had a lot to say, and a lot to feel. After all, I was in my mid-thirties by then and had plenty of years and messages under my belt. (This grief work went on for quite some time. However, on the day this happened this process started and I allowed it.)

Next, I checked in on what I needed. It turned out I needed comfort, and a new script to live with. This script needed to come from within, from my higher self, from my inner wise woman, from truth. Who I am and my worth have nothing to do with how I look or with my body. I am loveable, no matter what. I am enough. I am worthy. I am a child of Love. Did knowing this instantly change the shame?

Not by a long shot.

I am part and parcel of the culture I grew up in, which worships youth, not aging. I am exposed every day of my life to the messages my culture sends me about body, image, and age. However, shame had reached its pinnacle in me. It has never twirled me around in the same way since that fateful day. I see it now when I get exposed to shaming messages either from outside me or from my own inner dialogue. Seeing it makes it easier to intervene. I get to age and part of that is a great deal of body change. I get to be loveable and wise and wonderful and beautiful as I am. It has never been as bad as it was before I went through this process.

And by the way, I got to enjoy the rest of that vacation without having to take a torturing run. I got to sit around the campfire and enjoy the marshmallows. That young man that I had wanted to hurt was not even spoken to. He was the vehicle for the healing I wanted in my life.

I continued to work with my shame around body image and aging. I have learned to advocate for myself, how to be the best woman I can be and not get distracted with how I look. I have brought out my internal messages and examined them one at a time. I changed the ones that did not serve me and were not about truth.

This demonstrates an intervention on the rage/shame loop. I hope this example helps clarify the process. It certainly helped me.

> *Reflection: If we get under our shame, we can become aware of the unresolved issues that get to be healed. We get to have our feelings, address our needs, and advocate for ourselves in loving and nurturing ways.*

Days 61-90

Day 61
Tool

When we commit to something, we take a powerful step in manifesting what we are committing to. If we make a deliberate decision to have something be, then it will be as we decide. If we make a deliberate decision to consistently intervene on and heal our shame, we are sending a powerful message to the Universe and our inner selves. The shame may have a reaction. It resists the movement and "fights for its life." However, with commitment we are now able to see this reaction clearly and intervene on it.

To say: "I am no longer going to accept shame as a definition for who I am. From now on I will define myself as enough and worthy and loveable" is a commitment and affirmation that carries great strength. It is also an internal boundary. A boundary says what is or isn't acceptable. Learning to set boundaries is one of the tools that moves us in the direction of healing.

Mindfully living in "intention" is a powerful way of living in the world. It puts us in charge of our lives and empowers us through choices.

Reflection: We give our minds direction and empower ourselves through internal boundaries that no longer accept shame as our truth.

Day 62

Rule

Another rule that shame-based systems and people live by is that we must be "perfect." What we all know is that we can't be and so with "perfection" as our guide we will always feel like failures in some way. However, we continue to try and be perfect. We try to prove ourselves, and we strive to make up for our mistakes or perceived lack. It is a stressful and totally unnecessary way to live.

We cannot be perfect because we are human and humans make mistakes. When we are driven by perfection, we stop doing, never start, and pretend we are perfect, or compensate for our perceived lack. Whichever way we choose, we are doomed to failure and feelings of low self–esteem, as long as the tyrant of perfectionism is in charge.

It is imperative to recognize when the perfectionistic tyrant is in charge, and to look at what it is demanding of us. At times, when we are overwhelmed, we can grab paper and pen and write what our perfectionism is demanding of us. Then we can look at the list and realize the impossibility of this. At this point we get to begin to make conscious choice about what we are willing to do. We get to identify a different way, or ways, to get on with the task at hand, by utilizing a different choice. To begin to operate from choice instead of perfectionism begins to unlock the door to a healthier self-esteem. It embraces our humanness.

Reflection: Perfectionism does not give us choice. As long as we identify and operate from choice, and not the tyrannical demands of perfectionism, we will get to embrace our humanness with love and compassion.

Day 63

Shame Originator

As I have mentioned, often our shame is locked in place at a very young age when someone we had every right to believe was trustworthy, betrayed us. The interpersonal bridge between us was broken. At this point, we started to isolate and had trouble trusting others. We put up defenses so that we would not be hurt in this way again. In healing we get to the place where we begin to expose our shame with someone we have consciously chosen because they are trustworthy.

There are many tools to utilize in healing. Many of them have to do with tools we can use by self. We write, meditate, take walks, explore our inner self and develop our inner wisdom. These tools are very important, and at some point we get to heal our shame while interacting with other people. It is part of healing from the original betrayal. Learning our rights, choices, and boundaries empowers us to take care of ourselves with others. We learn how to be safe and take care of ourselves in ways that aren't just about pushing everyone away. When we do this, we find people we can begin to open up with.

Interpersonal relationships are an essential part of healing the original shame that resulted from betrayal. We don't need to start here, but we do get to move in that direction.

Group therapy is an amazing healing tool for shame because the parameters for safety are in place. We get to experience others hearing us. Often, we not only get loved and accepted as we open up, and we hear from others who have struggled like we have struggled. It is deeply healing to share our shame with another and experience being heard and seen with the eyes of love and acceptance.

> *Reflection: Eventually we get to bring our healing into relationships. There is no hurry in doing this, and we get to prepare for this.*

Day 64
One Thing Different

It is not egotistical to truly embrace all that we are, and love ourselves. It is not bad to see the magnificence of ourselves and live from those places. It is a different way to be in the world. It is living in a way that is the opposite of how shame would have us live.

When we live in our magnificence we will also see and embrace the magnificence in others. If we don't see this in ourselves or others, then we are seeing through the eyes of shame. Each of us is doing the best we can with what we have learned and experienced. Most of us have learned the way of shame. The way of the world is what has locked this shame in place.

Each of us is deserving of love and forgiveness. We may have a hard time forgiving because the behavior of others can be pretty horrible. However, our behavior is not WHO we are. Who we are is a piece of the divine, which is LOVE. Shame gets caught up in looking at the observable behavior, and does not look beyond that to the essence. We are not our behavior. Who we are is, LOVE. We are either showing and extending love or asking for it.

We get to practice looking beyond the surface. We get to say, "The love in me beholds the love in you." We get to call love forth, if we want. We get to call love forth in self and in others. Shame may try to convince us that we are wrong. In truth, shame is wrong.

Reflection: In the end, the only thing that is real is LOVE.

Day 65
Tool

I used to teach conflict resolution. In the shame-based world, we end up in a lot of conflict. Shame thrives on it. Clear communication is very important. There are two versions of the conflict resolution tool I used to teach.

Simple version:

    a. We start by saying "When you..." Follow this with exact information that is factual and will help the other person know exactly the situation we are referring to.

b. Next, we say: "I felt..." We stick to feeling words. Examples of these are: anger, sadness, happiness, fearfulness, and shame.

c. We now say: "I need..." We are very explicit about what it is that we need.

An example of this form of communication is:

"This morning when you left the house and slammed the door, I felt angry and hurt. I need to know what you were upset about."

Complex version:

a. This stays the same as the Simple version above.

b. We add a different 2nd step. It starts with the statement, "I started thinking..." We then add all the things that were running through our thoughts after the incident named in the Simple version.

c. This is, again, the same as the Simple version's B. We name our feelings.

d. We now say, "All the things I considered doing as a result of _____. (We must be thorough. If we leave something out, we may be leaving out the most important things to clear the conflict.)

e. The same as the Simple version's C. We name our need.

An example of this more complex form of communication is:

This morning when you left the house and slammed the door, I started thinking:

a. That you had left for good.

b. That you were mad at me.

c. That you did not even realize how upset you were.

d. That you were never going to tell me what upset you.

We continue this list with everything that went through our head.

I felt angry and hurt.

I considered many responses. They were:

-   Not bringing up the incident.
-   Packing your bags and changing the locks.
-   Calling our therapist.
-   Calling you at work and demanding you talk then and there.
-   Screaming at you in front of the neighbors.
-   Saying a prayer and letting it go.

But I decided the thing I most need is for you to help me understand what upset you so much.

These two forms of conflict communication use the "I" statements and are only our own personal truth. They are not about blame, but they are about understanding. We can get quite proficient at using these steps quickly when conflict arises.

Reflection: Good communication helps us take personal responsibility for our own internal conflict. It can keep us from going into shame. We can also use this tool for communicating when shame is engaged.

Day 66
Right

I HAVE THE RIGHT TO DETERMINE MY OWN HIGHER POWER

In the 12-step world, the word "God" is used in many of the steps. The term is meant to mean: Anything we can turn to that is, at that moment, "Greater than self." That can mean anything from a good friend, nature, the sacred Grandmothers, one's higher self, to a formal God or Buddha. However, just like in any other area of one's life, there is always someone that is more than happy to define what God means to them and think that is the same Higher Power we "should" have. I put "should" in quotes because using the word "should" on ourselves or others is a way of sending shame.

It can be helpful in healing shame to have some form of a "higher power." If we are immersed in shame and talk to someone safe, we can often find our way out of the shame lie and move into peace. That person, in that experience, could be called a "higher power." Another time when spiraling in shame it could help to get out and work in the garden and ground into nature. At that moment nature could be our "higher power." If we love music, we can play some music and find our way out of shame. The music is then our, "higher power."

The point is: We all have the right to define our own "higher power." We have the right to not believe in a "higher power." We all deserve respect for our beliefs. This respect means, non-judgment. Whether we believe in a formal God or not, we deserve respect. We don't need to defend our beliefs. If we get into defensiveness, we have most likely already been triggered into a shame loop. Instead of defense, we can just claim our right to our own beliefs. This can be done out loud or in our head.

Reflection: We always get to claim our beliefs without any defensiveness. We get to just "be."

Day 67
Rule

One of the rules that govern a shame-bound system is that some people are more important than others. This is called a hierarchy and it is an integral part of most every system in our culture. It is so ingrained that many would say that we have to have this kind of a system to function.

Is that true?

What might it be like if every system we were part of counted each person as equal in importance? What if each person was valued and treated kindly?

In a family, that would look like each person getting a vote. In a school, it would look like each child having equal value. Every child would be valued with the same importance as the teacher and principal. They all would be treated with dignity and respect.

Hierarchy is a breeding ground for shame. It says that some people are more valuable than others. It supports those who have money and power as more valuable and deserving of more respect. It shames those who are different, ill, or poor. It may preach that each person is important, but the laws and life styles would not back up those words.

Our culture supports shame. A hierarchy supports shame. We change from the top down and from the bottom up. We get to change the very foundations that support shame in order to have peace and love at the foundation of our world.

Reflection: Hierarchy supports shame. What messages do we get about ourselves when we are in a hierarchy and not on the top rung?

Day 68
Maude

Barb (B)—Maude, once we start feeling shame it seems we just go round and round in our head and heart. Why is that?

Maude (M)—It is important to know about how shame loops. To notice is how we begin to take our power back from shame. It does loop and loop and loop until we feel "loopy!" (Just had to say it!)

B—Well, most of the time we don't identify the loops as shame. The shame loop feels so familiar that we don't question it, never mind see the need to change.

> M—Yes, that is a part of why it goes on and on cycling. Once we get triggered, we get defensive and shut down our true feelings. Then we just loop in feeling "bad." We'll feel powerless to change the loop. When we feel powerless, we can be pretty darn sure we are in shame and a shame loop.

B—Let me give an example that I think fits with what you are talking about.

> M—Okay.

B—When we feel "stuck," many of us end up feeling shame. We feel we must be stupid or we wouldn't be "stuck." The longer we feel "stuck," the stupider we feel and the more "stuck" we get. We can't make a decision and we can't seem to get a solution. We just loop from bad to worse. Sometimes we force ourselves to make a decision or do something, just so that we won't be "stuck" any longer. However, when we make a decision in that way, we usually find we have made a pretty unproductive decision. We forced a decision before we were truly ready to make one.

> M—That is because shame is leading the way. When shame leads the way, decision-making doesn't work. Decisions we make, when driven by shame, end up creating more shame.

B—Well, what can we do at those times?

M—The first, and most important, thing to do is to realize that we are in a shame loop. We have to call it what it is: Shame.

B—Then what?

M—Then, I ask myself three questions:

a) If I weren't shaming myself for being stuck, what would I feel? (Anger, sadness, gladness, or fear?)
b) Once I know what I feel and let self-feel, I then ask: what does that feeling part of me need?
c) Then I ask self how I can take care of that need in the most productive way?

B—So, the shame isn't the feeling?

M—No, although we can look like we are really having strong feelings (see Appendix), shame really hides the true, vulnerable feelings. Therefore, shame keeps us from caring for ourselves.

B—Usually when we are stuck we feel scared.

M—Of what?

B—We get scared that we will never get unstuck.

M—That is tricky, but that is still the shame talking. It tries to convince us that things will never change.

B—Oh my gosh, I get it. Shame always tries to make us feel hopeless and powerless. So, when we look for feelings, it can be tricky.

M—Yes.

B—Okay, so if I am stuck, I usually feel lonely.

M—Okay, so we get to feel the feeling. It won't kill us.

B—It feels like it could. It feels like it could go on and on forever.

M—I know, but the fear of feeling the loneliness is much worse that actually feeling the feeling of loneliness.

B—So, I let myself feel lonely, and then what?

M—Well, I ask myself, "What does that lonely part of me need?"

B—I usually don't like to need. I end up feeling needy.

M—Yes, sometimes we feel shame for having feelings and needs. If that happens, we are in another shame loop.

B—It goes on and on.

M—Yes, it does. Continue to ask yourself what the lonely part needs.

B—Usually when lonely, it helps to have help or support. Sometimes, it helps to brainstorm ideas to help with the stuck feeling.

M—Looking at our choices with someone else can be very useful in helping us move out of shame.

B—Yes, it helps move us out of the idea that we have no choices, or have only "either/or" choices. It can feel so overwhelming and hopeless.

M—Sweet pea, that is the shame again. We can feel the shame that we are stuck, or when we have certain feelings or needs, or in asking for help, or when we can't come up with solutions except either/or. We keep naming the shame and moving forward with attending to the underlying feelings and needs. It may feel like we are stuck, and by doing the work of feeling the underlying feelings and identifying the needs, we are moving forward.

B—Thanks, Maude. Knowing we don't have to do this work alone helps more than anything else.

Day 69
Voice of Shame

Yesterday Maude made some great comments on how shame can trigger more shame. She talked about how we can have shame about the very things that can help us out of shame. For many of us, the shame gets going and, if left unchecked, it can go on forever.

We don't need to get completely overwhelmed and discouraged by this. We get to be thankful that we notice it and can name it. Without this, we could spin forever in this loop of hopelessness.

However, by naming the shame each time it comes up, we can then look for what we are hiding with our shame and actually find our way through it. We can make strides into our feelings and needs. We can take care of ourselves.

Fear of what we will uncover or of the intensity of our feelings and needs can keep us from moving ahead and through. Sometimes it is only trust and faith that keep us moving.

Unchecked shame does not just go away. It stays alive and well within us, ready to pounce on us with that old familiar feeling of "not being good enough."

We get to claim our inner courage to continue to bring our shame into healing. We can feel better. We can live a life where we know we are enough and where we feel good about self.

Reflection: We can choose to not let our shame go unchecked.

Day 70
Shame Indicator

Often when beginning our shame work we look for something outside of ourselves that triggers our shame. However, when we grow up in shame, it

"becomes autonomous." That means that shame does not need an overt trigger to become engaged. It can trigger inside our head. An example would be: We look at our day and realize we have more things to do than we have time for. We begin to feel like an idiot or stupid for scheduling so much. We drop into #4 in the shame loop (self-defeating thoughts or behavior) and don't get anything done because our shame has engaged. Nothing outside of ourselves happened. We internally triggered and went into a shame loop. We can identify this as shame. We can intervene on it.

That would sound like:

- My internal voice is beating me up.
- I must be in a shame loop.
- It seems it started when I looked at my "to do" list and found it was too much.
- That started my shame off.
- We can ask ourselves what we might have felt and needed if we had not gone into shame at that point.
- We may have felt a bit frustrated and needed just to reorganize our days, or we might have smiled and felt some humor that we had fallen into our old habits and then just shifted our days around.

More often than not, it is an internal "should" that gets our shame going. As we learn to identify those "should messages," we can change them to messages that are more human and loving.

Reflection: Internal messages can trigger shame.

Day 71
Model for a Shame-Free World

It is important to look at how our world could be different without shame leading the way. It gives us something to step into.

One thing that could be different is that we will live in community. Why is that? Because the origins of shame sit in having experienced betrayal by someone we thought we could trust. We have withdrawn. To heal, we get to experience relationships in which we are not betrayed. A place that this can happen is in "intentional community." This is a group of people who consciously set out to create community. It is not about keeping people out, but about welcoming people in. There is conscious choice around modeling and choosing functional relationships. This is:

- Talking about what is happening now
- Owning feelings
- Being respectful of others' feelings and needs and opinions
- Building trust
- Non-hierarchical structure, where each person is counted equally
- Taking responsibility for self and choices
- Rocking the boat
- Consciously choosing roles in the community
- Consistency
- Having the right to establish boundaries
- Respecting others' boundaries
- Flexibility
- Having rights and respecting the rights of others
- Room for each person to live in the essence of who we are
- Safety
- Kindness

This community will allow the shame to heal or not to develop in the first place. We will experience "loving presence."

Reflection: There are ways to live that are about kindness and love. We get to learn and practice and build community from this love and kindness and non-judgment.

Day 72
Shame Indicator

I was deeply touched recently when speaking with someone who said, "I felt erased in my family." That phrase captured how shame feels. At times people have described shame as feeling "invisible." But to feel erased means someone had a sense of ourselves at one time and then lost it. To feel erased is to cease to exist, or to be written off as unimportant. When we experience "feeling erased" we often cease having hope. Not having hope describes shame.

I believe we all need to be truly seen and heard. We need chances to tell our stories to someone who truly wants to hear them. When we do this, we can begin to be seen, and our erased or invisible feelings begin to heal.

We get to part of a family picture. If it is not our biological family, then it gets to be a family of choice. To choose a family and consciously become a part of it is how many of us are getting seen and heard. We meet the need of being a "part of" by choosing where that will happen and with whom we will connect.

We can also experience "feeling erased" when the family or people we are with see us as they want to see us, and not as we really are. Many of us grow into adulthood being seen by our families in "old" ways. We may have changed profoundly and yet continue to be seen as we once were.

> *Reflection: To pay attention to each person we encounter, to look someone in the eyes, and to take time to listen is how we begin to heal the feeling of "being erased."*

Day 73
Shame Defined

I have shared about rage and differentiated it from anger. I have equated rage with shame. But, there is more that needs to be added.

Many experience overt rage. We put our hands through walls, break things, and throw things. We say profoundly destructive things to other people. We look and "are" obviously out of control. However, many rage internally and covertly. It is still rage we are experiencing, but we have to be much more aware of it because from the outside we don't look full of rage.

Covert rage is the rage that goes on inside our head. It is the internal voice that beats us up because we made a mistake or did something we regret. It is the voice that plots revenge on others and wants to get even for things we have experienced from others. It is the internal rage that may never make its way out to the surface, but destroys our peace of mind and our relationships. That voice tells us stories about why someone did what they did and we believe that story and become rage-filled. We plot for ways to get even.

Covert rage is rage and it is shame. When we find we are looping in this internal rage, we can know we are in a shame loop. We attempt to see what triggered the rage. The trigger may be internal or external. If we find the trigger, we can work with the "resolving rage" steps in the Appendix. If we don't know the trigger, we can still look for what we may be feeling and needing that the shame is blocking, and find healthy ways to have our feelings, and take care of our needs.

Reflection: Covert rage is as deadly as overt rage to our relationships and peace of mind. It is shame.

Day 74
Tool

Boundary is a word used quite frequently in this day and age. What does it really mean? In Webster's Dictionary, it is defined as: "anything marking a limit." What does this have to do with healing shame?

Shame-based systems do not allow people to determine their own healthy limits, nor do they honor other peoples' boundaries. Some systems have so many boundaries that people feel there is no way inside. Other systems have no boundaries that help people honor their own preferences and needs. However, the boundaries, in both of these extremes are not determined by the individuals, but are established by the systems. They just are the way they are, and functional or not, they stay locked in place.

Part of healing shame is determining what our boundaries are. We determine what is acceptable or not for ourselves. We may change our boundaries as we heal, and we get to determine what they are.

For instance: We may feel uncomfortable with touch. We may not want hugs or physical contact from anyone, or only from certain people. We have the right to establish these boundaries. We may not know how to communicate the boundaries, but in this step we are just learning to determine what they are. As our healing progresses, our boundaries around touch may change, or they may not. We get to decide.

At times there is shame about having boundaries, especially if they are different from those other people around us seem to have. We can be aware if the shame comes up as we identify our "personal boundaries."

> *Reflection: We get to have boundaries. We get to say what is acceptable or not acceptable for us. At this point in our healing we don't need to worry about how to set our boundaries. We can begin to let ourselves determine what our boundaries are without shame.*

Day 75
Shame Indicator

We might feel humbled about this shame indicator. We might feel more shame because of it. However, no matter how difficult it may be to know, the truth is this: Growing up in shame stunts us developmentally. When we grow up in shame-bound systems, we spend much of our time on survival. We are trying to keep our heads above water. When shame leads the way, we are trying to prove ourselves, or prove our right to "be". In survival, we truly do not have time to progress the optimal way.

I remember reading a book about developmental growth when I was in my mid-20's. I recognized myself described in the books written account of a much younger person. It really confused me. I had been academically smart, but as far as relationships and developmental markers, I was way behind. Later, as I learned about shame and how it impacts us, I began to understand why I was so far behind developmentally. Shame had stunted my developmental growth.

It helps to learn about developmental markers. As we do so we can see where we have missed some key steps. I liken it to missing pages in a book. We learn what ones are missing and go about replacing those missing pages. It isn't impossible to do. It just needs to be done.

Reflection: Being developmentally delayed can be an indicator that we have shame in our cores.

Day 76

Shame Originator

Many of us learned to survive our addictive, shaming society by becoming "the rebel." We act out and appear to not need anything from anyone else. However, we often are trapped in the roles of rebels. We are the perfect "rebel." And just like anything driven by perfectionism, we are trapped in shame while looking like we aren't. This can be the same for any role we may be in. However, seeing the shame may be more elusive for the person in the role of "rebel."

When we are trapped in roles or behaviors, we are playing out a pre-determined image, rather than looking at our underlying feelings and needs. We may have had no part in determining the role. Many roles are determined by the family system as opposed to the individuals in the system. We fill a spot needed by the system. A rebel often fills the need of "scapegoat." The family can then focus on this person as the "problem" and not look at the underlying dysfunction in the system.

If we find ourselves with the label of rebel, and we can't "not be" in that behavior, chances are we were filling a spot needed by the family system, and we got stuck in the spot. This is how shame can get locked in.

We aren't seen for who we really are, but we are seen in the "role" we were given. We get lost in the role.

Reflection: If we have always been the "rebel," we may be locked in a role defined by a shame-based system and not know who we really are.

Day 77
Tool

We can have fun with this tool. We can utilize our creativity in a really fun and healing way.

Shame can feel all pervasive and omnipotent. Once we are in shame, it can feel extremely difficult to come out of it again. One way to take power back from shame is to create a character that represents our shame and then dress is up.

One of my shame characters is named: Olivia the Octopus. When shame hits me I feel like I can't get away. I feel sucked dry of all my energy. If I slide out of one shame crisis, another once can grab me. I feel like I am in the arms of an octopus. So now, if I feel shame, I can call it "Olivia." By naming it, I can take some of my power back.

After naming our shame-character we can draw them. We can make them into a cartoon character. We can dress them up and make them look goofy. If we aren't an artist, we can cut out pictures, or write a silly song, create a dance, or build a characterization of our shame figures. This helps us get our power back.

After we have done this, we can use this representation whenever we notice shame. It helps us feel less overwhelmed and gives us a tool to help us take our power back. We can call the character to mind when shame comes up. We still get to look at the feelings and needs underneath, and it is not as hard to do when we have the representation we created.

Reflection: Although healing shame can be serious work, we can have fun with some of the healing processes. This is one of them.

Day 78
One Thing Different

Part of what makes me so good at helping others heal from shame is the fact that I have had so much shame and have worked very hard to bring it into healing. This story is an example of the "pay-off" for the hard work.

For as long as I can remember, I had wanted to be an actress in a play. For many reasons, I had not fulfilled that desire. Some of the reasons had to do with shame and some had to do with practical reasons like not being able to get to rehearsals because of work. In any case, I finally had the time to get to rehearsals and decided to audition for a play.

I got a part in the play. It was a fairly big part. I was so excited. I had so much to learn! I was so far from perfect that I had to laugh. I knew Hollywood would not be knocking down my door and I knew I could do it. I didn't have to be perfect. I just had to show up, work, and do the best I could.

My shame wanted to get in there and keep me from "making a fool of myself." It wanted me to come up with a plausible excuse to quit. My shame warned me that I was way out of my league and too old to try something like this. On a night after a particularly tough rehearsal, shame got really insistent. My shame kept at me and I kept at the play.

I had NEVER been so happy to have done my shame-work, as when I performed in those plays. I had a cheesy smile on my face for days. I loved it. I had fun. I showed up and was there for others and knew my lines. I did it!

My reward for my shame work was my ability to have fun doing something previously unimaginable had I not done the shame work.

If we have a dream or goal, such as acting was for me, we use achieving that goal as an aim for our healing. We can get there. I know for me, I will never go back to the way I was when shame led the way! I am free from the demands of the perfectionist tyrant. My life is so much more spontaneous and enjoyable now.

Reflection: Healing shame means we get to have fun doing things we have always wanted to do.

Day 79

One Thing Different

Healing shame is a lifelong process. It can feel absolutely overwhelming. What we can do is focus on one thing we would like to do differently if our shame were not getting in the way. We focus on it for a day. We may focus on the same thing for a day or for months on end. However, focusing on one thing at a time helps us move forward.

For example, we may decide that we set self and someone else up when we have "expectations." We may have looked at how covertly destructive this is. We expect others to do certain things, and when they don't, we find fault with the other person even though we may never say it out loud. We begin to sabotage the relationship internally. We may determine the other person is "less than" in some way. Since 80-90 percent of communication is non-verbal, we are most likely sending the other person a shaming message without ever saying a word. (I attempt to pick examples that are fairly universal. My intent is not to send a shame message if we are setting expectations, but to use this as an example that many can relate to.)

We may decide that the "one thing" we are going to focus on is releasing our expectations of others. We may do this for "today." We may keep track of how often we do it. We may write our thoughts on paper. We may say "out loud" to the other person what our stories or expectations are. We may just keep score of how many times we do it. However, for that day we are focusing on one thing so that we can change it. We are changing our behavior of sending shame messages to others.

Once we notice we have set an expectation, we can then turn in a different direction. We can turn toward truth. What is the truth? Everyone has the right to live with dignity and respect and without criticism or judgment from others. So we notice our expectations and move forward into truth. One thing at a time for one day at a time can move us in a direction away from shame.

Reflection: We can focus on one change at a time and feel successful.

Day 80
Tool

It can seem like our inner guide is nothing but shame. We have talked about creating a figure to represent shame. Now we get to create a representation of "truth," or wisdom. In truth, "we all have inner wisdom."

Our inner wisdom is very different than our inner shame. It is very peaceful and quiet, as opposed to the loud and nasty voice of shame. It only empowers and it never attacks us or anyone else.

It can help to create a figure that represents this inner wisdom, find a figure that represents it, or imagine what that wisdom looks like. On January 8, I shared how I became aware of Maude, my inner wisdom. I also have several pottery figures that represent divine wisdom. They help me connect with the wisdom that I know is within me and within everyone.

Some of us have a connection with a figure from a major religion already in place. We can imagine going to that figure and seeking wisdom from that source. Some of us find that wisdom in an animal figure, in nature, or in some other aspect of our lives. We can also go out in the world, or into meditation and seek what that wisdom would be for us. I have known people who sought something they could turn to that represents wisdom and came back with a stuffed animal. It does not matter what that representation is. What matters is that it helps us keep calm and hear the wisdom within.

> *Reflection: Learning to "be still and listen" to our inner wisdom, to turn in the direction of peace, is a powerful tool in healing shame. It can lead us in a very different direction than shame would. Peace and wisdom is in each of us.*

Day 81
Poem

It is quite simple

Really

Yet I seem to want to make it so hard

Choose peace or war

Each moment

Every moment

Turn to the Peacemaker and ask

Show me how to love

Show me how to bless

In this you choose Peace

It is that simple

Barb Tonn

Day 82
Voice of Shame

I make a very bold statement in regards to shame. The statement is this: SHAME IS NEVER TRUE. Our behavior can be very mean and unkind, and that is about our behavior. Shame is about the essence of ourselves and despite how bad our behavior can be; the essence of self is love. It never changes. We may not be showing that love to the world. We may not know how, and our essence does not change.

Some choices I make may have dire consequences, but they do not make me bad or unlovable.

Healing shame means we align with a thought system that is completely opposite from what most people believe. Most people think there are times shame is true, or is needed, or will keep us in line. Shame does **nothing** productive or useful. It tries to make us believe that we are what we are not.

Some of the most brutal and harmful people have gone into healing and have been able to find the "loveable" truth about themselves and others. They have felt remorse for their behavior and been able to experience forgiveness and peace.

Some people who have had profoundly hurtful things done to them have felt hatred. Still, they have been able to find forgiveness and peace. They looked underneath the hated behavior and recognized the essence of love that truly defined the person. In that recognition, peace and forgiveness became possible.

We encourage people to speak to children about their behavior and not who they are. To say, "you are a bad boy" is damaging. To say, "I don't like that behavior and I need that to change" is not damaging. Shame always damages.

> *Reflection: Shame is never true. It damages. It hides the truth of the inner love in each and every one of us. There are no exceptions. We need to be careful and not confuse the essence of ourselves with behavior.*

Day 83
One Thing Different

LIVING IN THE POWER OF WHO WE ARE

The lovely part of healing our shame is learning to live in the strength and power of who we truly are. When shame leads the way, we live in the shadow land of "should" and other peoples' templates of what is right for us. As we continue to shed shame, we become more and more aware of our own personal truths. We begin to see what we feel and need and want and dream. As that "truth" leads the way we become more and more personally empowered to live out those truths.

One of the things that happens when we are little, is that shame becomes very established in our beings and we stop dreaming. We don't think we are worthy of the dreams we have conjured up. We get told that we aren't smart enough or good enough or worthy of these dreams. So, we let them go. We lose a part of ourselves when we don't dream.

My challenge for us is to take a long, meandering walk in a safe place where we don't have to be really aware of our surroundings, and let our minds drift. We can ask ourselves: "If I could do or be anything I wanted, what would that be?"

Jana Stanfield wrote and performs a song: "If I Were Brave." You can go to YouTube or Google to find the song. Listen to the words and dream about what you would do if you were brave.

Reflection: We get to dream.

Day 84
Red Flag

A red flag that we are in shame is when we are cycling in a self-destructive behavior or thought patterns. It means we are looping in #4 in the shame loop. (See Appendix.)

What is a self-destructive behavior? Let me make a list of some. My hope is that this list will increase awareness of what a destructive behavior is.

- Suicidal thoughts or pre-occupation
- Addictive behavior
- Inner critic that won't stop judging
- Rage at ourselves or others
- Being unable to make a mistake and forgive ourselves for it
- Being unable to start something we want to do because we know we won't be good at it
- Inability to let something from the past go
- Living in fear that prevents us from moving forward
- Setting standards for self that we are unable to meet and then beating ourselves up for not meeting them
- Stuck in compulsive behaviors
- Unable to interact in the world
- Isolation due to fear

This list is certainly not all-inclusive and it can get us thinking of our self-destructive behavior, and thoughts, as an indicator of shame. We can't intervene on shame if we don't call it shame in the first place.

Most of us have certain self-destructive thoughts and behaviors that we default to. We can begin to reframe those behaviors and thoughts as shame.

Reflection: When we are in a destructive loop, we are in shame.

Day 85
Voice of Shame

When we live in shame, we keep trying to "prove ourselves." We can do this in relationships, at work, to strangers, to friends. We live in a state of alertness. We can't seem to relax and just let ourselves be.

When I would begin seeing clients, I would give them an intake form with a list of possible problem areas. One of the areas was: "difficulty relaxing." That was underlined in almost every client I saw, despite what the presenting issue was. I believe this is because most of us carry shame and are vigilant in trying to keep it at bay.

Difficulty relaxing can come from always trying to "prove ourselves," or to be "good enough" at something or in certain situations. It keeps us very busy. We often work ourselves to the point of exhaustion and don't know how to stop. "Addicted to busyness" is something that Anne Wilson Schaef talks about in her addiction books. Workaholism is common and is endorsed in our culture. We can cancel or change plans because we have to work and it is acceptable. Yet, it can be as destructive as alcoholism.

The constant work often comes from shame and having to prove ourselves. When we are in shame we can't ever do it quite good enough, so we keep working harder. This loop can go on endlessly and in many areas of our lives at the same time.

What if we just got to be "good enough" as we are? What if we could learn to just "be"? That is what healing shame is about. We learn to get out of the never-ending loop of proving ourselves and learn how to embrace and encourage ourselves in loving and life enhancing ways.

Reflection: In truth, we are "good enough."

Day 86

Tool

We have a hard time stepping out of shame if we don't know we are in it. One of the ways we know shame is active is if we are "stuck." Shame gets going in our head and we lock down into self-defeating thoughts or behaviors. It is like a sticky web is over us and we just can't seem to move in any direction at all. We often can "know" a direction that would be helpful, but just can't seem to move there.

If we are stuck, we can see what our shame might be telling us about whatever it is we are attempting to figure out. For example: What if we can't decide if we want to get together with someone? We can't seem to make a decision. We are stuck in indecision. We can write out our thoughts to see what our shame is telling us.

- If I get together with this person my shame is telling me....
- If I don't get together with this person my shame is telling me...

- If I don't decide what to do my shame is telling me...

Then we can respond to the shame and look at all of our choices.

It doesn't pay to argue with shame. We can just look at it and hear what it is telling us and then look in the direction of what choice and compassion might tell us. That may look like this:

- If shame were not leading the way and telling me _____, my choices would be. (We can list them. We always need to come up with at least three so we don't get trapped in a shame-bind.)

We can claim a truth, whether we believe it or not. It helps movement begin again. The truth may sound like this: I am a good person and I will be a good person no matter what my choice at this time. I have the right to decide what I want to do with my time, no matter how others respond.

Reflection: Writing out what our shame is telling us when we are stuck can help greatly when looking at our choices. It helps us release from our shame.

Day 87
Shame Indicator

Shame can enter in many situations where we feel different from others. We can spend large amounts of time trying to decide how to "fit in" when we go to different events, or out in public. We do this to attempt to keep shame away. We don't want to look or act different. We can be very self-conscious. We might feel like all eyes are on us.

The hard truth is that we can't really keep the shame away by changing how we look. We can't make the self-conscious shame go away by being vigilant against it and changing our outside. Changing is an inside job.

Instead of looking outside of ourselves to determine what is correct in a particular situation, we begin to look at how we want to be. I remember a time when I was in high school. I wanted to look very cute and cool when I went to an outdoor football game. I lived in Minnesota and it was bitter cold. I wore what I thought would be attractive to others, and I froze.

I was so concerned with how others saw me that I hurt myself. I know teenagers are the epitome of self-consciousness, and I wish I could say it stopped when I grew up, but it didn't. My shame persisted in my looking more at what I thought would be acceptable, than in looking at what fit for me.

We can begin to look at what our own personal limits are. We can look at our boundaries to determine our choices. What is acceptable and what isn't? We may end up making choices we know will perhaps set us off from others, but they fit for us. We get more comfortable with ourselves and less self-conscious.

Now, when I go into an unfamiliar situation, or enter a situation where I do not really know what the "norm" is, I ask myself: "What works for me and my health and my budget and my style?" I realize what others think of me is not at the top of my list. This revelation is so freeing and helpful in realizing the progress I have made in healing my shame.

Reflection We can notice our self-consciousness and still make choices that fit for us.

Day 88
One Thing Different

BE VIGILANT FOR LOVE

Shame is vigilant for what is wrong with us. It looks for what is wrong with others. It is a constant negative. We find what we are looking for. If I am looking for what I don't like, I will find it.

I have mentioned that in our shame-based world we have everything backwards. Looking for and finding what is wrong is an example of backwards.

What if we were vigilant for Love and Kindness? What if that is all we looked for? What if when we saw someone who was not loving or kind we reframed it. We can reframe by saying: People are either extending love or asking for love. If they are asking for love we can respond with kindness.

Being vigilant for love completely reverses how we live in the world. We can set this as our intention each day. We can look behind the eyes of the people who are acting nasty and know they are asking for love. We can then respond with love. Most of us respond to nasty with nasty and feel somehow justified. What if we changed that?

We can't live in a shame-free world and keep our old habits. We must look at doing things in a very different way than we have. This is one of those ways. We look for love. We become love-finders. We seek only love. We look right past anything not loving and find the "call for love" underneath.

Reflection: We find what we look for.

Day 89
Voice of Shame

Shame is the inner voice that tries to convince us that we need to change things about ourselves in order to be worthy of love or respect or support. Part of the healing of shame is learning truly to love ourselves as we are. We will always be growing and changing and healing and becoming more and more the light and love that is our truth. However, we get to be enough in this moment. This is a great part of our work.

I GET TO BE ENOUGH JUST AS I AM. I get to live and not look back with regret because I made the choices I made when I made them. Each moment of my life, I have been enough. I do not need regrets. Some of my choices have caused me pain and some of them have had rough consequences. However, even if they were mistakes, that doesn't make me a mistake. I AM and always have been enough. This life is a classroom and I get to have "learning" be my purpose.

My husband is absolutely amazing with tools. He can build and fix almost anything. One of his favorite sayings is: "tools are our friends." That is very much the same in healing shame.

We can look at healing shame as a project and have a bag of tools to pick from to help us transform shame. The tools in this book can help us change an internal shame message into the voice of love. As we go through this book, we can learn to utilize different tools in different situations. We will have some tools we love and use regularly and some we take out occasionally. Our tool chest becomes our friend.

Reflection: Today I will pick a tool and use it.

Day 90
Shame Originator

Shame is often held in place with unresolved pain. Often unresolved pain is held in place with unresolved trauma. This pain or trauma is often not in our conscious awareness. However, many of us have a sense that we carry unresolved issues and are fearful to even approach the issues. Yet, the fear is bigger than what we experience if we bring the trauma into healing. It can feel like we will be "blown into tiny pieces," if we go into our pain. That is not the truth.

We cannot heal our shame/pain/trauma by staying unconscious. We can trust our inner wisdom to know when we are strong enough or ready to know what is buried under the surface. We can stay open to process and healing by being willing to allow our trauma to surface when it is time. We can claim the following: "I trust I will know what I need to know when I am ready to know it." That way we can begin to trust our healing process and inner wisdom to take us where we need to go to bring what is unconscious into consciousness.

We get to live in this willingness to build our support systems, develop relationships with people we can trust to be there for us, and utilize the tools we are learning in our healing. Then, if there is trauma, we will have the available resources to heal the trauma.

Many of us have such fear of what we will find buried beneath the surface that we shut down our willingness to be open to processing things. We can trust our deep wisdom to know when the time is right for anything that might be buried to rise to the surface.

Reflection: We are building the resources to heal our shame at all levels. We get to trust our process. We get to find a therapist to help us resolve our trauma.

Days 91-120

Day 91
Tool

If we are interacting with someone else and notice our shame has been triggered, it can be extremely helpful to acknowledge it, out loud, with that person. That would not be indicated if we were with a stranger or someone who would not understand what we were talking about.

Often, when working with couples in counseling, they have made agreements that they will inform the partner as soon as they notice shame has been triggered. If we are in conflict and our rage is coming up, whether covert in our thoughts or overt in our behavior, we can say, "my shame has been triggered." This lets the other person know that we are starting to spiral in shame. We often are disconnected from our feelings and in a defensive posture. We can also say, "I am feeling very defended right now." Either of these statements alerts the other person that to proceed in the current conversation would most likely be counter-indicated.

If we can inform the other person and take a "time out" to see what got triggered, we can then go back to the other person with important information. In relationships, we can learn so much about the other person and ourselves by taking this time to intervene on the shame loop.

We can make agreements with our intimate friends and partners that we will let them know if our shame is triggered, and take a time out. If each person will honor the time out, we can learn how to be more compassionate with each other as we heal our shame.

Reflection: Informing others that we are in shame and taking the responsibility to take a time out to see what our shame is telling us can bring us closer to each other.

Day 92
Multidimensional

Healing core shame is a multi-dimensional process. Shame is not just a feeling or a cognitive belief. It hits us on all levels of our being. We work on all these levels as we bring our shame into healing. The levels we work on are:

- Emotional—Under the shame are the emotions that we have not let ourselves have or have not felt. We are retrieving old buried feelings and learning how to identify and feel our feelings in the here and now.

- Spiritual—In shame we often feel disconnected, separate from others, observers, and not participants in the world. The spiritual journey is about finding our way into feeling "a part of." We find kindred spirits, values we share with others, and find a way to know we belong.

- Physical—Shame lives in the cells of our bodies. It impacts us physically. When we go into shame, our hands and feet will get hot or cold. We have a hard time making eye contact. Often trauma is locked in the body and when it is unresolved, we experience trauma in our bodies. We work with body techniques to release the trauma trapped in our cells.

- Relationship—Our relationships are areas that are deeply impacted by shame. We often struggle with intimacy, have a rough track record in our relationships with significant others, and are in roles (caretaker, rebel, scapegoat, etc.) that can hurt us. As we do our shame-work, we often need to do a lot to actively repair our old relationships, and learn healthier relationships skills.

- Intellectual—Here is where we do the cognitive work we need to do to heal our belief systems about ourselves and the world. We learn what shame has been telling us and work on changing our belief systems.

- Will—In shame we have no will. We are out of control. As we heal, we begin to put intent back into our lives and follow through.

Reflection: Our work when healing shame is multi-dimensional.

Day 93
Tool

I have talked individually about the importance of learning our rights, looking at our choices, and learning what our boundaries are. Often, we work with all three of these areas at the same time.

One of the most empowering tools we can utilize in our healing is to notice when we are in shame, or when we are going into a situation that often triggers shame.

We then sit down to write our:

- Rights
- Choices
- Boundaries

If we will take the time to do this work, we will often be able to be more compassionate with ourselves and others.

If we know ahead of time that we are about to go into a situation that often triggers our shame (knowing our red-flags helps with this), we can write down our rights in that situation or with these people, look at the minimum of three choices we have or can utilize for self-care, and write our boundaries (what is acceptable or not), before we enter into the situation. We can then go back and make a choice that honors our healing and abilities in this space and time. I used to do this before going into family of origin situations that could be difficult. After I started doing this, I took much better care of myself and also was much kinder to those around me.

It can also be helpful to do this if we are stuck in a painful situation and are not sure how to proceed. If we will take the time to write out our rights, choices, and boundaries, we can often make a choice that will be empowering.

Reflection: To write our rights, choices, and boundaries out and consciously choose is empowering.

Day 94
Shame Indicator

An indicator that we are in shame is when we are looking outside of ourselves for other peoples' reactions to us. We are giving our power to others to tell us how we are looking or how we are being perceived. If people seem pleased with us, we feel good. If they seem unhappy with us, we feel badly about self.

We often feel like we "should" be looking or behaving a certain way. When a "should" is involved we can be fairly certain that shame is involved.

This is another form of "external referencing" or "impression management." We are not comfortable defining our own truths and instead, we look to others to define it for us.

If we can catch ourselves externally referencing (looking to others to define our truth), we can stop, name the shame, and define what "our truth" would be if we were comfortable with "our truth." Sometimes we can look at our truth and still go forward in a way we think others will approve of. It is a many-staged process to notice when the "should" is engaged, to stop and look at our truth, and to risk stepping into this "different" way of expressing ourselves. We may not be able to examine our truth and change our behavior all at once. Knowing that change is slow, we can be gentle with ourselves in this process.

We get to be compassionate with ourselves as we learn to live more and more in the truth of whom we are. We may not be able to do this all at once.

Reflection: We can notice when we are looking to others to define us. It is a step in the direction of healing.

Day 95
Rule

As a therapist, I have learned how to ask the hard questions. I help people look at what is really going on in their lives, as opposed to just talking about the superficial. In our shame-based culture where the "no talk" rule is dominant, people often struggle with talking about the obvious and important issues others are dealing with.

I was with a group of my mother's friends once. One of the women had lost her husband within the last year. I was aware of how sad she looked. I said to her, "how are you doing since _____'s death?" The whole table of women grew quiet. I obviously had asked a question that "rocked the boat" of the status quo. The woman I asked started to cry and shared how lonely she had been and how hard it was. The women at the table responded with kindness and compassion. It was clear she wanted to share and could share with her friends. It was just that nobody had dared ask the obvious question that gave her the opportunity to share.

We don't need to be in therapy to share with our friends and loved ones. We do need to have the courage to talk about the obvious, to rock the boat, and share at a deep level. It allows compassion and kindness.

> *Reflection: We get to risk asking hard questions and sharing hard feelings when we care and are not letting shame interfere. If people aren't in a space to share we can give them the respect of letting them be in quiet until they are ready.*

Day 96
Tool

I lived in Minnesota for a long time. Years ago, while in Minnesota, I saw a T-shirt that said: "Don't Should On Me." I loved it. I was working with shame at the time. I realized how important it is when healing shame to not use the word "should or shouldn't" on self or other. I also realized that it is used a lot.

What is the big deal about the word, "should?" It is a word that delivers shame with it. If I "should" do something and don't, that means I am bad or stupid or inadequate in some way. If I "shouldn't" do something and do it then it means there is something wrong with me if I do it.

We use shame on each other or on ourselves when we are trying to control. What could we do instead? We could notice and take the word "should" out. Then we could put the word "could" in. It takes the shame out and puts choice in. When we are in choice, we are moving out of shame and in a world of respect for the choices we all have the right to make.

My challenge is for each of us to notice how often we use and hear the word "should." We then get to notice how we feel when we hear that "should." We may feel fine if we are in agreement, but if we aren't, we will most likely feel bad or defensive in some way. After we notice, we can put the word "could" in and see how that feels.

> *Reflection: "Should" is a word from the shame dictionary. I would love to see it removed from our vocabulary and replaced with "could."*

Day 97
Tool

When we are healing shame, we are encouraged to share in safe places.

When we have either shame-core issues, or have shame-triggers, we can bet that in our past there was some place in our interpersonal relationships where we felt shamed and/or betrayed. We live in a shame-based world where betrayal, (usually unconscious) happens constantly.

We can accomplish much healing by reading, journaling, meditating, prayer, and other solitary activities. However, because much of shame happens interpersonally, it also needs healing interpersonally. It is the sharing of our shame with another person that is the most important and the hardest. We are extremely vulnerable when we share with another. However, when we share our shame with others, and are seen with eyes of love, compassion, and acceptance, amazing healing happens. This type of healing can happen in therapy, both individual and group, as well as with a friend, a member of the clergy, a sponsor, and in healthy relationships where there is trust.

We can ask someone to listen to us by asking for what we need. We can ask that they listen with:

- Non-judgment
- No-advice-giving
- No "fix-it" ideas
- No interruptions
- Absolute attention to what we are sharing.

We can share that we are healing from shame. To tell someone what we are doing and ask for what we need is the ultimate of "self-care." It sets the stage for the part of ourselves that feels so defective and raw and feels certain of rejection where we experience the opposite of shame.

If we can think back to a time in our lives where we shared something in a way that we felt very vulnerable, and we were heard and seen with loving eyes, then we most likely experienced a deep connection with that person. It most likely felt healing and peaceful. This is what safe sharing creates.

> *Reflection: Safety is what helps us know healing and peace. It allows the part of us that feels so alienated from others to begin to feel a "part of" and "connected to." It feels like a miracle of love the moment we are "witnessed" as worthy, enough, and lovable. We deserve this. We get to claim it.*

Day 98
One Thing Different

Shame reminds us of our perceived flaws and deficiencies. It puts the focus on what we think is wrong with ourselves. What if the one thing different we did each day was focus on our strengths? What if we put as much effort into finding our strengths as we do in focusing on our problem areas?

As we move more and more into our healing, we begin to see how we have gotten it all backwards. We see that we can do things differently and have more peace in our lives. Instead of focusing on our flaws, we put focused intention in learning our strengths. There is a lovely website where we can take a free inventory of our strengths. The site is:

www.authentichappiness.sas.upenn.edu

This is a positive psychology website where many free inventories are offered. To do the "signature strengths" inventory can help us begin to look at parts of self we maybe never thought of as strengths.

We get to utilize these strengths in our healing journeys. We get to add to them and use them as we make decisions in our lives. It is a different way to look at our lives, and helps us navigate our way out of shame and into peace and healing.

Shame does not want us to see our strengths, so don't be surprised if a part of ourselves gets defensive and negative and can't find our strengths We get to keep looking for what makes us a wonderful human being who has the gifts and strengths to get out of shame and into life.

Reflection: We all have strengths.

Day 99
Red Flag

Many of us have people in our lives we cannot forgive. Many family systems have stories of people that have been written off as unforgivable. Often we have stories we tell that can get us as upset as they did decades ago. When we are stuck in pain and anger and are unable to forgive, we often find a situation or memory that is held in a shame-bind. We can't forget it and we can't forgive it.

We may not have thought of the situation for years, or we may think we have put it behind us. But when we start talking about it, there is still pain attached and we remember it in clear detail. This is what happens when a memory is locked in shame.

If we are actively healing our shame and we find one of these memories in our history or our family history we can name the shame that holds the pain in place and set the intention to release the buried feelings and move into forgiveness.

To release and forgive can be fear-filled because we often have used the memory of pain to rationalize continued anger and protect ourselves. To forgive can feel like we are vulnerable with someone who hurt us deeply. In truth, the continued anger and pain are hurting our peace, not the other person. We get to move into healing, and still keep our boundaries of not choosing to be around someone.

Shame keeps our memories in pain. We can set intent to heal and find peace. The memory laced with pain may be a red flag that we are caught in a shame loop, even if it is decades old.

Reflection: Red flags help us see where healing is still needed.

Day 100

Specific Shame-Based Issue

All shame is sad to me. It is such an integral part of our culture and so very destructive. The shame I am writing about now is the shame many people carry if we need psychiatric medication. If someone needs to use medication for depression or bipolar or anxiety, or sleep, they often feel deep shame. That shame can keep those of us who truly need a certain medication from taking the medication, and gaining back our quality of life.

Many of us who do not understand brain chemistry or chemical imbalance can spout opinions about "people just needing to get it together," or "pull themselves up by the boot straps," or "just needing to eat differently or take herbs, etc." There are times diet and herbs can be useful, and there are times medication is very important.

In truth, there are many of us who have our lives back and suffer less, while benefiting from the correct medication prescribed by a doctor. There is no shame in needing medication.

If someone has suffered, is not getting better, and is encouraged by a doctor to go on a medication, I hope we can give them support and love. I hope the person who needs the medication can set a boundary by looking those in opposition in the eye and saying, "I believe you do not truly understand when medication is useful. I hope you will release your judgment and support me in my choice."

Reflection: There is no shame in needing medication. It can be a wise and useful choice. It may give healing to brain functioning in a way nothing else can.

(If I can give one bit of advice here it would be: If we need help for a psychiatric diagnosis we can go to someone who specializes in mental health issues and psychiatric medications. This gives us the best chance of getting the most appropriate help.)

Day 101

Shame Indicator

We can be certain if we are involved in a self-destructive behavior that we are in shame. This can be a bit tricky, because the defensive strategy of denial can keep us from acknowledging that certain behavior is destructive. That coupled with rationalizing can keep us from seeing the shame that is driving the behavior.

This can be the arena of addictions.

Another tricky way we can keep from looking at shame is when we take a behavior that can be healthy or good for us, and carry it to such an extreme it becomes destructive. Examples of extreme behavior can be:

1. cleaning
2. physically working out
3. computer games
4. diets

If we look at what is driving the extreme behavior, we often find ourselves being driven by shame, such as, trying to prove we are good enough, impression management, feeling less than and trying to compensate, and using behavior to keep our real feelings and needs out of our awareness.

I grew up in a culture that worshipped the "God of thin." I had profound shame about my body and had no perspective on healthy body image and weight. I did not know a way to accept my body. I was preoccupied with "body image" and I was absolutely driven by shame. I never felt good enough or thin enough. The self-destructive behaviors and thoughts that I was involved in were over- exercising and obsessing about how my body looked. I took something healthy, like exercise, and used it in a destructive way. It was never enough. I never felt like I was enough.

In truth, under the denial and rationalizing we "do" know when we are out of control and engaged in destructive behaviors and thoughts. We "become willing" to be honest with ourselves when our thoughts and behaviors become destructive. We then look at the shame that is driving the destructive thoughts and behaviors and bring that shame into healing.

Reflection: Having self-destructive thoughts and behaviors indicates we are in a shame loop.

Day 102

Maude

Barb (B)—Maude, where does this shame come from? How can I be doing well, going through my day, and then feel like crap? Why does this happen?

Maude (M)—You know, Barb, we seldom get answers to "why" questions. We live on a really goofy, often very violent planet. Shame is what drives this violent dysfunction, this violence against ourselves and others. So, there isn't always an "obvious reason" for the sudden crappy feeling or for the violence. Shame is in the air we breathe. What is most important is to be alert to the shame that is under the crappy feeling and the violent impulses.

B—Does that mean we don't have to come from a crazy or addicted family to have shame?

> M—No, we don't. It is a crazy world. The more we know this and don't personalize anything, the more we can begin to "be" the love that we are.

B—I always like to figure things out.

> M—I know and it won't help. When we become more and more in tune with the love we are, the less we will find the need to "figure things out." We notice when the shame hits. We know because we feel like crap or want someone else to feel like crap. Those are indicators that we are in the murky waters of shame. We then send out a big prayer to whatever we pray to, for HELP.

B—It seems like so much of what I have learned is the opposite of what really helps.

> M—Yes, and so we need to unlearn what hasn't worked, and what hasn't brought us peace, before we relearn what does. We unlearn the need to figure it all out and we relearn the need to ask for help. We unlearn the need to know why and just notice. We notice when our thoughts or actions toward ourselves or others are mean and nasty and realize the "shame bug" hit us. Then, we choose again.

B—It seems so hard. In fact, it almost seems impossible.

M—I know how it seems. It is quite simple, but it is not easy. If we stay in our moments, we may notice when we aren't peaceful, and when it may be helpful to send out a call for "HELP."

B—Well, anything is better that feeling like crap.

M—Well, honey, many times we think that, but in truth, we'd rather be "right," or "special," or "look put together," or let "pride" get in the way of noticing and asking for help.

B—I get it. I think I want to have peace of mind rather than all this judgment and anger and hate and shame, but then I just can't seem to get to peace.

M—Yes, and we get to be honest and see that and then we have made a big, huge, gigantic step to peace.

B—Thank you, Maude

M—Any time!

Day 103
Poem

It isn't "me," alone and lost

I have a Love that guides me

Each and every moment

I need not struggle and effort and grunt with pain and exertion

I need only breathe and step back and let Love lead the way

I'll find the words come easily

I'll find I live in Peace

I'll know I am a child of Infinite Grace and Peace

I'll know I am not alone

We are one

We speak love

We live in peace

So Be It

Barb Tonn

Day 104
Right

I HAVE THE RIGHT TO MY OWN OPINION AND TO HAVE MY OPINIONS RESPECTED.

Growing up in a shame-based culture brings with it certain "politically correct" opinions. What our culture or subculture is can determine what those opinions "should" be. The culture can be very rigid about what opinions are acceptable and which ones are not. The subtle or not so subtle pressure to have certain opinions, coupled with outright shaming that comes from having opinions that differ from the "norm" can make it very difficult to believe we have the right to our own opinions.

It is not a matter of right and wrong. It is about being able to feel good about ourselves, for how we believe and think. If our opinion is not respected, we have choices about how we respond to the disrespect. Our opinions represent our beliefs. They are unique to ourselves. Shame does not want us to feel good about ourselves, and that includes our opinions.

Many of us need permission to determine our belief systems. We get to do that. We then get to make conscious choices on whether to share our beliefs and opinions. We get to decide whom we hang out with. If we are not respected, we get to decide what to do.

Reflection: We get to have our opinions and we get to be with people who respect them. We have choices.

Day 105
One Thing Different

I read an article once about a couple that had been robbed. Their business had been broken into and they lost virtually everything. What happened after that was puzzling. They found that nobody wanted to hear about what happened or to talk about it. They ran into "stony silence." I was curious about this. What I have come to know is that: when bad things happen to someone it sets off a fear in others that it will happen to them. We think that if we don't listen or acknowledge, or talk about it, we can maybe keep it from happening to us. Because of the fear of others, the people who need support experience feeling "shunned" instead of feeling supported.

Shunning can be experienced as very shaming and painful. The inability to be heard or seen can be very shaming. "Bearing witness" to each other can alleviate shame or circumvent it. In truth, bad things happening to others, does not make us a magnet for bad things to happen to us. If we are avoiding talking to someone because something bad happened to him or her, we get to notice and choose a more loving response. We get to look at how we might feel in their shoes and what we might need. We get to break the "no talk" rule.

Many of our responses that come naturally, reinforce shame. Our culture often does not know how to respond in a kind way to others. If we can't "fix" their problem we often feel powerless and this feeds shame. If we can't "fix" it we can still listen and respond with care.

When I was first a therapist, I thought I had to have a way to "fix" all pain. What I learned was that the greatest healing came from "listening," and "bearing witness" to the pain of others.

> *Reflection: Many times, our responses are shaming. It is another part of how our culture is a big pot of "shame stew." We get to listen, even when we can't do anything else.*

Day 106
Healing Action

Shame would try to convince us that we are different from everyone. In fact, it would strive to make us different and unique and unable to see the sameness in our hearts.

Shame lies.

Although in form we all look very different from each other, in content we are all the same. In our hearts, whether we acknowledge it or not, we all want peace. We all want to live in peace and harmony.

Shame does not want us to see that in each other.

One of the important facets of healing shame is extending peace. When we attack and judge, we are extending the opposite of peace. If we are thinking attacking and judgmental thoughts we get to choose again. We can decide if we would rather create peace or war. It is our choice to make. In fact, we make this choice each moment of each day.

A question we get to ask is: is this thought or behavior bringing peace? If not, we get to choose again. We can turn in the direction of peace each time we have chosen differently from peace. We can choose peace. If we don't know what that would look like, or how to stop the not peaceful thoughts, we turn in the direction of love and ask for help. It isn't easy, but it is quite simple. Shame would have us believe otherwise. Shame has nothing to do with truth or peace.

Reflection: We can choose peace in each moment.

Day 107
Tool

When we feel like we are a bad, unlovable, unworthy person, it is hard to take care of ourselves. Deep down we don't believe we are worth "self-care."

One of the hardest questions we can ask ourselves is: "what do I "need" right now?" Shame has not allowed us to really look at our needs. We can often feel shame about having needs. When we grow up in an environment where our needs are not acknowledged, we often develop beliefs that our needs are too much, not important, or bad and wrong. So, looking at our needs can trigger a shame loop.

In order to take care of self and heal shame, it is imperative that we begin to identify our needs and take care of them. Often a useful first step in this process is to do some writing about our beliefs about needs and people who need. It is common when shame is the leading voice in our head to have a fear of appearing "needy." Because of this we shut down our needs.

The second step can be doing some writing on this question: If my needs are okay, what might I need right now? It begins to open us up to needs without shame being attached.

When we first are working with our needs, it can be helpful to do this writing without getting caught up in the confusion of how to meet these needs. Getting comfortable with having "needs" sets the groundwork for learning how to meet them.

Reflection: Having needs and learning how to take care of them, is part of our healing.

Day 108
Tool

As I mentioned previously, shame is experienced in the body. There are physical responses to shame. Trauma is held in the body.

One day, I was experiencing shame. As I sat there noticing shame, I decided to go into it and see where it was in my body. I closed my eyes and let myself be led to where it was. At that time, it was in my arms. I felt like I couldn't reach out or touch. As I sat with that feeling, I felt drawn to writing about it. I did "Flow of Consciousness Writing" on what I was experiencing. "Flow of Consciousness Writing" is where we grab a pile of paper and a pencil and write without stopping. It takes us deeper into our psyche than stop and go writing does.

I wrote three pages. I let myself write about what my shame was telling me, what it felt like, and whatever came up about what my experience was at the time. At the end, I let myself claim a truth since shame is never telling the truth. As I completed the process, I noticed that I was no longer experiencing shame in my body or in my thoughts. I had moved through that level of shame.

We can all challenge ourselves to do this process when we are aware of experiencing shame. It is so easy to let shame take over and just fall into it. This process is a way to move shame through and feel empowered at the end.

I noticed that in shame I had a hard time reaching out for support. After the writing process, my arms were no longer heavy and I could reach out.

> *Reflection: Our body can lead us into and out of our shame if we pay attention. "Flow of Consciousness Writing" can help us when shame is in our body.*

Day 109

Tool

I have noticed that when I expose my shame to another, I feel very vulnerable. I am showing my underbelly. I am letting someone else know when I feel stupid or less than or unworthy. At that time, I am risking being misunderstood, and if that happens, I may re-experience my original shame. It helps to really have the awareness or our vulnerability when we share our shame. It helps us pick carefully whom we will share our shame with.

Early in my work as a therapist, I did not let people know when they shared their shame, mistakes, and history with me, that they may feel very vulnerable. So, I learned that people, after they shared, did not always know how to come back and see me again. I would have people come in and see me and share deeply. At times, they would do that before they knew me very well and before they had a trusting relationship with me. I would feel very honored they had shared with me and very puzzled when some of them did not come back.

What I learned was that after they had exposed their secrets and shame, they did not know how to come back. They were afraid I would judge them harshly. That is what they were already doing to themselves and so they projected that onto me.

I learned to tell people at the beginning of my work with them that once they started sharing with me in a deep way, they may feel very vulnerable and have a hard time coming back to see me. They may think I was judging them and would not want to work with them. I told them that I would not be judging them, that I would be very honored when they shared and that I would very much want to see them again.

Letting people know they would feel vulnerable was very helpful. I suggest that when we share our shame with people we let them know we are vulnerable and let them know what we need from them as we share. (Sometimes it helps to ask people to not interrupt, or to ask them to not judge, or to just honor that we are not blaming them, but just trying to heal our own shame.)

This is part of why I talk about creating safety around sharing shame and secrets. It is why we pick carefully when we share the stuff where we are really vulnerable.

Reflection: Sharing shame is a vulnerable process.

Day 110

Tool

I know you will hear me rant on about the word "should." I have already suggested releasing it from our vocabulary and consciousness. It just sets up shame. I am expanding and suggesting releasing the words "ought," "must," and "have to."

Why?

These words keep us from owning our power of choice. It is in owning our power of choice that we truly step into our own personal powers and out of shame. Each and every moment we are choosing our realities. We are responsible for the world we see. That does not mean that I am responsible for what others choose to do, but I am responsible for how I respond to them and the world. It is in owning our power to choose that we can begin to experience peace instead of upset. It is hard to really own this because we live in a shame construct in our world, which constantly reinforces the belief that we are the "victims" of the world we see. The way to stay a victim is to not own our choices.

This does not mean we beat ourselves up when we don't own our choices or find ourselves experiencing being a victim. It means we notice, turn in the direction of kindness and love, and look at our choices in responding.

Ask: Would I rather choose to be peaceful or upset?

We "gently" catch ourselves whenever we are using the words, "ought, should, must, and have to." We then change the word to "could" and look at our choices. We consciously choose. We then step into our power.

My hope, for all of us, is that we choose PEACE.

Reflection: We get to change the words "should, ought, must, and have to" to "could." We then step into our power.

Day 111
Tool

On Day 74, I talked about "boundaries." I said to explore them and not worry about setting them. Setting them means we need to learn how to empower ourselves to do things differently. Now, I would like to explore how to set our boundaries.

There are two kinds of boundaries. We can have "internal boundaries." These are decisions we make in our heads and do not necessarily share with others. The others are our "external boundaries." These are boundaries we share with someone as we set them. These are often scarier boundaries because we are risking having our boundaries be rejected by others.

Let me give some examples of internal boundaries:

- I will no longer let my mom upset me.
- I will no longer give _____ the power to make me feel badly about myself.
- I will give myself the choice to leave if I am uncomfortable.

- I will let myself know what my feelings and needs are and not let anyone tell me they are wrong.

These are things we are working toward, that we are conscious of, but we don't necessarily share with others.

Our external boundaries are ones we tell other people as we set them. Examples of external boundaries are:

- I do not want a hug right now.
- I am not comfortable coming over to your house.
- I have a right to choose how I spend my holiday and I want to spend it with friends this year, not with the family.
- I prefer voting in confidence. I do not want to share who I am voting for with you.
- I get to do what I want with my time and I do not need your permission.

Setting external boundaries can be very scary. We sometimes need a friend to support us, or a therapist to help us determine them and the best way to set them. We get to ask for support. We can also utilize the support of our inner guidance and wisdom.

Reflection: Setting boundaries moves us out of shame.

Day 112

Healing Action

An action we take to move out of our shame-based identity is to learn to be a human being with all our imperfections, doing the best we can, with good and bad days.

Shame is driven by perfectionism. Shame demands the impossible. It demands we be perfect according to a standard imposed on us by a belief system from the outer "should." Shame does not allow mistakes, the process of growth and learning, or forgiveness.

We get to consciously seek out our humanness. We get to learn how to be human, make mistakes, and know what "good enough" means. We get to start to do something because we want to, and not because we are good at it. We get to give ourselves the gift of having good and bad moments and days. We get to let ourselves learn what it means to have our own foibles, mistakes, wins, and potential.

When we take perfectionism out of the mix, we can have a lot of fun exploring what helps us feel happy and creative. We get to start and stop things. We get to try new activities and pick up old ones we left behind. We get to dream and move in the direction our inner selves want us to move.

A writing exercise we can utilize is the now familiar Flow of Consciousness Writing driven by the question:

- If I let myself be guided by my inner self, I would...
- If I didn't have to be good at it I would...
- If I could pick up an old dream it would be...

We can come up with our own questions and prompts and follow the writing thread to see where it takes us.

Reflection: Claiming our "humanness" is a gift of healing shame.

Day 113

Shame Indicator

I had someone I know describe shame as "wanting to shrink away." These words really felt true to me. If we find ourselves wanting to hide, shrink away, go to the other side of the street, drop thru the floor, or disappear, we are most likely experiencing shame. There is a sense of having been seen as less than, that compromises our sense of ourselves in some way, that we truly wish had not been witnessed.

In my years as a therapist, I have listened to people share many shame experiences. I can feel the vulnerability. I notice the person on the brink of wanting to run away and hide. I am feeling their shame. It helps to acknowledge the strength shame has, in that it convinces us that we need to hide. It tells us that we have been seen as lacking and might as well break communication with whoever saw us. Often, we attack them before we get attacked.

Shame lies. We think our only recourse is to disappear. We think we have made a fool of ourselves and that there is no coming back. We think we are seen as damaged goods. In truth, even if someone sees us as lacking in some way, or saw us embarrass ourselves, or perceives us as "less than," and responds negatively, it is not about us. We aren't on a stage needing to perform to others' satisfaction or approval. We are, in our lives, doing the best we can and that is good enough. If others shame us, we get to set an internal boundary that we won't let others determine our value or worth. If others judge, it is not about us, it is about them.

We all have moments or experiences we wish we could re-do. We all have things we don't want to bring out in the light of day. We don't have to make it worse by judging ourselves as needing to hide. We get to look each person in the eye, without apology. We get to show up and BE.

Reflection: Wanting to shrink away is a sign shame has entered. What shame tells us is never true.

Day 114
Rule

One of the rules of shame-bound systems is to live in denial. We can deny feelings, needs, dreams, abuse, and addictions. We can also deny how much shame we live with.

"Shame of our shame" is part of how we stay in denial of our shame. We are convinced that if people knew about our shame they would think less of us or go away. We fear rejection. This fear keeps us from sharing in a safe place and experiencing the healing of being seen with eyes of love.

Denial is #2 in the shame loop in the Appendix. It is one of the favorite defenses we turn to as our shame is looping. It insulates us from reality. Denial keeps us from looking at our shame and bringing it into healing. Denial reinforces the shame of our shame.

Denial is a major issue in our culture and in our homes. We can't do something about an issue if we cannot look at it. We get locked in the dysfunction with no way out.

If we know that "denial" is often in place in our shame-bound world, we can begin to explore it. We get to look at what we may be denying. We get to be curious about what shame is telling us that keeps us from bringing it into the light of healing.

The opposite of denial is openness. We can picture opening a door into the dark room of denial and shining a light into the corners to see what lights up. We can also picture opening a door into health and healing and see what is there. We can be open to "what is" and see with the eyes of love and not shame.

Denial compounds the shame that is already present. It locks us in the pain of shame.

Reflection: Healing opens the door of denial and lets us clean out the cobwebs.

Day 115
Tool

I have a simple tool I want to share.

The shame voice is speaking non-stop. Unless we isolate and listen to what the voice is saying, it will be impossible to intervene on it. Pick one of the following three topics and then listen to your inner voice. Write down the first three things your inner voice has to say to you on the topic of your choice from the three listed.

The topics:

* Your looks

* Your intelligence

* Your work

After you have written down the first three things your inner voice has to say, sit back and pay attention to how that voice sounded. Is it derogatory? Does it compare you to others? Does it bring you down? If it does any of those three things, you can be sure it is the voice of shame.

Now comes the hard part. Write down three kind statements about your chosen topic. You get to turn your ear in a different direction and listen to the still small voice of your sweet guardian angel or an inner wise woman/man, your own Higher Power, or love. What does that voice say? You can be sure that this voice will not compare you to another (either favorably or not). It may sound foreign to your ears. It will bring peace and a smile. When we first hear that voice, it is hard to believe and we won't necessarily believe it. However, for our own healing, and in order to honor truth, we get to become willing to turn in the "direction of kindness" and listen.

Now, we get to be still and let this in: SHAME NEVER TELLS THE TRUTH.

Sometimes, when we are looking for the kindness of truth, we need to claim a right. For instance: I have the right to look just like I look. I have the right to respect myself just the way I am. I get to have the intelligence I have and to have that be good enough. I get to be smart in the way that I am smart and have that be perfect for me. My work gets to be what is right for me. I deserve respect.

Those are some examples. We can't force our old beliefs away from ourselves, but we can gently and kindly turn in a different direction and become willing to believe kindness, compassion, and love.

Reflection: We can do this exercise to help us look at shame and what the underlying truth just might be.

Day 116
Tool

I often go to conferences. I also work with energy medicine, which deals with the body as an energetic system. During an energy medicine conference, I attended, I noticed that every presenter was working with color as a healing tool. I am sharing some of the information from that conference in this daily.

One concept I learned is the idea of "running color." We all know that certain colors appeal to us at different times. Some mornings we may pick an outfit solely because it is the color we want to have surround us all day. Many people paint their houses a certain color or pick a car because of a color preference. Color can impact us in many overt and covert ways.

A tool for healing is to notice where in our bodies we are feeling something uncomfortable. They can be emotional or physical sensations. Then, we sit, breathe, and relax and let a color come into our awareness. Notice the discomfort and then fill that area of discomfort with the color. We fill and surround ourselves with that color and pay particular attention to the area of discomfort. This is "running color." After we have done that, we can notice any change that has occurred from the color.

This tool can be used for moving discomfort, pain, negativity, and emotions out of our bodies and minds. We are left with the energy of the color we introduced.

I love this tool for releasing shame and other pain. One of the things I like knowing is that "running color" can't hurt me. It is another useful tool for our tool chest of moving shame out of our system.

Reflection: Color has energy. We can use it in healing.

Day 117
Shame Indicator

In shame-based systems, people do not get to change. We are held in a concrete vice of a certain role. If we make a mistake, we are reminded of it forever. We may have changed into a completely different person and the system will still see us in the same old way.

An example of this would be people who have been horrible alcoholics. They may have been in trouble with the law, or a fighter, or someone who had affairs. They sober up and become law-abiding, faithful partners, who are peaceful and kind. However, the system they are from may never see them in this way. The system does not know how to support change, or forgive.

As part of our healing, we can take the time to look at how we see ourselves and if we have acknowledged our own changes. Maybe we still are seeing ourselves in the same old negative, shameful way. Maybe we are integrating some of the changes we have made.

We can also look at how we have perhaps locked others into certain roles and not let them change. It can easily happen with family of origin roles. Have people changed and we haven't truly acknowledged the change or extended forgiveness?

When we get together with people, what are the stories we repeat? Are they the ones about stupid or embarrassing things they did? If so, we are perpetuating the shame. We don't need to shame ourselves if we do that, but we can notice and change. What would happen if we told the stories of change and healing and the lovely things these people did or do?

In truth, change is possible. If we are on a conscious path of growth, we are most likely changing a lot. We can know that others are doing the same. Sometimes I do not see how much I have changed unless I look back in time at how I would have handled something then as opposed to now. It gives me a lovely perspective on how much my healing work is paying off.

Reflection: We all get to change and it is so helpful to acknowledge the change.

Day 118
Shame in Our World

A particular shame I have noticed is what parents experience when their children struggle. This can be their young children or their adult children. I see the parents feel like "bad parents." They take it on and don't recognize the difference between being "responsible to" our children and being "responsible for" our children.

If our children have a hard time, we can take it on as being all about us. We can beat ourselves up and spin in shame. In that spinning, we are not able to respond in a useful way to what is happening with our children.

This is part of the dynamic in our culture of "blame." We can blame ourselves completely for something or blame another completely. Either way is not grounded in truth. It is one thing to take responsibility for our errors and mistakes as parents. We all make them. We make amends to our children, make commitments to be different, and make amends to ourselves for not being perfect. We then can give our children responsibility for their choices. We can step back and give them the dignity of having their way of being in the world or by acknowledging their personality, which may be very different than ours.

In truth, we have an opportunity to look at when we are feeling shame when our kids are struggling or end up making huge mistakes. We get to look at the "should" the "expectation," the "blame," and "perfectionism." We do this so we can have some peace, let go, and allow our children to learn and grow and take responsibility for their own lives.

When I do workshops on shame, I notice the first group to get triggered into their shame is the parents. The expectations we have of ourselves as parents, and the expectations we have on our kids can be loaded with shame. Parents are human too.

> *Reminder: We can take our "parent shame" out and shine the light of truth on it. We can see our children with the eyes of love and ourselves with the eyes of love.*

Day 119
Voice of Shame

I think it is worth noting that when we consciously start bringing shame into healing there is often, usually, most likely, going to be a backlash. If one is not prepared for the backlash, it can be really frustrating and often scary. Many people stop their healing process when this happens.

We have identified with shame as our truths for a very long time. That part of us has become our identity.

When that identity is threatened, it fights back. It is helpful to be aware of this.

It seems innocent enough to start affirming that we are lovable, and adequate, and worthy. After all, it is the truth of who we are. The part that believes we are unlovable, or inadequate, or unworthy, does not agree with the truth. So, the defenses come up, or the self-defeating behaviors seem stronger than ever. It is important to keep moving into our healing. So, we notice the backlash, name it, and keep moving in our new direction.

For a recovering alcoholic, it may sound something like: Wow, I have not craved a drink for years and right now I really want one. That must be the backlash that comes when we really start claiming my worthiness. I will get some support for my recovery and keep moving in the direction of "self-worth," even if I am craving.

One time I was in an intention group. We met and held intention for each other. I claimed that I was done with shame. I would no longer allow it to control me or be my truth. I left the group and went on my merry way, only to be slammed by shame. It came up all over the place in my life, and felt so true. I learned that although I cavalierly claimed my truth: I am lovable and worthy as I am, the shame was not at all cavalier about responding. I had read about the shame backlash previously, and was able to recognize it at the time. However, I was still stunned by the intensity of the old shame.

Reflection: Knowing there may be a shame backlash as we move into the new can help us navigate those choppy waters.

Day 120
Tool

We are one-third of the way through this year of dailies. Before we move forward it may be helpful to go back and do an inventory of the things we have learned.

We can look at:

- Our own personal red-flags
- Tools we find helpful
- Rules we are changing
- Rights we are putting into effect
- Choices we are learning we have
- Boundaries we are setting internally and externally
- Actions we are taking to heal
- Writing we have done and what we learned
- Shame indicators we identify with
- Where we are building trusting relationships
- How shame has attempted to hold us back
- How we are changing as we bring our shame into healing
- How we are looking at the world and ourselves with kinder eyes

- Our internal support
- Areas we struggle with the most in healing our shame.

It helps to give credit to ourselves for the work we are doing.

In truth, we will be healing our entire life. However, the more we utilize the tools, the less time it takes to intervene on our shame and the better we feel.

Reflection: An inventory of our progress is helpful in motivating us to continue our healing process.

Days 121-150

Day 121
Red Flag

Shame has been described as a "shape-shifter."

We can be feeling like a worthy, contributing member of society. We can be feeling good about ourselves. Then, for what looks like no apparent reason, we can feel horrible. We can feel like we don't belong, have nothing to contribute, and are not worthwhile or adequate. We have "shifted." We are a different person.

When this happens, we have most likely been hit by shame and are now in a shame loop. We may not know what happened. Our trigger may have been internal or may have been external. However, we can identify that we are in shame. This sudden shift from feeling good about ourselves to feeling bad about ourselves can feel so crazy. We can shift so rapidly and until we get very familiar with our shame, we may not know why.

However, now that we can name the shame, we can begin to utilize the tools that we have. We can begin to look at what just happened in our thoughts or environment that triggered the shame, and look underneath for the unnamed feelings and needs. We can know that shame always lies. We can write what the shame is telling us, and that whether we believe it or not, there is a truth underneath the lie. The truth will be the opposite of what shame is telling us.

Reflection: When we suddenly shift from feeling good about ourselves to feeling bad about ourselves, the "shape shifter" of shame has hit us.

Day 122
Rule

A dysfunctional rule that supports shame is: Don't Rock the Boat. When something is going on right in front of us, and we don't acknowledge it or talk about it, we are supporting this rule. One of the reasons we are not talking about something can be because we do not know how. Another reason is because what is happening is so filled with shame that we go into denial.

An obvious example of this is when someone we are with is drunk and we don't speak up. It occurs with abuse and with other addictions. It also happens when we see something that is shaming and keep it to ourselves. When we don't say anything, we are supporting the rule: Don't Rock the Boat.

There are times when this is not a big deal and there are times when it is a disaster for the people involved. By not talking, we are supporting the abuses and addictions. We are pretending things are okay when they are not. We are discounting feelings and human needs.

It can be very scary to "rock the boat." We may need the support of others to take this big step. We may be risking our relationships with others. We may not be liked. We may be abandoned.

Shame is supported by living in silence and not acknowledging what is going on around us. It is crazy and hurtful.

> *Reflection: We can learn how to rock the boat when hurtful things are going on. It helps us step out of our shame.*

Day 123
One Thing Different

My voice teacher, Patty Stephens, made a comment that is a lovely example of choosing "one" thing that can make a difference in healing shame. She taught me to say, "attempt," instead of "mistake." Now, when I hit a wrong note or haven't memorized something, I don't say I made a mistake. I say I attempted something. It makes a big difference. It feels empowering. I feel good that I stepped forward into an action, whether it was perfect or not.

A lot of the language in our world shames instead of encourages. The definition for mistake is: an action or judgment that is misguided or wrong. It is the judgment that supports shame. What if we released the judgment when it was not quite the way we had hoped it would be? What if we just acknowledged ourselves for the attempt and gave ourselves high-fives instead?

Many of us fear that if we didn't keep the critical eye of judgment on ourselves and others that we would fail or look foolish. I contend that the opposite is the truth. When we use words and thoughts of kindness and support, we have a much better chance of moving into excellence and feeling good about our processes.

We get to become conscious of the words we use to describe ourselves, others, and our actions. We get to change the words that undermine us into words that support us.

Reflection: We get to change our language and in doing so we release shame.

Day 124

Voice of Shame

All of my life I had been told I could not sing. It always confused me because I sang so well in cars or when my dog and I were hanging out. Ha! I always loved singing.

I took a challenge. There is a woman in Albuquerque who teaches singing. (She is mentioned in the preceding daily.) Once a year, she takes 12 people and works with them on singing. We only rehearse five times, in two-hour blocks. At the end of this, each person performs two solos in front of a live audience of at least 120 people, with a band back up. The performance is called, "Pyromaniac cafe." It is a fire walk.

I took the challenge. I wanted to sing. I was sick to death of my shame telling me I would make a fool out of myself. As if that mattered. I was beyond caring what my perfectionism demanded of me. I wanted to sing. I didn't need a record contract or to go on *American Idol*. I just wanted to get past the point where I was self-conscious about my singing. I wanted to belt out a Christmas carol and have fun.

I had truly had enough of shame getting in the way of me doing things I wanted to do. I had faced many scary things in my life, and this, by far, would be the scariest. It may have been because it was so public. But, I was doing it.

On the Ides of March, in Albuquerque, I performed at the Pyromaniac cafe with 11 other brave women. There were 120 people watching and there was a live band supporting us. I had a blast. I did it. It was only because of the work I had done on healing my shame that I was able to claim my voice and sing.

One of the songs I sang was: "If I Were Brave," by Jana Stanfield. You can Google it and listen to the words. The lyrics spoke to the bravery it took to walk through my shame and sing in front of a live audience.

Reflection: There are amazing payoffs in doing the work of healing shame.

Day 125

Voice of Shame

A shame that haunts many of us is, "body image" shame. We can stand in a grocery line and notice that almost every magazine displayed has an article on how to lose weight, how to look thinner, how to be younger looking, and how a famous person has become "fat" and what a shame that is. It is no wonder that so many of us carry shame about our bodies. It may be in how we perceive we look, or how we are aging.

What does this say about our culture and the priorities that are reinforced? If we look different from what the magazine is displaying, we have most likely felt shame for that difference. There is a certain, very narrow margin of what is beautiful and what we need to strive to look like.

An addiction that carries profound shame is, "overeating." We can't hide it. Every time we leave the house we are exposing ourselves as "less than," as judged by our culture. We feel shame. We feel judged. We want to hide. We are not "perfect," according to a standard that is unhealthy, unkind, and hurtful.

What do we do?

We name the shame. We begin to make friends with our bodies. We begin to expose the lies. We do not settle for what the shame tells us. We deal with the addiction if we have one. We identify and feel the feelings that are "eating at us." We learn to attend to our needs. We speak the truth that our eating covers up.

Reflection: Shame lies. The truth is: we are beautiful and worthy.

Day 126

Shame Indicator

Family systems can carry shame for generations. If a family has a secret that has shame around it, it gets passed on for generations, until the shame is brought into the light of healing.

An example of this shame might be when someone got pregnant before they were married. For some families, this is a huge shame. It is covered. Wedding dates are changed and secrets are kept. Babies' birth certificates have been changed, and the children told stories so they do not discover the truth. The shame is there. It is buried in the lies and secrets. It is felt even if it is never talked about.

This "felt" shame that is not talked about is passed on. We can know that something is not right. We can know that we are not supposed to bring up certain issues or question certain things. We just know that there is a "no talk" rule around certain topics. If it is generations old, we may never learn what the secret was. However, even if we do not learn what was there, we can claim that there was something and that there is shame around it. We can then claim the truth that shame lies and we refuse to carry the shame.

This secret shame in family systems can cause a family to feel "less than" without knowing why. We can sometimes learn a truth and bring it into the refreshing light of healing. That is a gift we get to celebrate. We can also celebrate whether we learn this truth or not. We can start over.

Reflection: Let's air the family secrets

Day 127
Poem

> I would want a swing,
>
> If I wanted a swing,
>
> That didn't know how high to go, and wouldn't learn.
>
> That welcomed the sweetness of the air flowing past,
>
> Saw the clouds upside down with new faces and pictures
>
> Where they hadn't been,
>
> Called to every old spirit that wanted to swing but hadn't or wouldn't and said,
>
> "Get on and fly into the sun with me."
>
> Yes,
>
> If I wanted a swing I would want a swing that drank in the sky,
>
> Drunk with Light!

Day 128

Voice of Shame

A question we can ask ourselves is: "Is it ever enough?"

I remember once when I was talking to a friend about losing weight, she said, "I don't think it will ever be enough." She was absolutely correct. When shame is leading the way, whatever "it" is will never be enough.

We will never feel good enough, thin enough, healed enough or smart enough, because shame will always interfere. If we are attempting to lose 10 pounds and achieve the goal, shame will say we really need to lose 15 or 20. The inner shame voice keeps moving the carrot further out, so we never feel success.

What happens is, we are attempting to reach a standard that is outside of ourselves and is driven by perfectionism. Unless we can develop internal standards driven by our own value systems, our struggle with our goals will continue to be unmet.

When we are struggling with feeling shame because we have been unable to meet a goal, we might entertain the following questions:

- What is the belief that is driving this goal?
- Is this a belief that I really stand by, or one that I have internalized that is not mine?
- If I were able to claim a belief that really fit for me in this situation, what would it be?

This helps us get more in touch with ourselves. It does not mean the shame voice will just disappear. However, it will help us catch it sooner and begin to live our life from the inside out, instead of from the outside in.

Reflection: Shame sets us up to be constantly disappointed. We get to define the truth that fits for us.

Day 129
Shame in Our World

There is a special painful place for the shame we feel when we believe we have failed in a relationship. It may come after a fight, after a partner has an affair, after a break-up or divorce, or after multiple break-ups and divorces.

We seem to think we "should" know how to have and be in healthy relationships. In truth, it is the opposite. We get to learn how to be in healthy relationships, and it may take a lifetime. If we truly understood this, knew this, and believed this, we could go through our healing processes and learn and grow and not feel like failures when we struggle.

What makes us think we "should" know how to be in healthy relationships? We have very few models for how to love each other in healthy ways. Sometimes we hear people say that their parents stayed together, so they should be able to. First, staying together does not necessarily mean it is really a healthy relationship. Second, it isn't the life path for all of us to just stay with one partner.

If one's path is to stay with another, then so be it. But, if it isn't, then we get to learn to embrace the changes, the endings, and beginnings without the cloud of shame that says we are "failures." We get to give ourselves the grace to learn and grow.

> *Reflection: Sometimes our biggest and hardest lessons are in accepting our own path, and learning how to love and forgive, again and again and again. Our paths are never shameful. They just are.*

Day 130
Red Flag

The shame loop, pictured in the Appendix, drops us into self-defeating behavior. Self-defeating behavior can be a strong red flag that we are in a shame loop. If we have a history of self-defeating behavior, we may never have looked at the roots of that behavior as being shame. Reframing self-defeating behavior and thoughts as being caught in a shame loop can help us enormously. We become curious about the shame that we are experiencing, that the self-defeating behavior is covering up.

Examples of self–defeating thoughts and behaviors are:

- Addictions
- Compulsive behaviors such as cleaning, counting, exercising (which can also be an addiction)
- Thoughts we can't stop

- Replaying an event or conversation in our heads
- Hurtful thoughts about ourselves or others
- An inner critic that won't stop criticizing

Whatever the self-defeating thoughts or behaviors are, we experience powerlessness over stopping them. We feel out of control. We feel trapped.

When we experience any of the above examples, we can be sure we are caught in a shame loop. We can begin to be curious about what triggered it either internally in our thoughts or externally by something or someone. We can then begin to hear what our shame is telling us. We can know it is not true, even if it sounds familiar and true. We can then look at the underlying feelings and needs and how to attend to them. We can share with a safe person.

Reflection: When we are powerless to stop self-defeating thoughts and behaviors we can know that powerlessness is a "red-flag." We are in a shame loop.

Day 131
Maude

Barb (B)—Hey there Maude. I have an important question for you.

Maude (M)—I am ready whenever you are.

B—What do you think the most important thing is in healing shame?

M—Good question. We have talked about the complexity of shame and healing on multidimensional levels. But, what is the most important thing? I think the most important thing in healing shame is "willingness."

B—Willingness to do what?

M—There needs to be a willingness to question virtually everything we have believed about ourselves and the world. We need to be willing to reverse our basic thought systems.

B—That sounds daunting.

M—Shame has really snared us into a world that is less and less functional. Our world is not working. There is very little internal peace. We feel like we don't quite live up to something we can't even name, and like we have to prove ourselves. Most of us are continually defensive and ready to attack in defense of ourselves. The world is more and more a place of war and pain. I believe it is grounded in shame. We have to be willing to turn it upside down to find the peace that is the truth under the shame.

B—So my prayer might be for willingness.

M—Yes, willingness to bring peace to our moments by turning in the direction of love as our guide, instead of shame.

B—Thank you.

M—In the oneness of one we are love, not shame.

Day 132

Shame Indicator

One of the things that can keep us from peace is to personalize. In his book, *The Four Agreements*, Miguel Ruiz has an entire chapter on "not personalizing." He talks about not personalizing anything. Whatever someone else says or does is about their scripts, their perceptions, what they've learned and their own templates of what is important or good enough. When we personalize, we make everything about ourselves.

This is very much the case with shame. If I have a shame-core belief that "I am not enough," then I will not only hear it wherever I am, but I will project it onto you and make it about you. So you behave in a certain way and I make it about me and give it the power to control how I feel about myself.

It is a sure way to be in hell and deny ourselves peace. And, it can be "extremely" hard not to do. I think it becomes harder in our intimate relationships. We have more of a tendency to make the other person's behavior about ourselves. Personalizing is one of those beliefs that we might want to scrutinize. First, we ask ourselves," is it really true?" Then we ask," is it is a belief I really want to hold onto?" Then we find a more peaceful belief to replace the original one.

If we can begin to move in the direction of not personalizing what others do and say, we have more control in our life. We don't give another the power to define us, upset us, or help us feel better.

Reflection: Don't Personalize Anything.

Day 133
Forgiveness

Recently, I heard some words from a wise woman named, Julia. She said, "forgiveness is not a huge magnanimous act, something you bring to another. It is acceptance of what happened."

I was struck by the clarity of her words. Often, we struggle with forgiveness. We feel it has to be a difficult process, and take a long time. We often do not know how to forgive, or even if we really want to. Shame makes sure we don't forgive because it is driven by perfectionism. If ourselves or others can't be perfect then they and we don't deserve forgiveness.

The simplicity of acceptance that something just "was," is helpful. We may never understand why it was, or how it could have been, or what the motivation was. We just accept that it happened.

When we can stop fighting and move into acceptance we can find the "still peace of acceptance." We don't have to bring forgiveness to the other person. We accept. Julia also stated, "The energy of acceptance is within oneself and it takes effort to accept. The words stated from one person to another, 'I forgive you,' often shift the focus as if it were a transaction. Yet, in many ways, it has little to do with the other person. The real work is internal."

Reflection: Forgiveness is acceptance of "what was, what happened."

Day 134
Rule

Loyalty to our family of origin may interfere with our healing process. Many of us were stewed in the belief that to say anything critical about our families is absolutely wrong and bad, and as a consequence would make us "wrong or bad." This family loyalty is set in stone.

If we experienced something painful growing up and do not look at it, it will fester, become inflamed and cause greater distress. Our fears of looking and naming something that happened in our families are often based on the belief that it would make us "bad." Bringing family secrets out in the open often feels like we are blaming.

What we can know instead is that it is not about making someone wrong or assigning blame. It is about healing the beliefs about ourselves that came from the decisions we made as a result of the actions and words of others.

Loyalty can prevent us from looking at something and bringing it into healing. If we are not honest about what happened, we can never bring that injured part or damaged belief about ourselves into the light of day.

Our families were doing what they thought was right and the best they could for where they were at that time. We don't need to blame them, but we need to look.

Shame often originates in trauma memories that are locked in our cells. We must look at these memories and be willing to release them. It may be trauma-work that is needed and so we do it. It may be looking at it with a friend or a therapist and taking responsibility for our feelings and the beliefs we hold. We look, we release, and we can heal.

>*Reflection: Loyalty to our families can keep us locked in our shame. We have a right to look and heal.*

Day 135
Healing Action

"Unless we can sit in the presence of ourselves and love ourselves as we are, we will act out in some way."

Barb Tonn

When we don't like ourselves, we live in shame and fear. We are fearful that others will see us as lacking, as not good enough, as imperfect. We are certain we will be discovered as frauds and be rejected. That thought is so painful that we hide it behind a myriad of disguises. We carry a level of anxiety that we will be seen as lacking.

We act out to divert our attention. We get trapped in that acting out, and often see that as our identities. We mistake what we do with who we are.

There are as many ways of acting out as there are people. Some of us have addictions and combine addictions, or switch from one to another. Shame is ALWAYS under our addictions. Some of us act out in our heads. We have a constant stream of criticism. It won't stop. It is painful. Some of us act out by distracting attention away from ourselves. It is too painful to be seen. Whichever way we act out, we are in our shame.

We can try to fool ourselves that what we are doing is just part of living in a busy world. We can deny. When we are acting out, we are trying to keep our shame away. It distracts us from healing our core issues.

We can learn to release the shame and learn to truly sit in the presence of ourselves and like ourselves as we are. We can, if we are willing to stop and look and are honest. We can discover the essence of ourselves is "love and lovable."

Reflection: We get to learn to sit in the presence of ourselves and love ourselves.

Day 136

Healing Action

HEALING SHAME IS A PROCESS

One of the questions I am frequently asked is: When will my shame be gone?

My observation is that as long as we are present on the Earth we will be dealing with shame. It is part and parcel of the very air we breathe. As humans, we are inundated with mental-shame constructs in our readings, our teachings, and our cultural and familial upbringings.

Healing shame is a process of increasing consciousness to become more aware of when we are receiving shameful messages from the outside and when we are self-triggering a shame message on the inside. At the moment of awareness, we can bring the shame into the light of truth. It is with this awareness that we are able to heal and transform shame.

As we grow more adept at noticing shame for what it is, we can more easily move and transform it. When will we be done? When we identify shame, shine the light of truth on it, and see it for what it is.

Reflection: Instead of trying to be finished with healing, we get to be aware of shame in the moment. It is the only place it can be transformed.

Day 137
Shame in our World

A dynamic I have begun to notice is the shame young adults often carry when they are not able to take care of themselves financially. In truth, whenever an adult is struggling financially is brings up profound shame. In this daily, I would like to specifically address the shame of the young adult.

Young adults grew up believing that by their early 20's, after college or some sort of schooling, they would be able to live on their own and be independent of their families financially. Instead, many have had to return to their parents' homes because they could not make their financial commitments. Some have not been able to leave their parents' homes because of finances.

The current economy is very different than the one that many young adults were accustomed to. However, the belief system that is in place from growing up in that economy has not necessarily changed. As a result, the young adult often feels profound shame that they are not financially independent. When I say, young adult, I am often talking about adults into their 30's. The ability to buy a home, pay off student loans, pay for insurance, and then meet the needs of their own children is often impossible in the current economy. This leaves them in a developmentally delayed adolescence. Consequently, they are struggling with shame.

The parents of these young adults are also often struggling with shame. They feel like failures. They feel responsible in some way. They are embarrassed that their children can't make it on their own.

All this shame is happening and we don't know how to talk about it. We don't know how to talk about our expectations and how things have changed, and problem solve without the shame getting in the way.

The "no talk" rule is a real hindrance to problem solving. We get to learn how to talk about our expectations, realities, struggles, finances, responsibilities, embarrassments and shame. We name the issues and acknowledge the shame. It can be hard to be in this situation and it does not need to be complicated by shame.

> *Reflection: If we are unable to meet our financial needs, it is not shameful. It may be hard and it does not mean we are less than.*

Day 138

Shame Loop

Some of us can identify with having a shame-core. This means a negative "I am" defines our senses of ourselves. Although we may not always be conscious of it, this shame will lead the way in our lives, and we will live trying to compensate for our shame. We will make choices in our lives from this core shame.

Shame of our shame makes it hard to acknowledge our shame. As a therapist, I have seen countless people who clearly identify with a shame-core but are unaware of it or deny it. Whether we acknowledge shame or don't, it is a cruel taskmaster. Unless it is brought into healing, it will be a constant source of pain.

There are many ways we defend against really acknowledging our shame. Defenses are #2 on the shame loop (see Appendix). Some of the ways we defend are:

- Projecting our shame out onto others and seeing in them what we will not look at in ourselves
- Deny that we have shame
- Rationalize and attempt to explain or justify the shame

- Intellectualize and avoid insight and emotion by analyzing shame intellectually
- Minimize shame by not acknowledging the pain it causes
- Block the shame
- Dissociation, which can vary from mildly disconnecting from one's immediate surroundings to complete detachment from reality
- Repression, during which we suppress the thought, feeling, or emotion attached to shame

Whichever defense we use, it keeps us from bringing our shame into the light of healing. We can become aware of our defenses and which ones we are most likely to use.

Reflection: Defenses are part of the shame loop. We use them to defend against the pain of our shame-core.

Daily 139
Tool

DOING SOMETHING HARD

When our shame leads the way, we can find countless excuses to not do what we know is ours to do, or what it is time to do. Shame drops us into a self-defeating behavior (#4 in the shame loop- see Appendix.) It becomes very difficult in our lives to do the healthy, healing, or positive thing.

When we are really struggling to do something hard and just can't seem to succeed, we get to look for the underlying shame and address it directly.

One exercise we can do when we are not moving forward is:

1. Claim some space and time where we will not be interrupted, and put a 'Do Not Disturb' sign on our doors.

2. Grab a pile of paper and a pencil. (We do this in writing, not on our computers.)

3. Start writing without lifting our pencils or pausing (flow-of-consciousness or "hot" pen) and put into words what our shame is telling us.

4. Write: In regard to what it is I am attempting to do, "My shame is telling me..."

5. Keep writing until we can't identify one more thing our shame is telling us. Shame can get really nasty and go on and on. Get it all out!

We then turn in the direction of what a voice of compassion might say to us or we can claim rights.

Examples of rights:

- I have the right to make a mistake.
- I have the right to claim my truth.
- I have the right to kindness, etc.
- I have the right to my own process.
- Or we can claim a truth: Whether I believe it or not, I am a good person, worthy of __.

It is imperative to reach a truth and/or a right. We don't want to stop with just what the voice of shame is telling us.

Pause and let the truth sink in. If we just cannot get to a truth, this is an important time we share with someone who is very trustworthy and let them help us find rights or truths. We write as many of these down as we can think of.

This can be extremely helpful when something is hard or we feel stuck in self-defeating behaviors or thoughts.

Reflection: Flow of Consciousness Writing is a powerful healing tool.

Daily 140
Model for a Shame-Free World

On Day 128, we talked about the shame we can carry if we have struggled in relationships. Now, I would like to look at ending a relationship, consciously, without shame.

The construct many of us carry when a relationship is over or we want it to be over, is that someone must be at fault. We blame. We make the other person wrong and ourselves the innocent victims. This is a shame construct. It does not have to be this way.

We can choose to end our relationships because they are no longer serving the intention of being a loving relationship. Many marriage ceremonies are now saying that the parties involved will stay committed as long as it is serving the highest good of both people. If that ceases to be, the two will go their separate ways, honor the time they were together, and honor what they shared and learned while with each other.

We can do a ceremony when a relationship is over. We can take responsibility for ourselves, our decisions, our choices, and moving on. We can honor each other in front of witnesses, including children involved. We can share what we learned and what we wish for each other. We can say "good-bye" or we can honor that the relationship has changed form.

The model for ending relationships can change when we no longer need to blame. This can be an important aspect of our model for a shame-free world. We can create ceremony for ending relationships in a non-shaming, loving way.

Reflection: We get to change the paradigm of shame.

Day 141
Right

I have the right to ask for what I want, but it doesn't mean I will get it.

First and foremost, we all have the right to think about and determine what we want and need. Many of us who are bound by shame do not even feel we have the right to want and need. Therefore, to ask for what we want/need feels impossible. (Asking is another step in the process. At this point, we are claiming a right. Later, we will learn how to ask for what we want/need.)

It is important in healing from shame to begin to look at what we want and need to take care of ourselves. We have the right to do that. This moves us beyond the mere survival of living in shame.

Often shame-based systems have certain people in the system that think they know what everyone else needs. They will speak for the people in the system. They have become the "voice" for the different people in the system. They tell the others what they need. This sets up a shame dynamic.

Having needs and wants often triggers shame. We can often get past that by prefacing our search for our needs and wants with:

- Whether I believe it or not, it is okay to have needs and wants.
- I have the right to identify my own needs and wants

Then I get to begin to look at asking for what I want and need. This was addressed on Day 128.

Reflection: I have the right to ask for what I want.

Daily 142
Personal Story

I have been a speaker at countless workshops. My topic is "healing shame." The following story is one I have shared at most of them. It demonstrates a covert rage/shame loop and how to intervene on it. It follows the healing steps on the shame loop in the Appendix.

The shame/rage loop at the hospital:

The following story demonstrates the quiet, covert shame loop, and the shame nobody sees, but, nonetheless, is destructive.

I was lead counselor in a psychiatric hospital, on a chemical dependency unit. I was in a meeting in which the counselors, doctors, and nurses get together and develop treatment plans. I was in one of those meetings when I became aware that the meeting was going on, and I no longer knew what was being talked about. I was not sure where I had disconnected, and all I could think about was fixating on wanting one nurse in the meeting fired.

To look at me you would never have known that I was plotting against this person, or that I was not really present anymore. I had been working on my shame; so it did not take me long to think, "Ah, I must be in a shame loop." My thoughts were destructive (I wanted someone fired), and I did not know what was going on (I had disconnected). Both of those are shame loop indicators. So, I went about the task of intervening on my shame, following the steps on healing the shame/rage loop in the Appendix.

1. What had triggered me? The last point I remembered was when I had shared something I thought was important and that nurse I was fixated on had cut me off. Okay, that is a good awareness. Now I could begin to get a handle on what had happened.

2. If I hadn't gone into shame when I was cut off, what might I have felt? Well, I would have felt

discounted and hurt. Okay, now here is the trick: I needed to feel the feelings. It is not useful to just identify the feelings. We have to feel the feelings.

3. Once I had let myself feel, I had to identify what the discounted part of me needed and what the hurt part of me needed. Both the discounted and hurt parts of myself needed to know it was okay to have an opinion and they needed me to advocate for them. How might I do this advocating? A rule of thumb I have is: if I have an ongoing relationship with someone, and something like this comes up, it is my job to do for me what most likely has not been done before and advocate for myself. I had an ongoing relationship with this person so I needed to advocate for me. That does not mean I make her responsible for my shame. The shame was mine to heal. I determined that the next time I saw her I would tell her what had happened and what I needed in the future. A couple of days later I ran into her and I said, "a couple of days ago when we were in our staff meeting, I said something I thought was important, and you cut me off. In the future, when I share, I would appreciate it if you would acknowledge what I had to say." I had a need to be acknowledged and I took care of it. I no longer wanted the nurse fired and life went on. It actually didn't matter if she did what I asked. What the hurt part needed was to be advocated for and her need spoken. That was done.

4. Besides dealing with our feelings/needs in the here and now," there is the "there and then" that needs to be dealt with in order to heal shame. So, I asked myself what this reminded me of? I looked at the issue and thought about growing up. I grew up with a very brilliant father. He often unconsciously cut me off. I ended up feeling inferior. Up until that day I triggered when I was cut off. So, I clearly had some Dad-work to do from my past. My inner self had never been allowed to feel her feelings about being cut off, had never been able to express her need to be acknowledged, or to be advocated for. I re-entered therapy to do more Dad work. The "here and now" shame loop had been effectively dealt with, but now I was working on the core issue of feeling inferior, and I was healing from past hurt and discounting. That was the "there and then" work that held the shame in place."

This is an example of intervening on shame and doing healing work in the present and on the past. It is a process. Feeling inferior is deeply rooted, and multidimensional. However, as I have taken responsibility for my own shame and healed it, I have found that incident by incident, and step by step I can bring my shame into the light of healing and process it.

Reflection: Recognizing when we are in shame and utilizing the "shame/rage loop and intervention steps" that are found in the Appendix are helpful.

Day 143
Rule

Shame-based systems do not know how to build trust. In order to trust, there needs to be safety. Safety is built on consistency, talking, sharing feelings and needs, and having them respected. It is built on "being our word." This means we are congruent. We share our truths in a kind and compassionate way. Trust is our knowing when we share we will be consistently treated with respect.

Shame-based systems are not honest. We may be angry and tell the other person we are not angry. We may be kind on one day and mean the next. We may be in an addiction and deny it. These all lead to a lack of trust.

To bring shame into healing, we need to have people in our lives we can build trust with and learn to trust. Learning who and how to trust is a process. We begin by acknowledging that we don't trust. We start learning how and who to trust. We become willing to be vulnerable in order to build safety. We become trustworthy. "Being our word" is about being honest, not gossiping, keeping confidences when asked, and using our words kindly, even when we are upset. This builds trust and creates an environment in which to heal.

Reflection: The "no trust" rule is locked into the shame-based system and keeps it unhealthy and lacking safety. We get to learn to trust. We need to have trust in our relationships to heal shame.

Day 144
Shame Defined

On Day 138, I spoke about those of us who have a shame core. Some of us have experienced "shaming situations," but the shame is not our core identity.

The following is such a situation:

We go to a birthday party of someone we don't know very well and for whatever reason we are left out of most of the party. We may even be made fun of. We are embarrassed and hurt. However, when we go home and talk to our moms, they understand, validate our hurt, and take care of us. If we never experience something like this again, we may not have shame core issues due to this experience. Our moms' responses helped us release the trauma.

However, if we struggle in situations that are similar, we may have some shame and need to bring that situation into trauma healing in order to really release the experience from our systems. We can do this by having our stories heard in safe environments, claiming and feeling our feelings, and hearing the truth, "it had nothing to do with you." If the situation still haunts us or impacts our current life, we can do trauma work on it. That work is usually done with a therapist.

Reflection: Some shaming experiences can be brought into healing and do not contribute to shame core identification.

Day 145
Specific Shame-Based Issue

Being unique can be shameful. In our culture, there is much emphasis put on "being normal." We are supposed to be like others and not stick out. So, if we have been dubbed "unique" or "gifted" in some way, we may feel shame for being different. It may be hard to talk about or even identify because we are "supposed" to be grateful for our gifts.

What if we aren't? What if we just want to be like everybody else? What do we do with that?

It can be helpful to talk to someone safe. This safe person is not going to try to talk us out of our challenges. They will listen and validate how difficult being gifted can be. This safe person will help us deal with our feelings and needs in productive ways. There is no shame in being gifted, or unique, and that can be difficult to believe.

I cannot tell you how common it is for me to hear the questions, from my clients, "is that normal?" or "am I normal?" I often answer, "there is no normal, it is an illusion." It is another of the constructs in our culture, which locks shame in place. Even making oneself look or act in a very different way from others, is often driven by shame. The shame causes one to compensate for perceived differences. The acting out does not come from a peaceful place. It comes from distress. That is shame.

While our culture is shame-bound, we can live in distress about just being the way we are. We have incorporated internal beliefs about what we "should" be like. When we don't match, and we seldom do, we feel shame and try so hard to be different. We have no peace. We keep "trying." Where there is effort to be something we aren't, we can know there is shame. It can be helpful to see what the belief is that is driving the anxiety, the need to behave the way we do.

> *Reflection: When we aren't peaceful about how we are, we most likely are carrying shame. It can be helpful to unearth the underlying belief that drives the discontent. Then we can decide if we want to live with that belief, or not.*

Day 146
Model for a Shame-Free World

Why do I make such a big deal about shame?

Sometimes I feel so obsessive about how I go on and on about shame. Then I really look at the havoc it creates in our world and in individual lives and I know I am not obsessive. I am just profoundly tuned into the pain it causes. I have been since I first began truly comprehending shame back in the 1980s.

At that time, I was working in a sexual addiction unit with Dr. Patrick Carnes. I was lucky to be one of the original therapists who trained with him when he started the sexual addiction unit. I would work with people who were very committed to their recovery. Many were repeating in sexual addiction treatment and many had been in treatment for other addictions. I kept wondering what we, the therapists and clients, were missing. Then I stumbled onto the concept of shame. I read all I could (not much at that time) and went to a lecture by Dr. Kaufman on shame. From then on, I have been so very interested in shame.

I believe shame is rampant in our culture. Shame not only underpins addiction, but most, if not all, mental health disorders. Shame wreaks havoc throughout all sub cultures. The belief that one is not good enough or constantly needs to prove oneself is in most people. It is not just in people with obvious challenges, but also in the inner beliefs of most everyone. Why is that? What is wrong? We have it completely backwards. Instead of believing that we are enough, lovable, and worthy, we believe we are fraudulent, or less than, or people would not think so highly of us "if they only knew..."

Shame is a constant construct. Perfectionism, blame, hierarchy, dishonesty, etc., are the hallmarks of a shame-based system. Does that sound familiar? It is the groundwork for most of our world, at least until someone gets conscious and truly works to make this different.

So, I keep at it. I keep working with understanding shame and finding tools to help intervene on it. There is not peace in a person's heart while shame resides in it. "Until I can sit in the presence of myself and love myself, as I am, there will be no peace." Instead, there is shame.

Please don't think it is just the other people who have it, or the "crazy" people, or the "addicted" people. It is part and parcel of the air we breathe and we need to heal it if we ever want peace in our world.

Reflection: We can refuse to look at shame and see how serious it is, and how much it has impacted our world. Shame is at the roots of our distress, our wars, and our lack of peace.

Day 147
Poem

Sitting in silence

I notice my thoughts

What direction do they lead me?

Peace calls- filled with love

I can't hear unless I listen

That will be my focus

Listening for the voice of peace

I am going home- at last

Only to find

I never left

I just thought I had

Peace

Barb Tonn

Day 148
Tool

On Day 140, we were looking at the "Right to ask for what I need and want." We were looking at having the right to identify our needs and wants. Sometimes we have a hard time identifying our needs and wants because we know we have no idea how to meet them. I wanted us to be able to identify them first, without getting stuck in the fear of not knowing how to take care of them.

Once we have identified our needs and wants, we get to learn how to "ask for what we need and want." Often we need to learn some new skill sets in order to accomplish this task. Some of those skills may include:

- Trusting ourselves to take care of ourselves
- Asking others for help or support in tough situations
- Learning to hear "no" and not give up all our power when we do
- Having different needs/wants from others and being comfortable with that
- Claiming our needs/wants despite others attempting to convince us otherwise
- Knowing we are in a process and not demanding perfection of ourselves in that process
- Knowing we always have choices

We have the right to ask for what we need/want and that doesn't mean we will get it. That is a truth we can learn and grow with.

> *Reflection: We get to put our inner child on our lap and help him or her learn their rights.*
> *Learning our rights is learning a new skill set.*

Day 149
One Thing Different

Compassion is the response to the suffering of others that motivates a desire to help.

I would like us to consider the importance of developing the ability to attend to our own feelings and needs, and have them be as important as those of others. Without being able to do this, shame will lock us down and we will not be able to keep our heads above water. To put our feeling and needs below others is one of the pitfalls we often run into in our shame-based world. We end up feeling selfish and bad if we put ourselves on the "important" list.

We need to take care of ourselves before we can be any good to anyone else. We need to have an awareness of others and how we impact them. When we have little children, we need to put their needs above our own. However, that can't be a permanent way of doing things.

Our shame-based world would have us believe otherwise. One of the signatures in our world is hierarchy. If there is a hierarchy in the needs category, nobody wins. What if all our needs were important? What if nobody's were more important than someone else's? What if we had compassion for our needs as well as others' needs?

Our world is short on true kindness. In true kindness, we all win. In true kindness, we are all sharing and loving and nobody loses. In kindness is compassion.

I read a story about a group of children in an underdeveloped country. They were put in a situation where there was some food put in the center of a circle. They were told that the first child to the center would have the food. When the children were told to "go," nobody moved. When asked, "why?" they all said that they couldn't be happy unless everybody shared the food. This is true compassion. The children all counted themselves and each other as important. In shame, we often count others and not ourselves, or ourselves and not others.

Reflection: "Self" is a part of the equation. We aren't better than or less than. We all are one. That is where compassion starts.

Day 150
Shame Originator

Many of us who are working on healing shame have trauma in our lives. Many things a child experiences as traumatic get minimized when we look back through the eyes of our adult selves. Trauma is defined as: an emotional experience or shock, which has a lasting psychic effect. Psychic is defined as: of the soul. So trauma is an emotional experience that damages the soul. We get to bring those experiences into active healing. This trauma work will help us heal our shame at the deepest level.

When we experience trauma as a child, we take responsibility for it. This is developmentally where we are at the time. We end up feeling "bad" because we feel responsible. A great deal of the healing in trauma work is around releasing the trauma from the body and our thoughts, in how we view ourselves.

We are fortunate in the plethora of techniques that have been developed to help us heal from trauma. Some of the techniques are: EMDR (Eye Movement Desensitization and Reprocessing), HMR (Holographic Memory Resolution), TFT (Thought Field Therapy), EFT (Emotional Freedom Technique), Somatic Experiencing, etc. As we bring our traumas into healing, we are also bringing our shame into healing.

It can be frightening to address old trauma and it is not as damaging as carrying unresolved trauma. What is helpful is finding skilled clinicians who are trained in trauma work.

Reflection: If we have trauma, we can give ourselves the gift of actively bringing it into healing.

Days 151-180

Day 151
One Thing Different

Part of the pathway out of shame is focusing on something different. Shame captivates us. We listen to shame constantly often unaware of it. We can change our thoughts by changing what we listen to. We can listen for the voice of love. What would that voice say to us? For some people, the voice of love has a name attached. It may be, Buddha, God, or Allah. It may be called, "truth," "source," or "peace." Whatever we call it helps us turn in a different direction. We turn away from the voice of shame in our heads.

What if that voice we have listened to is absolutely a lie? What if it has simply done its best to drown out the voice of love? What if we can learn to listen to a voice that will allow us to learn, make mistakes, be human, and forgive?

Shame is so loud and demanding that we don't often question it. When that internal voice shouts that we are idiots and inadequate or unworthy or frauds, we go right along with it. Why are we so intent on believing this? Sometimes I encourage people to say, "whether I believe it or not, the truth is: I am lovable, worthy, adequate, enough, etc.

There is a wonderful technique for changing our belief systems. As I have mentioned, if you Google: YouTube, "Donna Eden-Temporal Tap," you will see a demonstration of a technique for changing our core beliefs. I have used this technique for years and many of my clients have, as well.

The one thing we can do differently is to become conscious of the voice we listen to, and turn in the direction of a new voice. It may take a while to hear the new voice, and it is there. This new voice is the voice of love, not shame.

> *Reflection: We get to be willing to focus on something different. This may be a different voice. The new voice is the voice of "Love." It could just be the truth.*

Day 152
Tool

Healing shame can be such hard, heavy work. Let's have some fun today. Let's create a character that represents our shame. Then we can dress it up and make it look silly. It can help take some of the power back from shame.

- Go online and find images to download.
- Go into magazines and cut out images.
- Draw our own images.
- Picture an image from our nightmares and find an image that will match.
- Build something that represents our shame.
- Go to a thrift store and find an ugly toy or a toy that can be dressed up as shame.

- Go shopping and find an image of shame.

Once we get the image or 3-D object that represents shame, we take some time to really think how our shame triggers us. If shame has a big mouth, then we can exaggerate the mouth in our drawing or on our object. If it trips us up, we can represent that in an overly large shoe. If shame gives us the finger and is angry all the time we can represent that on the doll. The point is that we will exaggerate the drawing and/or object to help us recognize when shame is speaking in our heads.

After we have done this, and shame starts on its litany of criticisms, the drawing or object will come to our minds and we can smile and say, "there it goes again." It may take us awhile to smile when we hear shame, but someday we will get there.

Reflection: We can find ways to disempower our shame in creative ways.

Day 153
Voice of Shame

I was speaking with someone who understands shame. He said, "Shame is illogical." He knows that what shame is telling him about his worth is not the truth, and yet it can get to him.

We can know we aren't stupid when shame is telling us we are. We can know we are good enough and worthy and lovable, and yet shame can send us down the rabbit hole of self-doubt. That is what it does. Shame defies logic.

What we can do at those times is just notice, shake our heads, smile and say, "Shame got me again. I can't believe it got me again. I thought I was over this and it got me."

That is the very nature of shame. We can think we are in the arena of knowledge. We are certain we know better than to get hooked by shame, and it can still take us on for a ride.

What I can tell is, "It does not mean we have not made progress if we get hooked by shame. The fact that we notice when we are and can acknowledge that it took us on a ride, is progress."

We can always be hooked. However, as we progress in our lives of healing, we will truly catch shame sooner, intervene on it more quickly, and smile more frequently.

Reflection: Shame is illogical. We get to know that.

Day 154
Voice of Shame

I talk about "shining the light of truth on shame." The challenge is, we have believed shame is the truth. So, when I talk about turning to truth, we often don't really know what that means.

We may have had glimpses of the truth. We may have known someone personally who seemed to shine truth. That person saw us as the lovable person shame did not let us see. Truth has been reflected, whether we recognized it or not.

That person who reflected truth to us is actually an aspect of ourselves we may not recognize yet. We can't see ourselves reflected if we don't recognize ourselves to some extent. For instance, if we have never believed we were worthy and someone believed we were worthy and reflected that, we may not believe them.

However, we can build on what we have heard from others. The sweet kindness, the compassionate voice, the loving eyes, can be a template for building our own internal voice of compassion. That represents the truth we have been turning away from for so long.

I developed my inner voice of compassion by watching kind parents on a playground, and reading books written by people who represented kindness. I sought out quotes, poems, and books that helped my heart hear a different message from the voice of shame. Then, when I most needed to hear that voice, I could at least have some idea of how it might sound.

I can't define your truth for you. However, I can say that truth is NEVER the voice of shame, which is always mean and hurtful. We are in a process of learning and healing that allows us to turn away from shame and toward love.

Reflection: The voice of truth will always bring peace. If what you are hearing from inside or outside does not bring peace, then it is shame.

Day 155
Maude

Maude speaking:

There is a solid belief system on the earth plane causing more pain than any other. It is a belief that aligns us with the body and the ensuing belief that we are defective in some way. We are born into a world that supports this belief. Unless that belief is challenged and removed, it stays with us throughout our entire lives.

The belief that we are defective is false. The truth is that love created us like itself. We are not a body that is defective. We are spirit. As spirit, we are perfect, whole, and free. If we could see the destruction this belief in defectiveness has caused, we would drop it like a hot potato. Because we have not truly questioned the belief in our defectiveness, we have not seen the importance of changing our minds.

This book is about changing our minds. It is about living from a completely different concept of ourselves. It is about knowing that the body is not our truth. It is about turning in the direction of love to define us and motivate us.

The truth is: We are love. Love created us like itself.

...Maude

Day 156
Shame in Our World

If we wait for life to be "just the way we want" for us to be at peace, we will never have peace. The challenges and the gremlins keep coming. What can we do instead?

It seems to me that we can be in peace if that is our only goal. Usually peace is a nice idea, but it comes way down the list under all the otherworldly priorities. If peace is our priority, then it is not only possible, but also probable that we will have it.

I challenge all of us, to consciously set the intention, for even an hour, to make peace the only thing that matters. We can see what a difference that makes.

If peace were our only goal, our primary intention, then that would mean we would let go of being right.

Being right focuses on:

- focusing on what we do not like in ourselves, others, and our world,
- trying to prove our points or prove that we are good enough,
- living in non-forgiveness,
- not allowing ourselves to see that underneath we are all the same,
- being content with living in our resentments and anger.
- We get to be honest with ourselves if we are settling for less than peace. Only by honestly

noticing if we are peaceful are we able to keep moving in the direction of our intent: to live in peace, and not shame.

Reflection: We get to be clear about our intentions.

Day 157
Shame in Our World

As I write this book there are daily shootings going on around the United States. I see people living in fear, blame, and anger. It might be helpful to reflect very carefully at this point. It is easy to get outraged and look to something outside of ourselves to focus our feelings on, and "blame."

We live in a shame-based world. Part of what happens when we live in this stew of shame is that we end up feeling powerless. When people feel powerless, we lash out. We can blame our world, the gun laws, our families, and the insane people out there. Or, we can look at where we feel powerless and how we send that energy out into the world and contribute energetically to the mass consciousness of rage and shame.

We can examine our choices, see where we have not forgiven and/or blamed others for our state of mind. We can take responsibility for our choices and changes. We can empower ourselves to make choices that fit for us, and forgive ourselves and others. We get to take care of our needs in a healthy way, and make a difference in our world by being truly peaceful inside.

It can be so hard to step back and really look at our own consciousness. If we wait for others to change before we do this, our world just gets darker and darker, more filled with shame and rage.

I want to empower myself and all others to seek out the darkness in our own psyches and bring the light of healing and forgiveness to those dark corners. If we do not know how, we get to learn. We make it our priority.

Reflection: It is always tempting to blame something outside of ourselves. Let's not do that. Blame feeds shame and does not bring peace to our own hearts or the world.

Day 158
Healing Action

An action we can always take when our shame has been triggered is to "get quiet." After we are quiet we can take the action steps (see Appendix) out of our shame loop.

Shame sweeps us into a frenzy of fear, anxiety, and dread. It envelops us in hopelessness that can feel never-ending and as deep as the ocean. Once we learn how to identify shame, we learn the importance of getting quiet. We become willing to sit, look toward the light, ask for help, and wait for an answer.

After a shame loop starts, if we behave impulsively instead of getting quiet, we will be behaving in a "self-defeating" way. Instead, we notice and we quietly sit. We turn away from the shame and that means we turn toward love. We ask how love would respond in this situation. We wait. We wait until we feel clear about what love would say or do. We don't go off half-cocked and self-righteous. We sit in quiet and wait.

How many of us really do that? When shame hits we feel rage. That rage is loud. It is aimed at either ourselves or others. We want to push the shame far away. We don't want to feel the shame and rage. So, we push back as "fast" as we can. We clear the decks and we move "fast." We hurt ourselves and others when we do that.

Reflection: We sit, get still, and turn to love before we say or do anything.

Day 159
One Thing Different

Act as if...

What if for this day we acted as if we were absolutely worthy and enough? In truth, we are. So, we really aren't acting, but we are stepping into our truths.

What would be different if we lived our lives this way? I am going to do a brainstorm list.

If I acted as if I were worthy and enough I would:

- Feel more joy
- Make decisions without second guessing myself
- Feel confident and self-assured
- Feel a sense of having a place in this world

- Feel like an adult
- Know that I have rights
- Look at myself with respect
- Ask more questions and get more answers
- Have a sense of completion
- Trust myself and the world
- Absolutely feel more peace
- Give myself many choices and feel good about the choices I make
- Give my self-respect
- Give others more respect
- Cease arguing
- Feel empowered
- Look for the sweet innocence in myself and others
- Feel more joy
- Respect my rights
- Feel more grounded
- Find my purpose and live it
- Smile more
- Stop trying to prove myself and just let myself be

Reflection: We can "act as if" until we truly believe.

Day 160
Tool

On Day 65, we talked about a communication tool that is helpful, especially when there is conflict involved. Now we will use that same tool to communicate when our shame is triggered.

As I have suggested, it is helpful when we are in a relationship and our shame gets triggered to let the other person know. It can help circumvent going into a full-blown shame loop if we communicate it as soon as we get triggered.

Let's use an example of someone having raised his or her voice or yelled at us and we got triggered into our shame.

The format is:

"When you..."

"I feel..."

"I need..."

Short Version Example:

- "When I asked you when you would be ready to leave a couple of minutes ago, you raised your voice (yelled) at me when you answered."

- "I felt shame."

- "I need you to know that I have a right to ask you a question and I deserve respect." (Often claiming a right is very helpful in stepping out of our shame.)

In the long version, we add a new second step. We tell the person all the things we "thought" when they did what they did.

We also add a fourth step in which we tell the other person all the things we have considered saying or doing.

Long Version Example:

- "When I asked you when you would be ready to leave a couple of minutes ago, you raised your voice (yelled) at me when you answered."

- (New 2nd step) "I started thinking you thought I was a demanding, bad person, or that I had no right to ask you a question, or that I was demanding and not just asking."

- "I felt shame."

- (New 4th step) "I considered not mentioning this, or talking about this later, or making an ultimatum about not yelling."

- "I need you to know that I have a right to ask you a question and I deserve respect."

The short or long version can be an honoring and kind way to intervene on shame, for both people involved.

Reflection: In a relationship, we can circumvent damage by sharing when we are triggered.

Day 161

Healing Action

Healing shame is a spiritual process.

What do I mean by that?

We evolve from self-loathing to self-loving. Spiritual is defined as: having, relating to, or affecting the human spirit or soul, as opposed to material or physical things. Our spirit is healed as we learn to love ourselves.

How we do this is unique for all of us. We take our religious histories, family histories, and what we learned in our culture and find the way that works for us. Often we have to unlearn old ways of relating to ourselves and love before we can find ways to love.

Many of us identify with being recovering humans, Christians, Catholics, Jews, etc. If that is how we identify ourselves, then we get to heal the wounds that caused us to identify ourselves in that way. As we release from the old we begin to weave in the beliefs that fit for us and love again. We may have a formal God of some kind, or we may have an identity as light, or spirit, or some word that captures our essences.

Whatever way we do this work, we are healing our spirits, our hearts, the way we look at ourselves and the world. As we turn more and more often to the voice of love, we are in this spiritual process. It is essential work in healing shame. We can do it as agnostics or atheists. We learn to love. That is not a religious process, but rather a spiritual one. We may have a religion, but the process is spiritual.

Reflection: We are healing our spirit and therefore in a spiritual process.

Day 162
Right

I have the right to live without criticism or judgment from others.

The reality is that we will run into criticism and judgment from others around every corner. That is how we shame each other. We criticize and judge others in order to get them to be the way we want them to be. Judgment shames.

What we do with criticism and judgment from others is what makes a difference in the quality of our lives. We can give judgment and criticism the power to shame us. We can look at it and use it as a way to flush out what our beliefs truly are. We can use it as an excuse to rage and shame back. We can refuse to accept the shaming and go forth as we feel our inner guidance and belief system dictates.

We have the right to live without criticism or judgment from others means; we get to have choices if we are receiving criticism and judgment. We can:

- Ask someone to be with us without criticizing and judging us.
- Ask the person to stop the behavior or words they are speaking.
- Leave a situation where we are being criticized and judged.

- Take the time to express clearly how they are impacting us. ("When you...," "I feel...," "I need...").
- Claim our rights to live without criticism and judgment.

We get to choose whom we have in our inner circles. We can also share only in places where we know we are safe and will be honored. We always have choices.

Reflection: We can practice integrating this right into our day-to-day life and see where it leads us in our relationships.

Day 163
Red Flag

In order to bring shame into healing, we need to be aware we are in shame. I am going to write a short list of indicators that one is most likely in "shame." Any of these can be a "Red Flag" that we are in shame.

1. If we are experiencing being "stuck."

Often our shame has us in a double bind or a shame bind where we believe we should do this or that. When we only have two choices, we are usually not truly in choice, but are caught in shame. We get to open up into all the choices that are possible to release from this "stuck" spot.

2. If we are cycling in self-defeating behavior.

As we move into a shame loop, we always move into a self-defeating behavior (#4 on loop in Appendix). It can be addictions, an inner critic that leads the way, compulsive behavior that is a distraction, but not a help, etc.

3. If we "can't not do" something.

Often we move into a behavior that we know is not good for us, or is not helping us, but we "can't not do" it. We can often see a choice that would be helpful, but are unable to do it.

4. If we are living in "should."

Some of my earlier dailies talk about the word "should." I will be so bold as to say that if we are in a "should or shouldn't," we are in shame. We are not living from our truth but from a belief that comes from outside of ourselves that is dictating the behavior. If we change the "should" to "could," we will in all likelihood be able to make a choice for ourselves that moves us out of shame and into our truths.

5. If we are in a defensive posture.

When our shame is triggered, we move immediately into a defensive posture. When we are defensive, we look for what our shame is telling us.

6. If we can't get in touch with a feeling or need without feeling badly about ourselves. We often feel shame about having certain feelings and needs. So, when we have the feeling or need we feel shame.

These are some red-flag indicators of shame. It is not all-inclusive and it gets us thinking differently about thoughts and behaviors we may be familiar with and never identified as shame.

Reflection: Learning our own personal "Red Flags" empowers us in our shame healing.

Day 164

Healing Action

"What if each of us believed that we are as powerful and strong as we allow ourselves to be? What if we quit trying to be accepted by everyone and gave up trying to not alienate anyone, and let ourselves be as strong and powerful as we are? The most difficult part of any endeavor is taking the first step, making that first decision." -Robyn Davidson

Shame wants us to live in a belief that we are not enough and never will be. It keeps us perpetually living in a state of effort. We can't relax and rest and just be good enough as we are.

If someone does not like us, we may say it does not matter, when, in truth, it nags away at us. We feel uncomfortable with displeasure from others. This is shame.

We start shifting this by setting an intention to allow ourselves to be good enough. When we don't feel "good enough," we remind ourselves of our intentions. We move in that direction, even if it is a constant jerking back and forth between not feeling like we are enough and beginning to believe we are and then finally living in the knowing of our being enough.

The same can be done with our vigilance to see if others like us and approve of us. We set intention to let what others think of us be none of our business. When we find ourselves on the other side of this intention, we cross back over to what is our business. Our business is approving of ourselves and letting what others think take a back seat.

> *Reflection: It seems like a long road, and it surely can be. However, it is so worth the journey. To accept ourselves, be able to release the effort of always trying to be perfect, and to release the need to have others' constant approval is a path to freedom and peace.*

Day 165

Specific Shame-Based Issue

There is a deep, painful belief in much of our world, that being overweight is shameful. If we are overweight, it shows. There is often a self-consciousness about our weight. We are constantly aware of it and often feel shame about it. We feel like others see our imperfections and are judging us. It never leaves.

Shame is not about truth, and it feels like it is. I know it is easier said than done to shift our core shame. If we are overweight and feel shame, it is most likely this body image shame represents the core shame that we are not good enough. We then focus on our bodies and beat ourselves up for how we look.

The core work is focused on the feeling of not being good enough. We can't talk ourselves out of the belief that we are not good enough. The shame is in our core. This shame has most likely been there for most, if not all of our life. This kind of shame affects all aspects of our life.

I hope, if you relate to this, that you will see someone who specializes in healing shame and let them help you with whatever holds this shame in place. Going on a diet, hiding out, beating ourselves up, or focusing on changing our bodies are not the answers. Letting our shame and pain out in a safe environment is a helpful way to bring our deep hurt and our feelings of not being good enough into healing.

> *Reflection: To focus on our weight or changing our weight is not going to bring healing to our core shame. We all deserve to heal.*

Day 166
Shame Defined

I was reading a novel the other day and found a great description of shame. It was in *The Burgess Boys* that was written by Elizabeth Strout.

The character:

"would nod and keep walking, always with her sunglasses on, walking to calm that terror and also the sense of having done something so wrong that only on this muddied path could she feel unobserved in her sense of shame, deep enough that had she been among others they would have pointed at her, knowing her as an outcast, a criminal. She had done nothing, of course." (Strout," p.239)

The sense of self-consciousness can be so deep that it attaches to ourselves as an identity. It does not depend on anything having happened. It is just there. Shame is the sense of needing to hide, of not wanting to be seen, of deep humiliation.

Shame may not always be present, and it can surface at any time. The ability of shame to come at unexpected moments keeps us wary. We don't know when shame will hit, and when it does, it can knock us flat. We can suddenly experience what was described in the above quote. This is the nature of shame.

We may have experienced this much of our lives and not known what to call it. Our culture is finally finding a way to talk about it and a word that describes it. This word is "shame." We used to think of it as a feeling we felt when we had done something wrong. Now, we use it to identify that internal feeling of not being enough. It haunts many and diminishes the quality of every life it haunts.

Reflection: We get to name the experience in order to intervene on it. The name is, "shame."

Day 167

Shame Loop

I have been talking about a "shame loop." It is depicted in the Appendix. I want to talk us through what a shame loop would look like if it were not intervened on.

- Step 1 is where we are triggered. We may be triggered by something external or internal.

- Step 2 is where we move into a defensive posture of some kind.

- Step 3 is where we disconnect from our real feelings and needs.

(Steps 1, 2, and 3 happen simultaneously.)

- Step 4 is where we move into self-defeating behaviors or thoughts. The hallmark of step 4 is a powerlessness to stop the thoughts/behaviors or to see a way out.

- Step 5 is where we come up with some way to try to "make up for our perceived shame." We make up some plan to either pay penance for or punish ourselves for what happened in #4 or for being the defective person we perceive ourselves to be.

- Step 6 is where we have a sense of temporary relief. We have paid penance or punished ourselves so we feel a bit more in control. However, the shame is still engaged, because we have not addressed it directly.

We can have countless unresolved shame loops going at the same time. We can live in this shame loop.

Reflection: We can learn to see when we are in a shame loop, and where we are in that loop. We can utilize the tools in this book and tools that we have gathered elsewhere to intervene. The Appendix has a section entitled "Steps to Intervene on Shame/Rage Loop." If we follow

*these steps, we have a useful tool for
intervening on shame.*

Day 168
Poem

It comes in spurts

Like the hose when I first turn it on

Pressure is building

My creative juices don't flow constantly

They are full and rich at times

Quiet and calm- barely a trickle at others

No need to force

Just notice

Be still and know

Creation never stops

It rests and moves in different currents

Peace,

Barb Tonn

Day 169
Forgiveness

Regret is a feeling most of us have experienced. We
regret an action or words that we've said. We return
to it from time to time and don't know how to make
peace with it. We don't know how to forgive ourselves.

When we regret we are looking back at something, but with a consciousness different from the one we had at the time we are regretting. We are at a different level of consciousness now from where we were in the past.

Releasing regret can happen if we allow ourselves to dialogue between the people we were then and the people we are now. We can do that in writing or in alternate chair work.

On paper, we have the person we were then talk to the person we are now. We can identify one hand as the hand of our present self and the other hand as the hand of the self we regret. We switch the pen from hand to hand as we dialogue between these two parts. We can also do this with one hand. It can be useful to attempt it both ways and see which way helps us the most.

We can also set up two chairs. We can put the one who did or experienced what we regret in one chair. We can visualize him/her as we looked then. We put the current self in the other chair. Then we move back and forth between the chairs and dialogue about the issue we regret.

Both of these tools can help us understand our younger self and help us reach a point of self-forgiveness and release from the regret.

> *Reflection: What a relief it can be to reconnect with the self that made the choices we regret. We can find that our younger selves were doing the best they could with where we were in consciousness at the time we made our choices. We can forgive ourselves.*

Day 170

Specific Shame-Based Issue

A dynamic that happens with regularity as we actively step into healing, is the resistance we experience from the people in our environment. As we utilize the tools, we are rocking the boats of those around us.

Our family system, friendships, and work relationships, all have a balance that is like that of a mobile. We all have a certain weight in the system and certain roles. I have talked about how dysfunctional that may be, but it is in place, nonetheless. As we begin to behave differently, adopt new rules and roles, define some new boundaries, express our truths and live from our truths instead of the "shoulds" that we have lived with, we are rocking the mobile. Everyone around us is part of that rocking and rolling and he or she doesn't always like that.

Although we often hear verbal support from people around our healing and change, the fact that they often experience change in their relationship with us is not always welcome. Often this resistance is experienced at a very unconscious level. However, we feel it.

We know that we will experience this resistance from people. We will get the message that we "should" return to the way we were before. We often experience rejection from those we love. We get to learn how to navigate those painful and rocky waters.

We get to be clear that the work we are doing is important to us, or it will be extremely difficult to keep on our new path when the resistance hits.

> *Reflection: Receiving a "resistance response" from others does not mean they don't love us, and don't truly support us. It comes from the fear that they experience because they cannot predict how this "new" person will be in relationship with them. It is just part of the healing process, and it helps to know it is in all likelihood going to happen.*

Day 171
Rule

Many of us set our dreams aside. Many of us never dreamed. When we grow up in addiction, abuse, shame-based systems or cultures, we live in survival. There is no time for dreams.

In many systems, there is an unspoken rule that we are not supposed to be better than others in the system. This means that we aren't supposed to be more educated, earn more money, or do things that the top person in the hierarchy has not done. Dreaming would break this rule.

We can begin by claiming the right to dream and move in directions that are different from our culture or family. We can ask ourselves the question: "If I let myself dream, what would I dream about?" We can tentatively step into a different way of being. Our shame may try to shut us down, and we can notice the shame voice and keep turning in a different direction.

Dreams allow us to begin to expand, grow, and live with a purpose beyond mere survival. Dreams speak to our value and worth. As our shame heals, we open more and more to our dreams and to a different way of being in the world.

Dreams don't have to be about "doing." They can be about showing up in the world knowing we are lovable and worthy and having value as a person. They can allow us to move with more confidence in our day-to-day life.

Reflection: We get to dream and claim our dreams.

Day 172

Right

I want to write this daily about what is on my mind. I have been really busy. My work has been busy and my husband is out of town working. My dad died recently. I am traveling between four cities, working and navigating the waters of grief. I have had limited energy.

What I feel pushing on me is the possibility that shame wants to enter, because I can't do everything that I would like to do or others would like for me to do right now. I notice the shame sitting on the edges of my consciousness and wanting to pounce on me when I have not accomplished enough.

I need to keep reminding myself that I have the right to make my own decisions based on my internal guidance. I have the right to change my mind and reconsider commitments. I have the right to take care of myself in the ways that fit for me. I have the right to honor my energy as it is right now.

Claiming rights has made a big difference in my quality of life and living without shame. It has kept me from moving into the shame that just waits for an opportunity to pounce on me. Learning my rights has helped me care for my self at all times. I notice that when I am vulnerable, living in my rights helps to keep me from shame.

Reflection: Claiming our rights is a powerful tool in healing.

Day 173
Voice of Shame

I hear shame being spoken constantly. The most recent time was when someone was talking about the holidays. They were trying so hard to prepare perfectly. In the meantime, they were sad and having a hard time, but would not deal with the feelings because they did not feel they had the right to have them.

There is a lot of shame about having and sharing feelings. Examples of the shame-voice regarding feelings and needs are:

I "should not"

- Still be grieving the loss of my pet

- Feel so down when I have so much to be grateful for
- Need so much attention
- Be angry
- Care if others like or accept me
- Have such a hard time in relationships
- Be so fat
- Have done...
- Be so upset at my family
- Be alone

I "should"

- Go on a diet
- Make more money
- Be happy
- Care about...
- Divorce him/her
- Not divorce him/her
- Have been more practical about retirement
- Have said "I am sorry"

I could write pages of examples. Many of the things mentioned above are worthy goals. When they are preceded by a "should" or "should not" then shame is leading the way.

Nothing works when shame is in charge. We can work on changing our underlying shame, and we can also change our "should" to "could."

Reflection: We need to name shame in order to claim the right to our feelings and needs, and our way of being in the world. When we have a "should" or "should not" running the show, then we can know that shame is in charge. In the long run, shame never gets us what we want.

Day 174

Shame Originator

I need to make a comment on the belief that there are times when we "should" use shame. One of my friends was watching a national morning TV show. They were talking about using shame on children to get them to do what you want them to. One of the announcers mentioned that they think it is good to use shame in this way from time to time. Some books on shame talk about healthy shame vs. unhealthy shame. This is a place where our language is not consistent. What they are really talking about is healthy guilt. Guilt is what we experience when we break our own value system. If we feel badly about breaking our value system, it helps us know we can make an adjustment in our behavior that is within our value system. We make the adjustment and then we move on.

When we experience shame we don't move on. We spin inward, feeling like a bad person. It is not about what we did, but about the essence of who we are. We need healthy guilt, but not healthy shame.

To shame a child to get them to do what we want is damaging and controlling. It is the difference between, "you are a bad boy" versus "I don't like that behavior." If we are using shame to get our children to do what we want, then we are out of control and trying to use control in a damaging way to get control.

Having said that, we have all done it and will do it. We can catch ourselves when we do.

We can go back and say, "I am sorry. Mommy/Daddy was out of control and I wish I had not said that." What I will say instead is: "I need that behavior to be different. If the behavior is not changed I will need to give you some consequences."

We also need to forgive ourselves and not shame ourselves. We learned how to shame in our world. We did not learn how to differentiate between shame and guilt and choices/consequences. We just didn't. So, we forgive ourselves, make our healing statements, and move on. And, we don't keep using our shaming behavior.

Reflection: There is no such thing as healthy shame and there is not a time when shame is called for.

Day 175
One Thing Different

What do we stand for as opposed to what do we stand against?

When we live in shame we are at war with ourselves. From this internal war, we create war in our lives. War divides and then divides again. This is what shame wants. It wants war and division. Peace is too quiet for shame. It forces us to face ourselves and that scares our shame-based selves. So, we stay in conflict.

One dynamic I have noticed is that people often do not choose "for" something they want to stand behind, but choose "against" something. This puts us in a war dynamic. We are back in the shame-based world. We want things to go a certain way and use shame to try to get things that way. We are shaming whatever we are choosing against. We make the other side bad or wrong and fight against it. This is shame driven. It creates more war.

If I can change that paradigm to choosing "for" something I can stand behind, I can make a difference and not shame those who do not believe as I do. I am choosing my value system. I don't need to go to war with others over what I believe. I just get to live in my truth.

This can be effective in many situations, from politics, to eating as we want (vegetarian vs. carnivore), to living in a community with similar values, to going to a church we want or not going to a church because it doesn't fit for us, to getting our bodies pierced or not. I can stand for or live in what fits for me without making someone, who does it differently, wrong.

> *Reflection: Doing this "One Thing Different," standing for instead of against, can make a difference in our world. We are shifting the foundation of our world from one that is shame-based to one that is love-based.*

Day 176

Shame in Our World

On Day 174, I talked about there being no healthy shame. I would like to talk more about what using shame to control can set up. That way, if we choose to use shame to try to get another to do what we want, control them; we will have a sense of what the consequences may be for us.

Using shame to get another to do what we want may get us what we want in the short term, but in the long term, we set the groundwork for a "boomerang" effect.

When we do something because someone shamed us into doing it, we will carry resentment. We may not even acknowledge the resentment at the time. However, if we notice how we feel when someone shames us, tries to manipulate us into thinking or behaving the way they want us to, we don't like it. We can feel a range of feelings, from a bit put off to rage-filled. Granted, we are always responsible for our own decisions. However, when we are little, or are in a relationship where there is a power imbalance, we may not have the ability to make our own choices. So, we go along with what the other person desires, but we don't like it.

Eventually, the desired response the person who used shame thought they got from us will boomerang. The long-held resentments, the feeling of being manipulated, having to sacrifice ourselves for others' approval or for safety will erupt. The boomerang turns back to the person who delivered the shame. The underlying resentment we feel is now focused on the person who manipulated us with shame.

Reflection: If we use shame to try to control others, we get to be aware of the boomerang effect. We get to decide if the choice to control is worth the consequences we may experience from the boomerang effect.

Day 177

Forgiveness

Over the years as I have studied shame, I have become intimately aware of the pain it causes us as individuals, and the long-term effects in our culture. However, the biggest sadness I have for the shame that dominates our world is that the shame we carry keeps us from truly being able to forgive ourselves and others.

To forgive is to be able to see past the actions of ourselves or others to the innocence of the heart, of the spirit beneath the action. I don't think we learn how to forgive unless we truly get tired of the lack of love in the world and decide there must be another, better way to live. We then become willing to live in a very different way.

The new way will seem harder at first, because we get to unlearn or release from our old judgmental way of being. We get to open to living our lives from the heart. We get to focus on our own choices and let others be responsible for their choices. We get to focus on the innocence in our hearts and project that out to others.

This "new way" sets the stage for forgiveness. Forgiveness sounds something like, "the innocence in me beholds the innocence in you." "The innocence in me beholds the innocence in me."

Reflection: No matter what the behavior, if we walked a mile in the shoes of another, we would release judgment and embrace their hearts.

Day 178
One Thing Different

I just returned from walking a labyrinth for solstice. There must have been at least 100 people on the labyrinth at any given time. We were all walking in our own ways, at our own speeds, saying our own prayers, to our own Gods. And yet, I truly experienced us as one. We were "one walking in the oneness of one."

It was one of the most peaceful periods of time I have ever had. It felt timeless. It felt like love extended outward in every direction. It was peaceful.

I could feel a kindness filling the room. I could feel love and peace moving.

This peace is the opposite of the competition and judgment of the shame-based world we are usually in. It was lovely to have had a reminder of what peace feels like.

It will make it easier for me to notice when I am not in peace and when I am.

It may not be walking a labyrinth that reminds us of peace. It may be floating in a canoe on a lake, or sitting in a park and listening to the birds. I don't know what it is for each of us, but it is there. When we experience peace, we are reminded of what is there for us each moment as we relinquish the shame-based ego at our core and step into the love that is our truth.

> *Reflection: It is worth it to experience peace.*
> *We will all find it in different ways.*
> *Experiencing peace will remind us of our*
> *connection to each other through love.*

Day 179
Healing Action

For a long time, I lived in a state of utter unconsciousness. I did not realize that when I lived this way, I hurt myself.

One of the ways I lived unconsciously was when I was an active alcoholic. After I went into recovery, I realized that one of the things I did with my drinking was, not deal with feelings and needs. In truth, I did not know what I was feeling most of the time, and I certainly did not know what I needed.

For example, I went through a divorce. I was hurting and I felt insecure. I needed support. I did not know how to address any of those feelings and needs in a productive way. I felt shame about going through a divorce, and I felt like a failure. So, I drank. I didn't deal with the feelings and needs trapped under the shame of feeling like I was a failure. This hurt me.

After I went into recovery, I realized how much I hurt myself by not learning the language of shame. I learned that under the shame were feelings and needs that were starving for attention. It was overwhelming at first. At times, I defaulted to other acting out behaviors. However, it became apparent that if I truly was going to have a life I could feel good about and find peace in, I needed to learn the language of shame. I needed to deal with my feelings and needs in a productive way.

Reflection: We get to put off our healing for as long as we want. We get to step into healing when we choose.

Day 180
Tool

We will never feel as vulnerable as when we bring our shame into healing. We will be stepping out of our comfortable old slippers of shame and into the power of loving ourselves. We will stop hiding our lights and playing small. We will stand in the essence of who we are. We will stop letting shame tell us we "can't" and step out onto the stage of life and live from our truths.

When we turn from our shame and move into love we will reach out. We will bring our sisters and brothers with us as we move from judgment to acceptance. We will open to all the ways we can creatively and openly express ourselves.

We will know what it is to be vulnerable. We will never look back. Once we step out, move through the vulnerable feelings, and into the embrace of loving acceptance of ourselves and others, we will jump for joy.

I feel like creating an anagram from the word "vulnerable." We can all see what ours would look like.

- **V** is for finding our "voices."
- **U** is for "us" as we join together.
- **L** is for the "love" we will begin experiencing for ourselves and others.
- **N** is for taking care of our "needs" in a healthy way.
- **E** is for extending forgiveness to "everyone."
- **R** is for giving our shame a "rest."
- **A** is for letting love be our "answer."
- **B** is for the "bravery" of leaving the old and moving into the new.
- **L** is for leaving every old construct of shame.
- **E** is for opening to "everything" from our heart.

That was fun. We can make up our own healing anagrams and it will help us remember our tools.

Reflection: This journey out of shame will take the rest of our lives. We may as well have fun with it.

Days 181-210

Day 181
Red Flag

There is a physical response in the body when we go into shame. I heard someone recently talking about observing someone. They said they knew the person they were observing had gone into shame because they'd turned beet red and wouldn't make eye contact.

As I mentioned previously, our bodies' limbs will get cold or hot when shame hits. We also flush in the face when our shame is triggered. Flushing is what an observer will notice that may be a cue that a person is in shame.

Flushing can be a very clear signal to the conscious observer that it is time to back off. When we are in shame we are usually incapable of having a clear and coherent conversation. It is like we shrink to a much younger age. To attempt to talk rationally with a triggered person is usually self-defeating for all involved.

At times, the person who is flushing hot will notice and be aware that they have gone into shame. It may be a good time to name it (if in a safe place), or to find a way to leave the environment and see what might be going on. In a safe environment, we may be able to say, "My shame has been triggered and I need to stop for a while. I will let you know when I am ready to talk again."

If partners or close friends have developed a language of shame, we can let each other know we are in shame or that we are seeing shame in another.

Reflection: Flushing red and hot is a cue that we are in shame.

Day 182
Voice of Shame

I have met many people who feel absolutely devoid of being helped. They have been given the message that they are hopeless, their lives will never get better, the world will never get better, and they will never change. This is what shame feels like.

Shame is NEVER true.

I have had people put "Shame is Never True" on their screen saver, write it on their bathroom mirror, make a t-shirt out of it, and send themselves a card that tells them this.

Shame is NEVER true. We can't be reminded of this too often. Shame feels true. We have felt like failures, or like we are not enough, or unlovable for as long as we can remember. Oh, we have had moments when it seemed to go away, and then something triggers us and we are back in it again. So, we think it will never change.

That is because we have not known how to consistently work directly with our shame. We have not unlearned the belief system shame supports and learned a new belief system. We have not integrated the tools that will help us when we are triggered.

Shame is NEVER true, and we can bring it into healing. We get to be tenacious. We get to learn that healing is a process. We get to acknowledge we are in a shame-based world and healing shame is the opposite of what most of us have learned.

Reflection: Shame is NEVER true. It is not our identity.

Day 183
Shame Originator

I have recently been writing about not using shame to motivate others, and how it can backlash and boomerang on those who use it. As often happens, I was speaking with someone who shared a story that will help me demonstrate my point. They were struggling with feeling shame when they were late. It turns out their parent had used shame to try to keep the kids on time, especially for church. She held great resentment for that and felt vicarious abuse (when you see someone abused and are powerless to intervene) from watching her sister be shamed and abused for running late.

At the time the abuse was happening, the parent may have had some success at getting her children out the door in time for church. However, the backlash was the trauma the child experienced and the resentment at the parent who used the shame.

Was it worth it? Did the shame help?

A case can be made for the fact that the mother got the children to church in time. However, the long - term consequences were grave. Could it have been possible for the parent to use positive reinforcement, or kindness to achieve the same results? In fact, that mother was in all likelihood using the same methods that were used on her. This is how we pass shame down through the generations.

This writing is truly not about shaming us as parents, because we have in all likelihood used shame to get the desired results. It is to help us become conscious of something we may not have thought of, so that we can make some changes. We all do it, and we can all change it.

Reflection: We all tend to pass shame on unless we begin to see the dire effects.

Day 184
Tool

It is time for me to remind us of one of my favorite tools. I have become clearer and clearer about the absolute help we can give ourselves if we look at:

- Rights,
- Choices,
- Boundaries.

If we are struggling in a relationship, or if we are going to be in a situation that we are uncomfortable with, or we are spending time with our families and are anxious about it, or we just don't know what to do about something, we can sit down and write our rights, choices (always more than two or you are just in a shame-bind), and boundaries. We write them out or speak them to a trusted friend to clarify our thoughts and calm our anxiety.

What are boundaries? What determines a healthy boundary? Boundaries determine what is acceptable and what isn't. They are personal, based on how we are feeling and our needs in a specific situation. Everyone gets to determine his/her own boundaries.

We can have overt and covert boundaries. The overt boundaries are ones we say aloud in a given situation. Example: I do not want a hug right now. I do not want to room with someone else in this hotel. I need my own water bottle. I don't want to be sexual. Covert boundaries are ones we have in our own personal thought bubbles, but do not necessarily say aloud. Example: I will no longer give my power over to _____ to upset me or ruin my day. I am in charge of my choices and will make the best ones for me.

I utilize a mantra that helps me. When I am stuck or going into a situation I feel uncomfortable with, I say, "rights, choices, boundaries." This empowers me. It helps to write them out, and we can also call them up quickly if we have thought them through ahead of time and/or shared them with someone.

Reflection: This tool honors ourselves and others. It reinforces love. It can't be good for one and bad for another.

Day 185

Tool

INDEPENDENCE DAY

Let's use this day to declare our independence from shame. Here are some suggestions for ways we can do this.

- Write a "good-bye" letter to our shame.
- Write our own "declaration of independence" from our shame.
- Write out our own "Bill of Rights" to live free of shame and the shaming influence of others.
- Make an art collage that highlights our lives without shame as the driving force. Instead of shame, we get to live with love motivating every thought, word, and action.
- Write a letter to our inner wisdoms, asking for help in living independently of shame.
- Declare our intentions to live free of shame with someone we trust who will hear us and affirm our thoughts.
- Ask someone to help as we navigate our way out of shame. Tell them exactly what we need and how they can help us. We make sure it is someone who has the language of shame.
- Spend a day celebrating our independence from shame in a way that fits us.
- Dance or sing or twirl sparklers to honor our intention to, one day at a time, keep moving away from shame.

Reflection: This is the day to "Declare" our independence.

Day 186
Shame Defined

Shame is an illusion.

That may feel like a really strong statement. However, what is really strong is the illusion of shame. From the time we are born, we start believing that we are damaged goods. Then, we spend the rest of our lives trying to prove we are good enough. Major religions often talk about "original sin." So, we start out with that belief. It isn't just a religious thing. It is a people thing.

What if shame is the opposite of what is true? What if we, in the essence of our being, are only love, only perfection? What if, the truth is, we are born in the perfect likeness of Love? Then, shame is the opposite of what is true.

Years ago I watched a movie called, *Cocoon*. There was a scene where beings from a different galaxy thought they were alone, so they unzipped the skins they were wearing that made them look human. Inside they were this incredible light. What if that is the same for humans?

What if the body we wear is just a cover-up for the essence of who we are? We get distracted by our bodies and the not so nice things we do to each other. But, the essence of who we are is not that body or what we do. The essence of what we are is love. Love created us like itself.

What we get to do is remove the blocks we carry in our thoughts and in our beliefs that keep us from seeing our own essences and the essences of others. "The loving essence of me beholds the loving essence of you."

Yet, we have it completely backwards here. We think we are the bodies and the terrible things we do to ourselves and others. When we take our blindfolds off, we see that shame is the illusion.

The illusion is very strong. We have a very hard time believing that we are lovable, good enough, adequate, worthy, etc. We get to challenge ourselves to turn away from the illusion of shame. We turn toward the compassionate love that created us like itself.

We get to challenge ourselves to look past our behaviors and the behaviors of others to the love that is the essence of who we are. When we look into our own eyes in the mirror we look deep into the soul, the essence, the love that is there.

We don't need to prove ourselves as worthy, enough, lovable, or adequate. We get to love ourselves and never question that again. What we need to question is the shame we have believed for so long.

Reflection: Shame is an illusion. We are not shame. We are love.

Day 187
Maude

Barb (B)—Maude, it seems important to put this book together. I have spent my career learning about shame and how it completely alters our existence and causes such profound distress. When we feel less than in some deep way, we are unable to feel connected to others, to God, or to ourselves. Can you comment on this, please?

M—I agree. It is tragic seeing so many people feeling depressed and anxious, feeling so very alone, and having no sense of personal value. That is what happens when shame is what we identify with. We end up feeling like we are not lovable enough, or worthy, and we have to prove ourselves constantly. When we identify with anything but love as our essences, we are not in truth. When we are not in truth, we will not be able to feel our connections. So, if we do not feel connected, like we are always on the outside looking in, then we can know we have identified with the wrong teacher. Our inner teacher either teaches love or hate. Hate shows up as fear. It is good, Barb, to have focused on this in your work, because you can teach others to change their teachers.

B—What does it mean to change your teacher?

M—Most of us have listened to the teacher of hate and fear. This teacher lives in constant judgment of ourselves and others. It is a continual drone in the background of our thoughts. We listen to that voice 24/7, and it is always lying. So, we can literally turn our heads in a different direction and begin to listen to the teacher of love.

B—What if it isn't there? Or what if it brings up fear that I am not good enough and will be rejected by the inner teacher of love?

M—The voice of love is always there. In some studies, it is called, "the still small voice." This voice is always there and we can learn to listen for it and to it. As we begin to listen for it, we begin to develop the ability to hear it. We get to learn that the fear is not based on truth.

B—The voice of love must be pretty hard to hear.

M—Actually, it is the most natural thing we can listen for and hear. We do have to learn to hear in silence and be still. If we are running around busily, we will have a harder time hearing even though it is always there.

B—Are you sure everyone has it?

M—Yes, it is the inner teacher of love. It is always there for everyone. Always.

B—If I hear judgment and hate of ourselves or others, or put-downs, is this the wrong teacher?

M—Yes, and you can turn in the other direction and listen, actively listen, for love. You can also ask, "What would love say?" Then, listen.

B—Well, I can see how important that is. That must be why I have dedicated my life's work on healing shame. Thank you.

M—Yes, my sweet one, anytime.

Day 188

Healing Action

Years ago, I read a chapter in a book that really stuck with me. The book is, *The Dynamic Laws of Healing*, by Catherine Ponder. Chapter 12 was titled "Chemicalization, A Healing Process." In it, she talks about what happens as we set spiritual intention. She teaches us to prepare for a predictable shame backlash.

The backlash she is talking about is our experiences when we begin to consciously identify shame and question its' truth. As we begin to move away from our shame, our shame gets louder, nastier, seems more convincing, and all and all can be very frightening.

I remember one time I was talking to a trusted friend. I told her I was going to release all the shame that I carried. I innocently set out from that conversation ready to release shame. Well, the shame that I carried took that as a direct threat and hammered me. I was assaulted by my old shame messages, new shame messages, and situations that reinforced the belief that shame was the only truth of my existence. Luckily, somewhere during the next couple of weeks, the memory of the information in the Catherine Ponder book crept into my conscious mind and I realized what was happening. I was experiencing a backlash from saying I was going to release all my shame.

We can set our intentions to move out of shame, and we can be conscious of the negative reaction, "backlash," of the shame to that intention

> *Reflection: We get to be aware that our shame is quite invested in our staying shame based. We may have experienced this when we claimed our independence from shame a few days ago.*

Day 189

Shame Indicator

When our shame triggers us, we go very internal. We disconnect from those around us. We loose awareness of people and our surroundings. We find ourselves in a dark and painful place. We are convinced if we share what is happening to us with others, we will be ostracized, abandoned, and hurt.

It is at these times that it is the most important to share with a safe person. Community is essential in healing shame. If there is not community, we can hire a therapist, or turn to a trusted clergy.

Our shame lives and thrives in the secret of our thoughts. Shame's life depends on never being exposed to the light of kind, accepting eyes. When our shame is triggered we need to be heard and discover that people will not run in the opposite direction. We get to experience that instead of running away, they can relate to us and love us. We hate ourselves at times, and project that outward. We assume others will hate and reject us as we have hated and rejected ourselves.

Part of healing is developing a support system of loving, human people. I say "human" because the people we choose need to be in touch with their feelings. They can then reflect their knowing because they can relate to the struggle we feel so alone in. It may take time to develop this community of support, and it is well worth the time and effort.

Reflection: To reach out and connect is one of the hardest and kindest things we can do in our healing journeys out of shame. Reaching out to others, connecting, and experiencing kindness, brings deep healing to our isolated shame based self.

Day 190
Shame Indicator

We have been talking about choices and I keep saying we need more than two options for it to really count as a choice. When we only have two choices, we are in a shame bind. This is most commonly called a double bind. When we are in a shame/double bind, it will sound like "either/or." If I am only looking at two choices, I will most likely feel shame, no matter which I choose. Being in a shame bind and feeling shame no matter what we choose is a "Shame Indictor."

We get to look at the shame message that is under each choice in the shame bind.

If I do _____, my shame is telling me _____.

Once we isolate the shame messages on each side of the bind we can look at what the truth is. In that way, we expose the shame. We can then look at all the other options our shame has not been letting us see.

I will give an example. I need help. I am in the bind of either getting help or not. This is an either/or shame bind. If I isolate the shame further, it will look like:

- If I get help, my shame is telling me: (I may be too vulnerable, or I will look like a loser, or nobody will want to help me and I will be rejected)
- If I don't get help, my shame is telling me: (I may be a failure, or not finish and be a loser).

Whether I ask for help or not, I feel bad, I feel shame.

What is the truth if these two shame messages are not about truth?

The truth may sound like:

We all need to develop support systems to turn to when we need help. It is part of being human.

- There is no shame in needing help and no shame that we get to take the time to develop a support system.
- There is no shame in doing things alone.

It isn't the options that are the problem. It is the shame driving the options that lock us into inaction. Once we expose the shame and claim our truths, we can choose one of these options or find others.

Reflection: To identify that we are in a shame bind is half the problem. To identify what the shame is telling us and turn in the direction of truth is the other half. We, then, are free to choose what truth fits for us or look at options the shame would not let us see previously.

Day 191
Tool

An anagram used in the 12 step communities is: HALT

- H- Hungry
- A- Angry
- L- Lonely
- T- Tired

We are encouraged to HALT when we feel them.

We can use the same anagram for working with our shame as we do for addictions. If we experience various shame indicators, such as, feeling badly about ourselves, behaving in destructive ways, not feeling peaceful, or struggling, etc., it may be a good time to halt. We then get to attend to whichever HALT behaviors (hungry, angry, lonely, tired) we are experiencing.

Halting helps us get clarity about what is going on within us, and what our needs are. The "HALT" provides breathing time to step out of the shame. It we halt and attend to our needs, it gets us into the here and now moment. Only when we are in this here and now moment can we truly take care of ourselves in an effective way.

If we are not taking care of ourselves in an effective way we are at higher risk to trigger into shame. If we are already in a shame loop we will have a harder time releasing from it.

Reflection: HALT is a useful tool when we are struggling with shame.

Day 192
One Thing Different

Don Miguel Ruiz wrote the book, *The Four Agreements*. In it, he writes about four things we can focus on to increase the chance of bringing peace into our lives. The four agreements he mentions are:

1. Be impeccable with your word
2. Don't take anything personally
3. Don't make assumptions
4. Always do your best

The book is a lovely expression of some principles for living in the world that support love and not shame. I highly recommend the book.

We can take each of those agreements and focus on them one at a time to make the shift away from shame, or we can make a study of all of them together for an extended period of time. Either approach provides structure for living in the world differently. These structures can help when we feel overwhelmed by the changes we are stepping into, or when we don't know where to start.

We get to create the structure for healing which best fits our personality and lifestyle. There is no "one" way to go into healing shame. There is the way that fits for us individually.

Having a book to lean into can help us develop a structure, and a language for healing. Although the Ruiz does not use the word, "shame," he is definitely talking about healing in a way that is supportive of releasing shame.

Reflection: We get to create our own healing paths.

Day 193
Rule

I focused my graduate work on shame and the impact of the "no talk" rule on reinforcing shame. When a family, work, or government system is experiencing problems, or has addictions, or abuse, and those issues aren't talked about, they become shame bound.

If I am angry or upset and don't know how to talk about it, the anger becomes destructive to myself and/or others. In the "no talk" system the obvious can be denied. It is not talked about. This "no talk rule" reinforces shame.

When we have grown up in systems where the "no talk" rule prevails, we don't know how to share. We have to learn. We often don't know how to talk about the obvious. It can be frightening to share. Often the feelings we are experiencing aren't acknowledged and come out in abusive or destructive ways. For mental and emotional health, we get to learn to talk about what we are feeling and experiencing. We get to talk about the obvious.

Talking with safe people, sharing in safe place, expressing without fear of reprisal are all integral parts of healing shame. We get to challenge the "no talk" rule. We get to bring our shame out into the light and talk about how it has impacted us. If we are in a system that does not support the change to a system where individuals get to share, we get to make choices about our proximity to that system.

Reflection: Talking is essential in healing shame.

Day 194
Right

I have the right to say "NO."

We have the "right to say, no." However, we often have a hard time practicing saying it and sticking to it. In saying "no," we are risking criticism and rejection. Both of those things are difficult for shame-based people.

Saying "no" sets a boundary. Saying "no" tells others what is acceptable or not acceptable for us. It delivers a need. Saying "no" may set off more shame. Therefore, we may be reluctant to say, "no."

For now, we get to start with knowing that saying "no" is a right we all have. We may have to learn how to say it. We may need support to say it. We may not be able to say it for a while. We may have a hard time hearing it from others. But, we have the right to say it.

There are songs written about "no" being a complete sentence, or "what is it about "no" you don't understand?" The fact that those lyrics show up as songs demonstrates that many people struggle with either saying "no" or honoring when someone says, "no."

As we continue in our healing processes with shame we can begin to teach our inner child the truths, whether we believe them or not. Learning our rights is part of that process.

Reflection: We don't have to start with practicing our rights. We can start with learning them.

Day 195
Healing Actions

Shame	Healthy sense of self
1. No rights/ No choices	Exploration of rights/choices
2. No Limits	Set limits/Set boundaries
3. Objects count	Personhood counts
4. External Judge	Internal Judge
5. Hierarchy	People count equally
6. Blame	Appropriate responsibility
7. Feels dishonest sense of others	Feels more honest (internal Knowing who I am and trusting my
8. No reconciliation	Forgiveness possible (of self and others)
9. Value for what we do	Value for who we are

Each characteristic of shame has a corresponding Healthy characteristic. These lists show the movement out of shame and into a healthy sense of self. It represents an on-going process of healing.

Day 196
Healing Action

I am going to be referencing Day 195 for the next few days. It helps us get an overview of the process we are in.

In #1 on Day 195, the movement is from not knowing we have rights or choices to exploring and learning our right and choices. In the shame-based system we do not know that we have rights or do not know what our rights are.

Knowing our rights can be extremely empowering. In shame-based systems the intention is to "not" support each other in stepping into our power. Living in our power can be very threatening to the dynamics in the shame systems.

Often when we are in a situation and don't know which way to turn, one of the most helpful things we can do for ourselves, is to learn our rights. At times we need legal assistance to learn our rights. Sometimes we can go to human relations in a work environment. We can read about healthy systems and how people in those systems support each other by honoring rights. In this book, I have been writing about rights and will continue to do so.

We have been reading about choices. We can talk to others to brainstorm choices. We can identify when we are in a shame bind and expand choices beyond the either/or. We can write choices out and then consciously choose. We can set intent to build the skill sets we need in order to act on our choices. Learning our choices and consciously choosing moves us from victim to self-empowered. It moves us beyond the shame-based system.

> *Reflection: We all have rights and choices that help us move beyond the shame and into our personal power.*

Day 197

Healing Action

In #2 on Day 195, we move away from not knowing our limits into learning what our limits and boundaries are and feeling empowered to set them.

We have looked at the concept of limits and boundaries. This is how we create safety for ourselves. This is how we move from victim consciousness to our power.

What are our limits/boundaries? Do we have any? Do we ever share them or set them with others? Do we notice when we are angry and then look at the possibility that our limits or boundaries have been crossed? Maybe this is because we never set limits in the first place.

Our anger can be a great red flag for learning that we need to establish boundaries. We can notice our anger as a way to determine where we need to set limits.

We can look back at times we were angry and notice what boundaries would have been helpful. We can make decisions about where we set boundaries in the future.

We start exploring our boundaries by talking with friends, our therapists, and safe people. We get curious about how our lives might be different if we set some clear limits with people. We practice and get empowering support.

Reflection: Exploring limits and boundaries can be extremely empowering in our healing processes.

Day 198
Healing Action

In #3 on Day 195, we begin to value people and relationships more than objects and things.

I will share a story to demonstrate this. Someone I knew from an alcoholic system experienced the following: There was a fire in the home and they were directed to start saving "things or objects." They ran around grabbing electronics and objects deemed important while risking the lives of the people. The fire was getting worse and they were not allowed to leave until they had rescued what was deemed "important." In most shame-based systems, the people, their feelings, their relationships, and health are not valued as much as the things in the system. This is the same in the business world as in the family institutions.

As we move into our healing, we begin to value the people in our lives, the relationships we have, the health and welfare of friends and family, above our driven desires to acquire more and keep our feelings in the background. In the business world, the stability, health, and relationships in the work environment are valued and attended to.

We have become human "doings" instead of human "beings." Workaholics get a pass for missing time with friends and family because work is valued above relationships and people. We get to do that differently.

Reflection: It is helpful to look at what we truly value and how we support what we value with our actions.

Day 199

Healing Action

In #4 on Day 195 we are moving out of our focus on the "external judge" and into developing our own "internal judge."

If we listen to the voice in our head we find that we are primarily concerned with how we perceive others view us. We worry about what "they" will say about us. We look outside of ourselves, to an external judge, to make decisions in our life. We often attach to certain belief systems without really discerning if the teachings fit for us. Do we really want to live in the way that is being determined by the belief systems we are attaching to? Do we give ourselves choices?

The movement in the healing process is from being all consumed by what others think (the external judge) to what we think (the internal judge). We take time to get conscious of the choices we are making and how we feel about those choices. We get curious about what we might think if we weren't concerned about how others would judge us. We take a look at what we are valuing and if we feel good about those values. We write out our beliefs. We then ask our self if we want to keep those beliefs or change them.

This is a critical step in the healing of shame. Shame is an outside construct we adopt as our own, most of the time very unconsciously.

Reflection: What do I believe? What do I stand for? How do I want to live my life? Who am I trying to impress? Is it getting me what I want in my life?

Day 200

Healing Action

Number 5 on Day 195, is the movement out of hierarchy and into counting each person equally.

Our culture thrives in hierarchy. There is consistently someone more valued than another. My challenge to those of us who are reading this book is to look at every system we are part of and become aware of who is valued more than another. Then, we look at what this honoring gets those higher in the hierarchy and what it gets those who are lower. We can do this without making the systems and people in the system wrong. This is what we have learned. We have not known any other way. Hierarchy supports shame. Some people are valued above others.

We can begin to get curious. How we would do things differently if each person in the system were valued equally? What if each of us was valued? What if our value was not determined by how much money we made or what color our skin was, or our sexuality? What if we were valued because we are intrinsically worthy? What if we constantly knew our worth and never questioned that? Can we even begin to see how different our world would be?

What if we could disagree with others and still value them? What if we, each of us, could count equally? We would have more dignity. We would be more respectful of each other. We would be kinder.

> *Reflection: The movement out of hierarchy is a major paradigm shift. We get to start by exploring options*

Day 201

Healing Action

Number 6 on Day 195, is the movement out of blame into taking appropriate responsibility for our words and actions. It is indigenous to all shame-based systems. Every shame-based system is about blame. We rarely hear someone in a shame-based system take appropriate responsibility. We blame our partners, children, government, teachers, political parties, minorities, majorities, weather, churches, leaders, men, women, food, wealthy, impoverished, criminals, nationalities, genes, biology, science, the unknowns, our weights, addictions, being misunderstood, childhood, old age, guns, other nations, global warming, our personality flaws, our sex drive or lack of sex drive, to name a few.

To take appropriate responsibility is not part of the equation in our shame-based world. There is always something we can blame and we do so, even when we are pretending to take responsibility for our part in something. Deep down we blame. Deep down we either blame ourselves for everything or nothing. In either case, we are not taking appropriate responsibility.

What if we started saying "my part in this situation is ..." Then, we earnestly look at what we are responsible for in that situation. We don't take more than our part and we own our part. We refuse to blame anymore. We own our part and let go. Whether the other side takes their part is their responsibility. We can't make someone else take his or her part. We own what we are responsible for with compassion and care. We own our part. Period. End of story.

Reflection: Blame is about shame. It does not bring peace or help our world work.

Day 202
Healing Action

Number 7 on Day 195, is about the dishonesty we feel in the shame-based system. Things do not feel right. Things do not feel honest. Things are not as they appear. From the outside, things can look fine, good, perfect, and from the inside it feels wrong, dysfunctional. A shame-based system can look good and feel bad.

As individuals and systems go into healing the movement is toward integrity and honesty. Words match actions. We begin to trust our perceptions. We begin to trust that what we are seeing and hearing is the truth. We also begin to be more honest with what we are thinking, feeling, seeing, and needing.

As we begin to bring ourselves and systems into healing there is more honesty and fewer secrets. We bring things out into the open, into the fresh air of truth. We hold ourselves and others to a standard of honesty that we can build on.

This, as in all aspects of healing, is a process. Those of us who have participated in step work in the 12 step programs have seen the steps take us from the dishonesty of early recovery to a deep sense of integrity and honesty as we work the steps and expose our secrets in the sacredness of the step work. This is the process of healing we all are in.

Reflection: Shame has us living in secrets and dishonesty. Our healing moves us into the peace of openness and honesty.

Day 203

Healing Action

Number 8 on Day 195, is about moving from an unforgiving frame of mind to forgiving ourselves and others. As I have talked about previously, because shame is fueled by perfectionism, it makes it difficult, if not impossible to forgive.

In order to reconcile with those we have resentments and judgments toward, including ourselves, we need to look through the eyes of kindness and humanness. We need to be able to put ourselves in another person's shoes. We need to want peace above "being right." Shame does not allow any of these mind-sets.

Shame is unrelenting in its search for perfection. If we make a mistake, it keeps that mistake alive in our thought bubbles. In systems, we remind the other person of their mistakes for decades to come. It will not allow us to make amends and be forgiven because it is not about an action; it is about the essence of self. So I did not just "do" something unforgiveable, I am "unforgiveable." I am a "mistake." This is where shame hits us. Without addressing what the shame is telling us about ourselves, we cannot reach a place of forgiveness. We need to let the shame speak so we can really hear what it is telling us about the other person or ourselves. We, then, can choose if we want to live with the shame beliefs, or consciously bring them into healing and change them.

As we address the shame messages about a mistake, and about the person who made the mistake, we can truly begin to see that we can never be good enough for shame. We get to see that we can live our lives in different ways.

The different ways we live our lives will allow us to be human, make mistakes without them reflecting on the essence of who or what we are, address the mistake, make amends, and move on. We are not our actions. The loveable essence of who we are never changes, even when we make a mistake.

Reflection: Shame demands perfection. In that paradigm, we don't get to forgive. We don't get to be good enough. We get to choose if that is how we want to live our lives.

Day 204

Healing Action

Number 9 on Day 195, addresses the movement out of the shame system where we are only recognized for what we "do," or not recognized at all, to a system where we are recognized and valued for "who" we are.

Part of the driven nature of our culture is a constant need to "do" more in order to prove we are good enough or worthy. It drives the workaholic mentality. It leads to exhaustion, resentment, defeated mentality, and illness.

When I have asked people what they were recognized for growing up, it is usually something they did, or achieved. It can be anything from cleaning their room, to playing the piano well. Those are achievements that are lovely to have accomplished. Yet, they do not honor who we are. It is the difference between, you are lovable no matter what, and you are lovable when you "achieve" something.

Recognizing the essence of a person may sound like, "I see you and honor you as a lovable person, no matter what. I value you in this world. I value you in this family, or work environment, or wherever we are." Our value is not attached to achievement. We are honored just because "we are." What we do is what we do, but it does not define us.

Reflection: We get to be honored for being "human" and for showing up in the best way we can.

Day 205
Red Flag

I have talked some about anger and rage and I want to say more. Understanding the difference between anger and rage is critical in discerning when we are in shame.

When we are in rage, we are in shame. Saying I am in "rage" can feel very shameful. What distinguishes rage from anger is that it is "always" destructive. If I am "thinking" thoughts that are destructive to my self, property, or others, or I am "acting" destructively toward my self, property, or others, I am in rage/shame.

THIS CONCEPT IS PROFOUNDLY IMPORTANT IN HEALING SHAME.

What does destructive mean? Webster defines "destructive" as tending or likely to cause destruction, tearing down, destroying. Synonyms are ruinous, detrimental, or fatal.

Rage goes on and on, seeming to have no end. There seems to be no way to resolve it. This is because rage comes from feeling like we are damaged goods. Rage can be triggered by something outside of ourselves and it can be triggered by our own internal thoughts. If we find ourselves in rage we can know immediately that our shame is engaged.

When we are in anger we feel like something has happened to us that crosses our boundaries. It is about an action, not about ourselves. It is finite. When we notice we are angry, we can take an action to correct a boundary invasion. Once that has happened we no longer feel the anger. It is now over.

Reflection: Rage is a red flag that we are in shame.

Day 206

Forgiveness

I found this prayer once and I think it speaks to the healing of shame and the need for forgiveness in our world.

Forgiveness Prayer

> If I have harmed anyone in any way either knowingly or unknowingly

> Through my own confusion, I ask their forgiveness.

> If anyone has harmed me in any way either knowingly or unknowingly

> Through their own confusions, I forgive them.

And if there is a situation I am not ready to forgive, I forgive myself for that.

For all the ways that I harm myself, negate, doubt, belittle myself, judge or be unkind to myself through my own confusions,

I forgive myself—Author, Unknown

We can only do the best we can at any given moment. That is enough.

Reflection: We usually have to work consciously to break the paradigm of "unforgiveness" in our world. This prayer may be helpful.

Day 207

Model for a Shame Free World

Today I want to encourage everyone to honor the courage it takes to break the old shame paradigms we carry. It takes courage to:

- Look shame in the eye and turn in a different direction.
- Choose to live by an internal "truth" instead of the external "should."
- Feel our feelings.
- Address our needs.
- Consciously choose the beliefs we want to support and live by.
- Choose forgiveness.

- Choose peace over the shame need to "be right."
- Live consciously.
- Ask for help.
- Establish boundaries for ourselves.
- Look at our choices and choose what fits for ourselves.
- Empower self through choices, rights, and boundaries.
- Love instead of hate.
- Continue to turn over the paradigms we have lived in that support war with each other and within ourselves, and move toward peace.
- Continue to release shame so we can live more fully.

Reflection: We get to honor the courage it takes to release shame and live in the world in a loving way.

Day 208
Poem

Letting go can seem so hard

Pry those tightly clenched hands open

Raise them to the sky

Give "Love" a High Five

Another

Now live and fly

Let Go- Let Love- Fly Home

Barb Tonn

Day 209
Shame in Our World

One of the questions I am frequently asked is, "when will my shame be gone?"

It has been my observation that as long as we are alive on the Earth Plane we will be dealing with shame. It is part of the very air we breathe. As humans, we are inundated with mental shame constructs in our reading, our teachings, and our cultural and familial upbringings.

Healing shame is a process of increasing our consciousness to become ever more aware of when we are receiving a shaming message from the outside and when we are self-triggering a shame message on the inside. At the moment of awareness, we can bring the shame out into the light of truth. It is in this awareness that the shame is brought into healing. We can then allow it to be transformed.

As we grow more adept at noticing shame for what it is, we can release and transform it. When will we be done? When we identify shame, shine the light of truth on it, and see it for what it is.

Reflection: Instead of trying to be finished with healing, we get to be aware of shame in the moment. The moment is the only place it can be transformed.

Day 210

Tool

The term "thought bubble" is active in our culture as I write this book. It is helpful as a tool in healing shame.

It brings up the cartoon image where thoughts are isolated in a bubble. If we can isolate our thoughts into bubbles we are then able to identify what our shame is telling us. Now we are in the role of observer. As observers, we have a bit more distance from the shame. In the observer position, we may not be as activated by the shame. We can sit and write out our thoughts and surround them in a circle to indicate a thought bubble. The bubble can indicate that it is our shame talking and we can clearly see what the shame is telling us.

We can actually write a cartoon script and draw in the pictures that go with the words in the bubbles. It is a way of taking some of the power and intensity out of the shame.

Although our cartoon script is not funny, it helps us isolate our thoughts. Isolating our thoughts allows us to see clearly how mean, unloving and hurtful our inner words are. We then rewrite the script with the dialogue we choose.

> *Reflection: Finding different ways to hear, observe, and change our shame messages helps in the healing process. Some processes are more helpful than others. Drawing a cartoon with*

"thought bubbles" is one way we may find helpful.

Days 211-240

Day 211
One Thing Different

What we perceive as coming from others is what we first felt or experienced in our self and would not let ourselves acknowledge. If I believe you have judged or rejected me, then I have first judged and rejected myself. If I do not let myself look at my own rejection and judgments of my self, I will be convinced they are coming from you.

I remember when I was leaving my marriage my husband said, "you never believed I loved you." At the time, I thought he did not love me. What I see now is that I did not love me and I projected that onto him.

We can project constantly. If I am angry and will not look at my anger, I will be convinced it is coming from someone outside of me. It may not be a person, but a nation or a political party or a minority group. If I perceive anger outside of me, it may be helpful to look at my own anger.

The world is a mirror for our inner conditions. What I consistently see in others may be a reflection of what I feel about myself and am not willing to look at.

In the "new age movement," I consistently see people denying their own hard emotions. "I am not angry, I am happy. I will only focus on the happy thoughts." That is all well and good, but if there is anger there, and we won't look at it, we will see it reflected around us. If we honestly deal with our feelings, we are in our personal power, and have choices. If we don't, we will project them onto others and will end up feeling powerless.

> *Reflection: What we deny we project. If we are surrounded by "shaming" or "angry" people, we may want to be curious about how we are shaming ourselves and not letting ourselves deal with our own anger.*

Day 212
Shame Loop

Often when we are beginning our shame work, we look for something outside of us that triggers our shame. However, because our world is shame-based and we grew up in it, we have internalized many shame messages and identified with them. Shame becomes autonomous. We can trigger into it without any outside influences or overt triggers.

An example of an internal trigger could be that we are stepping into our day and realize we have more things to do than we have time for. We have made more commitments than we can fulfill or have double-booked our time slots. If our shame engages, we may begin to feel like an "idiot" or "stupid" for not catching this sooner. We may feel trapped and ashamed because we made a mistake. We drop into the "self-defeating" spot of #4 on the shame loop (see Appendix). In this place we can spin in the shame and actually not get anything done, or avoid taking responsibility for our error and making appointment changes. Nothing outside of us happened, but we feel shame. We internally triggered into a shame loop. If we can identify this as "shame," we can intervene on it. That might sound like:

- My internal shame voice is beating me up. It is telling me I am _____.

- It seemed that voice started when I looked at my "to do" list and found I had scheduled too much for my day.

- If I hadn't gone into shame at that point, I might have felt a bit frustrated and needed to reorganize my day or I might have smiled and felt some humor that I had fallen into my old habits. At that point I could have shifted my day around. (These are the steps for intervention found in the Appendix.)

- We are now productively advocating for ourselves and intervening on the shame loop.

Reflection: Noticing the shame when we internally trigger allows us to intervene on the process and not move into a full-blown shame loop.

Day 213

Shame in Our World

There is a phenomenon in the world today called, "bullying." We are reading about it happening in schools, online, in work places, and in homes. Urban Dictionary defines bullying as "abuse."

Bullying results from a power imbalance that is the mainstay of shame. It takes advantage of a group mentality that supports a hierarchy and minimizes the worth of certain people in the hierarchy. Bullying is the epitome of shame. It causes profound distress in those being bullied rendering them incapable of stopping it. A complete sense of worthlessness and powerlessness ensues. When bullying is not stopped, victims may resort to suicide.

Our culture has become increasingly shame-based and it is for this reason bullying has become such a common occurrence. Efforts to stop it have been fairly ineffective and even if it stops, the wounds the victim suffered are deep and difficult to heal. To be abused and treated as less than by one's peers is painful and very difficult to repair.

There is not a quick cure for bullying. It is entrenched in our culture. However, when looking at how our systems support shame, this is a marker. Often when bringing bullying into the light, the first response is to blame, another hallmark of shame. What we can do instead, is name the shame, and take our individual responsibility for our own thought systems that continue to support hierarchy, abuse, and blame. We can then take responsibility for changing our own thoughts and actions that support shame and bullying.

When we carry shame, we often bully ourselves, and at times we bully others. We support bullying when we don't look at how we participate.

If I bully myself, I abuse myself. During my active eating issues, I used to pinch my fat all the time to determine if I had gained weight. I used to beat myself up if I had gained weight or clothes did not fit right. Those were ways I bullied myself. Maybe we can at least be curious as to how we bully ourselves and look at the consequences. Are these consequences we want to live with?

> *Reflection: Bullying is abuse and we often do it to ourselves and others in ways we never would have called bullying. However, if it is bullying, we can do something about how we treat self and others. We can change from bullying to kindness and compassion.*

Day 214
One Thing Different

Sweetness/Light/Highest

"The sweetness in me beholds the sweetness in you."

"The light in me beholds the light in you."

"The highest in me beholds the highest in you."

Saying any of these moves us in a direction other than shame.

When we are mirroring our shame-based world we usually are saying something akin to, "the worst in me beholds the worst in you."

We grow up being taught to be discerning. What that often means is to make sure you notice if someone is leading you down the wrong path or is about to hurt you or take advantage of you. So, we look for the worst in others. Well, I am not saying to walk down dark allies, or to not have an awareness of evil intent.

What I am saying is: "When we are seeking to be more loving in this world, seeking to be in relationship, then the 'One Thing Different' we can do is: look past the surface to the sweetness, light, and highest that is in everyone." If I seek that, look for that, watch for that, then I must first see it in myself. I extend from that light in myself and find the light in others.

The way we live in this world, at least until we are truly on conscious healing paths, is the exact opposite of loving. We are pulled off love by failing to look beyond the surface of others or ourselves.

We can take care of ourselves and have discernment and still look for, or seek, the best in others. If we did this for a while, starting with ourselves, we would begin to see through completely different eyes and see a very different world.

What if the essence of who we are is love? What if we looked for that and took care of ourselves from that perspective?

> *Reflection: Next time we are around someone who seems particularly difficult, we get to say, "The highest in me beholds the highest in you." We get to notice what happens. We get to be curious and decide if we like the results.*

Day 215
Shame Originator

In our culture, we put a lot of stock in "figuring things out." We believe that if we can figure out shame, where it comes from, and what our triggers are, that we can eliminate shame from our lives. It doesn't work that way.

Shame can be solidly in place by age two. We often have no memory of our lives before two and we had limited language with which to describe our experiences, feelings, needs, etc. This lack of memory makes it difficult to figure out shame.

Shame is often communicated with the eyes. Say your mother got pregnant without planning to, in a way she feels shame about it. She had no way to deal with the shame. Every time she looked you in the eye as an infant she communicated her shame. You, the child, felt the shame and you had no way of knowing where it came from.

We may feel more in control if we can figure out why we have so much shame, but that will not change it. So, what do we do?

Even if we have the information that would help us understand where our shame originates, just having the information is not enough to heal it. Shame hits us on every level of our beings. We experience it emotionally, spiritually, in our relationships, physically, intellectually and with our lack of "will" to change it.

Therefore, we begin to work on our shame on all of these levels. We address the core issue of feeling and believing we are not enough.

Reflection: Even if we understand where shame comes from, merely understanding shame does not change it. We heal the core shame on all levels.

Day 216
Forgiveness

It was gay pride week in Albuquerque, where I live. The gay pride T-shirt for the year said, "Love is Love." It struck me as such an important concept in the healing of shame. We just get to love what/who we love. We get to leave others alone if they love in a way we don't.

Years ago, I was facilitating an inpatient alcohol treatment group. We were supporting each other in reclaiming dreams lost during our active addiction years. One man claimed a dream of having a "trap line." It really put me to my own personal test. I, personally, do not support trap lines. However, I did not want to shame him. One of the forgiveness tools I use in my own work is:

I forgive _____ for _____, because the truth is _____.

In this case, I said to myself: I forgive him for wanting a trap line because the truth is his belief system supports trap lines.

I don't need to make others "bad" for believing differently than I do. I may not ever want a trap line and I don't feel it is my right to shame others who think differently than I do. I can make a stand for something I believe in without attacking the worth and essence of a person who believes differently than I do.

> *Reflection: If I walked a mile in your shoes, I would do what you do. Shame is shame. Love is love. I want to support love. I can support capturing animals humanely, or not at all, without shaming those who believe differently than I do.*

Day 217
One Thing Different

Why Do I Focus on Shame?

I have worked with many recovering people who could not stay in recovery or just switched addictions. I have wondered what we were missing that their recoveries were illusive. I realized that until we can love ourselves we would act out in our addictions, or truly struggle in our lives. So, I began my search for what keeps us in our struggles, and realized it was shame.

Shame is developmentally in place at a very young age. It is often in place before language. We don't have common language for shame so many people do not identify with having it. However, my belief is that most, if not all people are identified with a false self, a negative self, and an ego self. Identification with these false selves keeps us from having peace in our lives. These false selves are shame.

So, I focus on shame because I believe without healing our shame, we will always struggle.

Reflection: Shame locks us into unhappiness and despair. We get to work directly with our shame to change it.

Day 218
Shame Defined

My husband had a bumper sticker that read "Don't Believe Everything You Think." I think that is so wise and helpful in healing shame. The thing is, we do believe what we think. We get attached to our belief systems and don't really look at our beliefs. If we really looked at what we believe, we could begin to question where the belief originated, and if we really believe it or want to believe it.

Shame is based on the presumption that we are damaged goods. The words may differ. We may feel like we are not enough, or not worthy, or not lovable, and we don't really question the belief. Or, we will argue in the defense of the belief without really taking a look at what it is based on.

We often will cite that we are not enough because of things we have done or have not done. We look at our actions and our mistakes and come to a conclusion about ourselves. Our behaviors and actions are not about the essence of who we are. We will always fall short of the "perfection" standard of shame. However, this is not who we are.

Who/What are we? What do we not see about ourselves and others? We, in our essences, are love.

When we define ourselves by our actions, we will feel less than or greater than, but never equal to.

> *Reflection: We are love. We make mistakes and mess up and it does not change the essence of who or what we are.*

Day 219

Shame Originator

We develop our boundaries as we grow. We learn who we are and what we are comfortable with as we look at ourselves in proximity to others. We are vulnerable as we grow. We aren't formed yet and we depend on others to help us learn how to care for ourselves.

When there is abuse, we learn we don't have the right to boundaries. We learn that we are defined by others and are there to meet their needs. The abuser dumps their shame on us and we are left feeling shame. We don't know the shame is not ours. We carry beliefs that we are less than and there to meet the needs of others. We do not have a sense of self that sustains us.

We grow up with the victim-stance. Victims often become the perpetrators. We don't know that the original trauma holds the shame-based belief in place. We just feel bad.

We get to bring our consciousness into healing. We get to begin to question this "badness" that we feel and bring it to the light of love. We become willing to question the belief in our badness and heal the traumas that hold it in place. We get to take responsibility for the victim consciousness we carry or the perpetrator behavior we perpetuate and know it is not the true definition of who we are. We get to change.

Reflection: When we are little and bad things happen to us, we let those bad things define us.

Day 220
Shame in Our World

Too often, in our shame-based world, being different has become shameful. There is an external norm that we often seek that does not match ourselves. Because we don't match, we often feel shame.

This difference can be in the form of:

- Our sexualities
- Our cultures
- Our personal habits
- How we dress
- What is important to us
- Our education
- How we speak
- Handicaps
- Our intelligence

- Our religions
- Our belief systems
- Our value systems
- The ways we spend our time
- Our activities
- How we look
- Our body parts

This is not an all-inclusive list. However, it represents the pain many feel when we are or think we are different than those around us. Often the pain comes in from making internal comparisons. Sometimes it comes from outside comments and bullying.

Different does not need to be shameful. Maybe one of the things that we will see change in our healing is a shift out of shame when we perceive we are different, to feeling peace.

Reflection: We get to learn to respect ourselves as we are and others as they are. That is what healing shame can bring.

Day 221
Right

I was just reading the book, *The Gift of Years*, by the author Joan Chittister. She wrote about a right that I love, and I want to share. As I have mentioned, one of the ways out of shame is to know our rights and to live with them as our truths. The right she mentioned is "I have the natural right to live till I die!"

That is perfect. We are being reminded of the fact that it is up to us to live our lives and to claim them as our own. We get to live as our hearts dictate. We get to live all of our lives in the way that fits for us, all the way until the end.

Shame does not support living our own lives in the way that our hearts would love. We live by "should" and the demands and dreams of others, whether those things fit for us, or not. We can begin to claim the right to live our lives, all the way to the end.

Living with the awareness of claiming our own lives and truths can deeply enrich our lives. We get to have dreams and ambitions and bucket lists that are unique to us.

Since I moved to New Mexico and am not caught up in constant travel and busyness, I have been claiming dreams. I am having so much fun and sharing joy. I am writing and singing and acting and about to be in a triathlon. Those dreams fit for me.

By lifting my energy, I make a different contribution to the world. I see that as my gift back to all of you wonderful people who are part of my life. Since we are one, it is my gift back to life to live in joy.

Reflection: We can begin to claim our "rights" at any age. It is never too late.

JOY!!!

Day 222

Healing Actions

I repeat myself in many of these dailies because some of the points are so essential in healing shame.

We have to name shame, so it has been given many pages. We need to be mindful of when our shame is leading the way or we can't bring it into healing.

We loop in shame. When we learn that loop, we can catch shame earlier and utilize the appropriate tools for where we are in the shame process.

The fact that shame is never true is repeated. The world would not have us believe that shame is never true. It would try and convince us that there are times we "should" feel shame. I believe there are times our behavior is hurtful to self and others, but that is about our behavior and "not" about the essence of who we are.

I look at certain tools many times.

- Writing out our shame and then a truth.
- Claiming our rights, choices and boundaries.
- Developing the ability to listen to our inner wisdom
- Being aware of when we are more vulnerable to being triggered.
- Having a list of our most frequent shame triggers.

Many shame triggers are repeated because they are the foundation for our healing. So many insights and tools go against what we learn in the world. Daily reminders of our tools help us continue in our healing.

Reflection: We can develop our own lists of important insights and tools for our healing.

Day 223
Healing Action

Getting out, gardening, being in nature, can definitely be a healing technique. We get out and focus on something outside ourselves. We get our hands dirty. We smell the earth. Shame takes us to internal places. Gardening can take us out of those internal thought spirals that can be hard to break. If we are in a shame loop and can get outside and do something in nature, it takes us out of ourselves, out of the loop. It doesn't have to be gardening. But, whatever we are doing, we focus on that project. It can make a lovely difference in our day!

It is Saturday and a lovely day in Albuquerque. I still cannot believe I live here. After 27 years in Colorado it seems so strange.

I am learning about the local plants. The plants are very different here than at 7800 feet in elevation in Westcliffe, Colorado. The ground, however, is not very hospitable to a vegetable garden. So, I am building some above ground gardens for the vegetables. I am quite excited. I was traveling so much before that I could not do a garden. Now, I can.

There is a plant here called, Broom brush. It has the most amazing yellow flowers that smell like heaven. The day my husband and I bought our home we purchased a Broom brush to honor the occasion. This morning, I noticed the first of the blossoms was out. The bush will bloom for about a month. So, that is quite exciting for me.

For me, to get out and work in the gardens is very therapeutic, and fun. I have a yard full of projects that will take years to complete. That's fine with me.

Reflection: If we are in a shame loop, it can be very helpful to focus on something in our environment outside of ourselves.

Day 224
Shame Defined

I recently heard the term, "Type B Perfectionist." As I have stated, perfectionism is the number one symptom of shame. It keeps us in a constant state of vigilance to do better, keep things under control, work harder and harder to heal a perceived defect, to impression manage, and to never let our guard down.

One might think that perfectionism would only drive actions for the "driven" Type A people. In fact, it can also be the driving force for the "kicked back," Type B person. Type B people can appear to not care, to not be bothered by what others think, and to rebel against the perceived norm. However, deep down Type B people may be struggling with the nagging shame core belief of "not being good enough", and may be kicking themselves for perceived mistakes or inadequacies.

Shame does not want us to notice it. If we notice shame, we may attempt to heal it. Shame likes to fly under the radar screen. It doesn't want to be in the light of truth.

Type B people can be tied in knots of shame just as Type A people can. It may not be as evident to those around us, or to ourselves, but shame crosses all boundaries and makes its home in all personality types.

Reflection: Perfectionism has a home in shame and can live in Type A and Type B people alike.

Day 225
Shame in Our World

It is amazing that once we become aware of shame, we see how often we inadvertently shame each other. We see how easy it is to express our judgments toward people who do not believe or act as we think they "should" or how we think anyone sane would act.

I was humbled the other day. I am someone who says that I won't talk politics with people. I thought I would be open to however others believe. Then, someone close to me voiced an opinion that was different from mine and I was absolutely aghast that they would think that way. Then, they laughed at my response and I was furious. Ha-the joke was on me. I see that despite all my talk about not judging others, I had judged mightily and could not laugh at myself. I was shaming that person. I was not practicing what I preach. I either continue to work on non-judgment and non-shaming, or I don't.

We can think that anyone would believe as we do, without realizing that our opinion is just that, an opinion. Many people, for many reasons may not believe as we do. If we truly want a shame-free world, we get to catch these judgments and hold ourselves responsible for the messages we are sending out.

We can easily send the message that, "surely you agree with me, and if you don't, then there is something wrong with you. You must be (stupid, unworthy, less than...) if you think differently than I do." If we do not like to receive such a message, then we get to hold ourselves responsible for changing our judgmental messages.

> *Reflection: Sending shaming messages to others who believe differently than we do is something we can be aware of and change. Holding ourselves accountable is a way we can make the world a less shaming and more loving, peaceful place. We all have the right to believe what we believe and to live without criticism and judgment from others.*

Day 226
Shame Indicator

Many of us live with an underlying sense of fear and anxiety that we try to alleviate with control and manipulation. We most likely have not looked at that fear and anxiety as an indicator that we are shame-based. I am suggesting that looking at the shame under the anxiety and fear may be extremely helpful in healing at the core level.

We may feel shame that we have anxiety. We may not have identified that this horribly uncomfortable feeling we carry is anxiety. Shame may cause us to feel defensive about looking at how we try to control and manipulate others in order to manage our anxiety. However, this does not change the fact that we are highly anxious and that we feel shame because of it. We may also feel very powerless to change the anxiety.

Many people have tried to manage anxiety through their own chemical addictions and pharmaceutical drugs. Often the root of the anxiety has not been explored. Prescribed medication can be helpful in managing symptoms, and we can still do the core work to release our anxiety.

If we feel less than, not enough, or many of the other shame descriptors, we live with a sense of not measuring up in the world. We will feel anxious that this inadequacy will be discovered and we will be judged and rejected. So, we attempt to keep others from seeing how anxious and fearful and inadequate we feel. We do this by trying to control and manipulate.

Looking at the shame directly and bringing it into the light of truth helps us accept ourselves as we are. As we learn to accept ourselves, we become less anxious and less in need of trying to control how others perceive us.

There are two therapy techniques that can be extremely helpful in working with anxiety. They are:

- Thought Field Therapy
- Emotional Freedom Technique

Those can be researched and learned either in a class or with a therapist who knows how to work with them. They are non-intrusive, non-chemical, and very effective ways to begin to rewire our nervous systems.

This and working with our shame can help us make powerful shifts in the anxieties and fears we live with.

*Reflection: Anxiety and fear are strong
indicators of shame core issues.*

Day 227

Shame Loop

One of the important terms I repeat in this book is "shame loop." It can be extremely helpful to understand the loop in order to effectively intervene on our shame. We can learn this by identifying when we are in shame and where we are in the loop. We then find the steps (in the Appendix) to intervene on the shame loop.

Unless shame loops are intervened on, we can live in shame. We can have many overlapping loops happening at the same time

As we learn about shame loops, we begin to see what our common triggers are. We identify many things in our lives which trigger shame and have not been resolved. We become aware of our most common "red flag" triggers and the "tools" that are most helpful in intervening on our shame loops. We see that we can't intervene just by cognitively identifying shame. We need to learn to heal on many levels. We learn that certain responses and defenses we never called shame, are in fact shame. We learn to take responsibility for our shame and bringing it into healing.

Once we are triggered the shame loop is predictable and is a tool we can use for the rest of our lives to help us stay on a healing path.

Reflection: We can learn the shame loop and how to intervene on it.

Day 228
Red Flag

When shame is engaged we live in a reactive/defensive state. When something happens and shame is triggered, we react defensively. At that point our feelings and needs get trapped underneath the shame. We can be triggered repeatedly and live in shame without even knowing we are in a reactive/defensive state.

This constant reactive state creates chaos. Shame loves chaos and lives in a constant state of chaos. This keeps us out of the present moment, which is the only place where we can really respond to life and identify shame.

If we notice we are reacting and that we are chaotic, we can see that we are in shame. This can be a red flag to slow down and identify what triggered us and ask our self how we would "respond" instead of "react." We can look for the feelings and needs that are trapped underneath the shame reaction.

We give our power away when we live in reaction. We let others determine our emotional states. You say or do something and I give you the power to upset me or put me in fear, shame, or anxiety. I do not respond with what my truth is or have an awareness of my feelings and needs underneath the reaction.

> *Reflection: If we are reacting and not responding, we will not be in our personal power. We can be in shame and be unable to identify it and bring it to truth.*

Day 229

Healing Action

I am someone who needs a fair amount of time to be by myself. I am fairly introverted. I pray and meditate, journal, and study in silence. I used to feel like there was something wrong with me for being so introverted and needing so much time to myself. I accepted other peoples' judgments of me when they thought there was something wrong with me.

When I have identified what my needs are, and I have become comfortable with them, I have been able to consciously take care of my needs. I no longer give my power to others to upset me, if they think there is something wrong with what I need.

We all have different needs. Some of us are more outgoing, or more in need of social interaction. Some of us are very introverted, or some combination thereof. The point is that we all get to identify our personal needs and take care of them in the ways that fits for us. We can also respect others who differ from us.

We do not have to accept others' shame. Others may not understand me and that is not my issue. I have the right to my needs and to take care of those needs. It is up to me to honor my needs and to take care of them. It is not my responsibility to get others to understand why I need what I need. If my needs interfere with your needs then I can talk to you about that and we can reach an understanding. However, if I don't honor how I am wired and what I need, I will end up resenting you and the world that tries to impose its judgments on me.

Reflection: We get to determine our own personal needs and take the responsibility to care for them.

Day 230
Shame in Our World

I was speaking to a woman the other day. She mentioned how she was aware of a deep-down sense of needing to be perfect to make up for being a woman. We have talked about "perfectionism" being the #1 "driving force" of shame. However, we have not talked about many of the things that drive perfectionism. Let me just do a brainstorm with myself and see what comes.

What drives perfectionism?

- Men having to prove they are macho or strong.
- Children having to prove they are smart and worthy.
- Women having to continue to look young and prove they aren't aging.
- A continual striving to do whatever we are doing perfectly so that we don't look like a fraud.
- Women and minorities having to be perfect to make up for being perceived as second-class citizens.
- Having to prove we are the perfect parent.
- Having to prove we are healthy by attempting to match some template that does not let us have human feelings, get sick, have bad days, etc.

Shame does not discriminate. It targets all of us, despite our ages, sexes, nationalities, religions, sexual orientations, sizes or shapes.

Reflection: The list I started is just that, a start. We can be curious about what our perfectionism is demanding and what it is striving to make up for.

Day 231
Red Flag

A red flag that we are in shame is when we "avoid certain people and situations." Shame can be linked to a person who was present or a place we were when we experienced shame. It may not be from a conscious shame memory. However, we cannot seem to motivate ourselves to go where a certain person is. We will cross the street if we see them coming. We may move from a city, church, job, recreational area or activity, and have all sorts of rationalizations for why. What we may not look at, is the shame that is driving the move or the avoidance of a certain place or person.

In the 12-step world, there is a phrase "geographical cure." Many times, we move to a different location in order to feel better. However, we aren't necessarily looking at what is motivating the move. We may have shame that is associated with the places we left. If we look at this red flag, we may not have to move so often. We may take the opportunity to heal where the shame sits. We may be able to look at the shame that motivates the "geographical cure."

If a person or environment has become "shame-toxic," we can bring that shame to the light of truth. Maybe we can't imagine resolving something, so we leave. We may be so embarrassed and caught in a shame loop that we live in step #4 in the shame loop, self–defeating behavior. In that place, we can't face ourselves, make amends to ourselves or others, or move into our changes. Our self-defeating behavior is the constant moving away from conflicts without ever resolving them.

> *Reflection: Constant movement away from people and places can be a red flag that unresolved shame might be motivating the move.*

Day 232
Multidimensional Healing

On Day 215, we looked at needing to work with shame on all levels. Just figuring it out will not shift shame. We often can't figure it out.

An area that gets neglected in much healing work is when shame impacts us on the physical level. As we get familiar with our shame and observe it in ourselves or others, we notice an automatic physical (body) response when we go into the shame loop. It is instantaneous. Our hands and feet will change temperature, our faces will flush, and we will not look people in the eye. We can't. We will pull back. We may have other physical responses to shame that we can become aware of. All of this happens when we move into a shame loop. We can't figure or think our way out of the physical response.

Noticing our physical responses validates shame. It exposes shame as something that happens and can't be understood away. However, as we do our healing work, there are many tools and techniques that can help us move shame out of the body.

One technique that I learned is called holographic memory resolution, or HMR. It is a tool that goes right into where trauma is held in the body and can help resolve it at its roots.

Another technique is called Eye Movement Desensitization and Reprocessing, or EMDR. It is a trauma technique that works with the many levels our trauma and shame are held in (including the physical).

There are many more techniques. We can work with massage, acupuncture, dance, music, sound therapy, somatization work, and yoga, among others.

Healing shame on the physical level is an important part of healing. Where our bodies have aches, pains, and illness, may be where we have unresolved healing that holds the shame in those body parts. We can benefit from the many techniques available to us today to heal shame on all levels.

Reflection: We benefit from healing shame on the physical level. Many of above-mentioned healing techniques need facilitation with a skilled therapist. We can find therapists credentialed in the techniques mentioned.

Day 233
Shame in Our World

We live in a shame-based culture.

It is easy to get stuck trying to figure out where all this shame comes from. I have worked with countless people who do not have a discernible shaming incident in their background, but feel deep shame about their selves. Why is that?

1. We live in a shame-based culture. (At least in the western world.)
2. What do I mean by that?
3. Our culture is steeped in:
4. Perfectionism.
5. Blame.
6. Not knowing our personal rights, choices, and boundaries.
7. Hierarchy.
8. Basing our worth on what we do.
9. Spending more time looking at what we "should" do than looking at what fits for us.
10. Levels of dishonesty in most interactions.
11. Not knowing how to truly forgive.
12. Believing that we are flawed in some way and need to constantly prove ourselves.
13. Having an external template for most of our roles and feel shame when we don't match it.
14. Not knowing that the essence of ourselves is truly innocence and love.

These behaviors are "shame-based" behaviors. They reinforce shame as our essence. They are the stew that we grow up in and die in. Unless we see that and completely reverse the way we see ourselves and others in our world, we will remain in shame. That leaves us in a very agitated state. As we learn to intervene on our shame, consistently shift the paradigm of our life to that of love, and utilize our tools, we move more and more into peace.

Reflection: Just growing up in our shame-based world is reason enough to struggle with shame.

Day 234
Red Flag

Another indicator of shame is the strong sense of wanting to disappear. We feel so embarrassed or exposed that we want to drop through the floor and never come back. Not all shame is this strong, but when it is, it is profoundly painful.

This can happen in a moment when we feel absolutely exposed as flawed in some way. We have been exposed as less than. It feels intolerable.

A profoundly shaming experience can have this kind of effect on us. I have had people share shame from their pasts. The experience continues to feel as strong and painful as when it occurred. When the person shares it they feel it as if it is happening in the here and now. It is burned in one's memory. These experiences can be resolved by previously mentioned trauma techniques. To do that, we need to be willing to bring them out in the open in a safe place with someone who has the expertise to bring healing to trauma.

If we have one of those experiences in our backgrounds, we can be sure that shame is attached and anchored in our systems. We can know that there are ways to heal that shame and leave it behind us.

Reflection: Trauma can hold our shame. We can begin to know that those painful memories hold the keys to healing our shame.

Day 235
Voice of Shame

I was talking to a brilliant woman today. She had gone into shame over something and immediately felt like a fraud. When shame hits, it can take us out at the knees. It can convince us that we don't know anything about something we are quite knowledgeable in. Shame can get into our heads and interfere with any forward movement in our life. It can speak in a voice that is familiar and sounds true. If we don't identify that it is the voice of shame, it can have its way with us. If we can catch that it is shame, we can use our tools to intervene on it. We need to remember that shame is never true.

Let us identify the shame and what it is telling us. Then we can claim a truth, whether we believe it or not. It may sound something like "Whether I believe it or not I am a knowledgeable, competent person who knows a lot about _____."

My shame always goes for the jugular. I can make an ordinary, human mistake. I can have a human experience. However, if it is a shame button for me, then my shame says that I am a fraud, should not be working in the field of counseling, and need to stop at once. Shame just does not do anything in half measures.

What I knew for my friend and what I can know for myself and for all of us is that we all mess up and we are all deserving good people. We are not frauds. We are honest, human, and lovable.

Reflection: Shame is the lie.

Day 236
Tool

Many of us apologize for ourselves constantly. We feel the need to say, "I am sorry." If we really looked at how often we apologize, we will see that we often are apologizing for just taking up space, breathing, needing, and wanting a life that is fulfilling.

We don't need to apologize for being. We get to take up space. We get to impose ourselves on the world. We get to look people in the eye, without apology for who we are and how we feel and what we need.

Shame is communicated through our eyes, and it is healed through our eyes. We learn to look into our own eyes in a mirror, without apology. We get to see ourselves with our own eyes of compassion.

Mirror work can be profoundly healing for those of us who apologize for who we are and for looking, feeling, needing the way we do. We can look deep into our own eyes; connect with our soul and say, "I love you just the way you are. I am going to stop apologizing for the way you take up space. I love you."

We also get to practice looking others in the eyes. We can practice kindness through how we look at others. We can sit and look out at the world through kind eyes.

Kindness is not part of shame. Often, we get to practice being kind to ourselves and others. I sing in The New Mexico Peace Choir. We sing the song, "We Can Be Kind." Google the song and listen to it. It shows us a way to bring our shame into the healing power of kindness

> *Reflection: We don't need to apologize for taking up space, having needs and feelings, and\or being who we are.*

Day 237
Red Flag

A red flag that we are in shame is when we," have a persistent feeling of being on the outside looking in." We don't feel connected to others or a part of things. We feel alone and feel extremely lonely. We can experience this, even when people, friends, and family surround us. Shame says that nobody really wants us around, especially if they really know us.

A way to deal with this is to acknowledge it. By doing this we put ourselves in the role of observers. Now, instead of being in the middle of the shame, we are observing it. In that position, we can more easily see the shame as a lie. This begins the movement out of the shame.

Being an observer means to watch what is happening. As a therapist, I used to have people do this when they went to join their family of origin for an event. I would have them sit back as if they were a newspaper reporter watching the family interactions and also how they interacted. It was a way for them to not get as hooked into the shame dynamics, and to keep a healthier perspective. Family events can be some of the loneliest and most shame inducing. This was a way to report on the process and not get so mired in it. It also helped see the shame from a different perspective.

> *Reflection: When we feel like we are "on the outside looking in," we are often in shame. This is a red flag that we are in shame.*

Day 238
One Thing Different

I have been looking at my own belief system concerning "retirement." I haven't looked at that much in my life. I recently realized I felt some shame about that. I had someone say to me, "why didn't you save more?" It sounds like an innocent enough remark. I don't know if they meant it as judgmentally as it sounded, or if my own self-judgment made it seem that way. The thing is, it wasn't shameful that I didn't prepare for retirement in a traditional way. It wouldn't be shameful if I didn't prepare in any way. In truth, I didn't really see it as relevant and I did not know how to prepare. That may have been a mistake, but it isn't shameful. It is important to see the difference between making a mistake and feeling shame because of it.

We each have our own processes, our own reasons, and our own responsibilities in making the choices we do. We get to live with that. We can do that without shame or negative self-judgment. We just get to be.

I made my choices and I take responsibility for the consequences. When I do that, I don't feel shame. If I am judged for my choices, I don't need to take that on. I know that if each of us walked a mile in the others' shoes, we would do the same things, make the same choices. We can be aware of the messages we give ourselves and others. We can be kind to ourselves for the choices we make. It certainly won't make a positive difference if I shame myself.

> *Reflection: I can own my choices and consequences. No need for shame. It just is. I just am. You just are. We have the right to make our own choices. No blame, no shame.*

Day 239
Voice of Shame

When I was an active therapist, people would ask me, almost on a daily basis, what "normal" was. They would ask if what they were thinking was normal. I began to recognize this as a code word for shame. We have some obscure idea of what normal is, and few of us feel like we are it. If we aren't normal, then something is wrong with us.

Even when we want to feel good about dancing to our own drummer or finding our own ways, we are often, deep down, feeling some shame about choosing a different path.

The truth is, there is no normal. There is a lie that there is a normal that we "should" try and achieve. In subcultures, we determine what is normal for that subculture. This determines if one gets to belong to the subculture. This perpetuates shame of not belonging and being different.

Striving for "normal" is a quest that is seldom, if ever, satisfied. It leads to discontent, pain, a sense of not belonging, and increased shame. Part of healing from shame is realizing we get to find a path that is ours. We get to determine what fits for us and feel good about those things.

Reflection: If we are striving for "normal," we are often feeling shame about ourselves and trying to be different than we are. We can notice, stop, and claim the rights to determine what fits for ourselves, with no apologies.

Day 240
Rule

Part of what makes trust so hard in healing shame is that we often have not experienced reliability or consistency. The rule we have learned is that the world and the people in our world are unreliable and inconsistent.

Shame-based people are here one minute and gone the next. We have a feeling or need and don't know what to do with it so we often just disappear from the relationship. Our shame gets triggered and we go away. We may be present physically, but not emotionally.

We are unreliable to ourselves and others. We usually have other unreliable people in our lives. We often come from family systems that are inconsistent. We do not have a model for reliability and consistency. We are consistently inconsistent. We are reliably unreliable.

We get to learn how to be our word. We get to learn how to be consistently reliable. We get to be consistent.

We get to define a new rule for ourselves. That rule would be, "we get to be reliable and consistent." We can learn this for ourselves and ask it of others. We can hold ourselves accountable and instead of just leaving when we don't know how to deal with something, we can learn to stay and blunder through until we have a solution.

One of the amazing things in the 12-step community concerns this very issue. We take responsibility for the messes we have made of our relationships and go back and make amends. We face our unreliability and become reliable.

Reflection: We can learn to be reliable and consistent. It helps in healing our shame.

Days 241-270

Day 241
Red Flag

Those in the addiction world, or who are adult children of addiction, have often become aware of the roles we have taken on in our family systems. The roles are often a result of birth order and jobs that need to be taken to keep the family system alive. The more dysfunctional the system, the more we are apt to be cemented into the role we were assigned when we came into the family.

The roles we most often hear about are hero, scapegoat, lost child, and mascot. If we identify with the role and we find ourselves in one of those roles in whatever family we are in, we can most likely identify with the dysfunction of the system that assigned the role.

What makes it so difficult for us if we are in a role is the inability to get the role to change. Once we are the heroes, we are always the heroes. Once we are the scapegoat, we are always the scapegoat. Whatever the role it remains the same. We can change, be a very different person, and still be seen in the same old light.

What becomes important is seeing ourselves in a different light. We can identify the role we have always had. We can see if it has worked for us, and if we want to continue in that role. We can then directly address the issues with ourselves and others in our families.

> *Reflection: The people in our lives may have a hard time seeing us in a different light, and we can begin to identify the roles we choose to take in our different systems. We can then release the shame that comes from the roles we were unable to release previously.*

Day 242
Multidimensional

On Day 215, we were talking about the different levels in which we get to heal our shame. One of levels is in the spiritual. We often see our higher power in the same light we saw our parents. Since we all grew up in a shame-based culture, we see our higher power in this shaming way. This contributes to our sense of being inadequate and disconnected.

Many of us react against a higher power because we refuse the one we grew up with. We disconnect from any matters of the spirit and forge on alone. We have the absolute right to do this. We can also look at our beliefs, where they came from, and begin the process of releasing from those we do not want to accept. We can then begin to look at what we want in our lives instead of the old methods that did not work.

An example may be someone who grew up in a family and/or religion that was abusive, shaming, full of anger, blame, and pain. We can begin to turn in a different direction for what we would want to replace that with. It may be connecting with something bigger, like nature. It may be refusing to accept anything that speaks unkindly and/or internalizing a loving voice that we can always turn to.

Healing the spiritual is a part of healing the shame. It doesn't have to look a certain way and it is a part of the healing process to consciously determine what love or a higher power might look like if it was different from what we had grown up with.

Reflection: Healing our spirit can be an important part of our healing.

Day 243
Shame Defined

If we would take the time to really look at our belief systems, we would realize that we all have a blueprint for how we think we are supposed to live and how things are supposed to be. We pick them up, usually without knowing, from our lives and experiences. We believe that we should, and you should, and couples should etc., do certain things. With this "should mentality," we have the blueprint for shame.

If we look at these "should" beliefs, we will see that they rarely represent our true belief systems. When we don't take the time to look at our belief systems, we listen to what the "should," voice dictates. When this happens we rage against it because it is driven by the shame "should."

If I have not examined and changed my belief system to one that fits for me, I risk living in constant shame. I will believe that others and myself are not measuring up.

I get to develop the belief system that fits for me. I get to establish what is the best way for me to live. If I want to be alone, married, gay, sleep alone, or if I prefer to be vegan, or an atheist, or have a religion, or don't, it is up to me. I get to determine that. I get to have my own beliefs.

> *Reflection: My life gets to be mine and your life gets to be yours. I get to determine my value system and live by it. I get to give you the grace to live by yours. Shame does not enter in unless I choose to put your beliefs on me.*

Day 244

Voice of Shame

CHOOSE PEACE

There is a very simple way of determining if we are listening to the voice of shame or the voice of love.

If what we are hearing brings us peace we are hearing the voice of love.

Shame speaks first and never brings peace. Love simply is and speaks the language of peace.

Shame always is about "doing" something. When we listen to shame, we get more agitated, confused, and less contented or peaceful.

When we listen to love we settle down, feel clear, contented, and more peaceful.

Sometimes we make things really hard.

I love to keep things simple. Love equals Peace.

Reflection: We most likely have not heard the voice of peace very often in our lives. That is because we didn't know to listen for it and because shame spoke first and drowned it out.

Day 245
Shame Loop

When our shame gets triggered a very predictable and destructive shame loop begins. A shame loop can last for decades. The time we loop in shame can be shortened if we learn to identify it and intervene.

What I mean when I say, "our shame gets triggered" is that something either internal or external sets off the old shame core beliefs that we are not enough, or inadequate, or unlovable. If deep down I have a belief that I am "not enough," then something someone says or does, or something I think can trigger the old feelings of not being enough.

It would not be so bad if we knew when we were triggered. However, most of the time when our shame gets triggered, we don't know it. That coupled with shame of our shame makes it really hard to stop the ball from rolling down the hill and becoming more destructive and more intense as it rolls.

Once our shame gets triggered, three things happen simultaneously. We are triggered, we move into a defensive posture, and we shut down from our real feelings. We may look like we are having all sorts of feelings. However, the shame reaction is really a cover-up for the underlying feelings. We may be ranting and raving and look really angry, but underneath we may be really hurt or scared. The hurt and scared do not show to the outside observer or ourselves.

Once these three things happen, we drop into self-defeating behavior. The really hard thing here is that until the shame is resolved (hard to do if we don't know we are in it), we live in these self-defeating places. The things we could do that may be productive or helpful elude us. As we live in the self -defeating space we reinforce the shame. The indicator we are in this self-defeating space is feeling very out of control. Our behaviors may be out of control or our inner critic may be out of control.

Eventually we try to get control again. We make plans and strategize or make amends or send flowers, but we haven't come to terms with the shame that triggered the shame in the first place. So, the strategy of getting control may bring temporary relief, but we are destined to trigger shame again.

The shame loop is shown in the Appendix.

Reflection: We can't bring shame into healing unless we name it. Learning the shame loop can help us identify where we are in the loop.

Day 246

Specific Shame-Based Issue

I have become aware of a specific shame that I want to share. I spoke with someone who does not believe in a god. She is frequently in situations where people assume she does, or assume that anyone who has any common sense would believe in a "god." She does not share her lack of belief in a "god" because she fears judgment and the ensuing shame.

The assumption that we believe in something specific, or believe in a certain way can lead one to make statements that inadvertently send a shaming message to someone if they believe differently. It can happen re: gods, political persuasions, sexual preferences, whether one knows certain music, literature, books, etc. The assumption is where we go amuck and end up shaming.

We don't need to accept the shame if we receive it, and it can be very uncomfortable. One of the "Four Agreements" in the Ruiz book I mentioned earlier is: "Don't Make Assumptions."

It is important in our new paradigm of living to respect that we may have different beliefs than the person we are speaking with. We can be curious about what someone else believes and support each other in having the right to believe what we choose. We learn to live without criticizing and judging others.

Reflection: We all get to believe as we choose. Wouldn't it be great if we didn't shame each other, no matter what we believed?

Day 247
Rule

Shame-based people and systems have rules around feelings. Some feelings are allowed and some are not.

Often the first step in identifying our rules around feelings is to learn what feelings are. We can Google "feelings lists" and learn the words that identify feelings. We can find many lists of feelings. As we look at the lists we may find:

- We don't have the language of feelings.
- We don't have certain feeling words in our vocabulary.
- We are locked into noticing only certain feelings and the rest go un-noticed.
- We feel shame if we have certain feelings.
- We don't know what to do with certain feelings.

Once we identify feeling words, we get to notice what our rules around those feelings are. We get to see if we allow certain feelings, feel shame about them, or just do not know how to relate to certain feelings.

In truth, we all have feelings. Sometimes we repress the feelings because we have not had healthy models for expressing them, or it has not been safe to have them. We may not have learned that it is through having and sharing feelings that we make our deepest connections. The extent we repress our feelings is the extent to which we feel disconnected.

Reflection: We get to have feelings, learn how to express them, and not experience shame for having our feelings. Our "feelings" allow us to connect to others and feel connected in the world.

Day 248
Red Flag

I was speaking with someone who had a child just diagnosed with Asperger's. She was stressing the point with her child that there is no shame in having that diagnosis. She reinforced this message by telling her child that it would not be a secret. They have had many discussions about not feeling shame for having a brain that is wired in a different way. She mentioned that a relative had a child with the same diagnosis who was making sure that nobody found out. We both felt the shame of the other family and how the shame of the diagnosis was reinforced by the secret.

I wanted to share this because it is such a lovely example of the difference between responding to something in love vs. shame. Our secrets can be the red flag that we have shame around something. Those are the very things we can benefit from bringing into the light of healing.

If we look at the day to day things we don't want anybody to know about and/or the long-ago secrets we never wanted exposed, we will see things we may carry shame around. This discovery can help us look shame in the eye and make a different choice.

We each have those unique features that make us who we are. We each have experiences that are different. However, in our hearts we are the same. We each want to be loved as we are, and accepted as we are. Sharing our secrets with others helps us connect with what is the same in all of us.

When we discover the things we are keeping secret, we can find ways to share them and bring them into healing. Sometimes, just having someone safe hear our secrets can be healing. Sometimes we have to redefine what we have kept secret.

> *Reflection: Looking at our secrets helps us discover the little or big pockets of shame we carry. We can bring those out with safe people and bring shame into love and acceptance.*

Day 249
Red Flag

I want to continue on the same note that I was on yesterday.

I was speaking with someone with whom I talk to regularly. She had not been available for about a week. She said, "I was sick again and I didn't want anybody to know. I guess I was feeling shame." She has had a rough winter and has been frequently sick and obviously felt embarrassed about that. That embarrassment is shame. So, because of that shame she has kept herself isolated and not gotten the support she deserves. Or, she may not want support, but she at least deserves to feel okay about herself and not embarrassed.

This is a small example of what we do day in and day out. We have some kind of unexplored beliefs we carry that determine what is acceptable or not. If we don't live within this belief system we can end up feeling shame. In this example, there was a belief that said that there was something wrong with her for being sick so often. So, she didn't want anybody to know.

When we don't want anybody to know things about us because we are fearful of judgment, we are in shame. It may not be a big thing, and it gets in the way of our loving ourselves, no matter what. It can also keep us from getting the help we deserve. Shame is so sneaky. We may think, "What is the big deal? We all have it." Yes, we all do, and it interferes with our love of ourselves and others.

> *Reflection: We get to be aware of those things we don't want anybody to know. We get to then name that we are feeling shame and look at redefining the shame. We then examine our choices. In the case of my friend, just sharing the thing she felt shame about was enough. She felt better after the sharing!*

Day 250
Shame Defined

I want to revisit what shame is. There is so much misunderstanding about shame that we can be experiencing shame and not know what to call it. If we can't identify the shame, we have a hard time bringing it into healing.

Identifying with shame is like zipping a skin over our soul's essences and saying, "This is who I am." That stuff about me being loveable and worthy and enough is what is false."

The false skin we identify with seems real and, although everyone has different words to describe their false selves, the words usually sound like:

I am not enough.

I am bad.

I am unworthy.

I am stupid.

I am a fraud.

I am defective.

We relate to these beliefs as our truths. We can't be talked out of them. We spend time trying to cover them up so that nobody really knows how damaged we are. We spend our lives trying to make up for or compensate for the defectiveness.

We often feel like we are being seen in this defective way. It is like constantly having an unloving god watching us, and finding us wanting. No matter what we do, we feel like it isn't good enough.

*Reflection: Although shame sounds true, familiar and beyond doubt, it is **NEVER** the truth. Sit with that a moment. The truth about* *us is that we were created by love and we are love*

Day 251
One Thing Different

When we have an expectation of someone and they do not live up to the expectation, do we have a right to be angry and send shaming messages?

I ask couples I work with to become conscious of their expectations of themselves and the other person they are in relationship with. I encourage bringing those expectations into the open and talking about them honestly. This open dialogue allows the couple to agree or come up with an alternative solution. This process helps prevent the unconscious behavior of sending shaming messages to each other.

We often have these expectations in all or most of our relationships. We think we know what others "should" do if they are a partner, child, friend, someone we work with, or have an on-going relationship with. We often don't voice our "shoulds" and get angry or upset when they are not met.

It is possible to communicate our expectations to others. We then have an opportunity to agree or disagree. We can then negotiate with each other, agree to disagree, agree, or go in different directions.

I had a friend once who was consistently at least half an hour late when we were to meet up. I had voiced my need to have her let me know if she was over 15 minutes late. She just did not live that way. We ended up going in different directions, but without shaming each other. We just had different needs and expectations when it came to time. I did not need to feel shame that I wanted to be timely, and she did not need to feel shame that it did not matter for her. We just had a differing way of being with appointments and time.

> *Reflection: If we are upset with another, we can see if we are operating from unvoiced expectations. If so, we can talk about them instead of sending shaming messages.*

Day 252
Red Flag

If we feel an inordinate amount of guilt, we are most likely shame-based. What do I mean by that? If we apologize for taking up space, having needs, and feeling the way we feel, we are feeling shame.

We often use the word "guilt" when we are really talking about shame. In doing this, we aren't able to utilize the tools for bringing shame into healing. For some, it is an automatic response to say, "I'm sorry." We feel like the responsible ones if anything goes wrong. We might call this guilt, but it is shame core issues that precipitate the constant need to apologize and feel responsible and/or guilty.

Guilt is feeling badly about a behavior whereas shame is feeling badly about ourselves. Constantly apologizing would indicate we feel badly about ourselves.

If I feel guilt over a behavior, or for doing something that breaks my value system, I can take responsibility, make the appropriate amends or repair, and feel better. I can leave it behind. When we have a constant sense of guilt that we are somehow not living up to some standard, there is no basis in our behavior and there is nothing we can do to fix it, then we are talking about shame. It feels constant and like it will always be there. It lies to us and tells us we are a mess and need to apologize for whatever is not going well with others.

If we can correctly define shame and differentiate it from guilt we can utilize tools to bring this shame into the light of healing.

Reflection: Guilt is not shame. It is about an action. If I am persistently guilty I am dealing with shame. Shame is about "self," not an action.

Day 253
Voice of Shame

The other day I heard someone say, "my shame is judge, jury, and executioner." That statement accurately describes shame.

Shame judges ourselves or others as bad, unworthy, unlovable, or some equally unloving judgment. It then puts ourselves or others on trial and will allow no defense. Love is not allowed anywhere near this trial. Shame speaks to the jury, goes on and on without truth being at all a part of the arguments. It knows how to present the arguments in a way that "sounds" true, but is not true. The judgments involve: "they say," "should," and "prejudice and bias." Anything that would not agree with shame's arguments is presented as part of the problem.

After the shame presentation and arguments, the jury has no recourse but to convict the person as guilty of being less than in some way. The punishment is some sort of torture. It is some form of punishment that involves suffering. The person who has been tried is found unworthy of respect, love, forgiveness, care, or concern. There is no end to the sentence. The one found guilty of being less than fell short of perfection. Thus shame is the harshest of jury's and the sentence is always some form of living hell.

Reflection: We all have the right to be heard and supported by love. Shame does not agree with that. If shame is putting us on trial, we might consider bringing love into the courtroom and seeing what it has to say.

Day 254
Model for a Shame Free World

As I wrote my book, I've become aware of how shame has become an acceptable part of our culture. As I just listen to people talk in the locker room at the gym, or in grocery store lines, or out and about, I hear shaming comments continuously.

The most common way I hear shame is in people putting other people down for behaving in ways they do not understand. They go on and on about how stupid some person, or group of people are. Another common thing I hear are people who think if others would just do what they think they "should," then the other person would be much better off.

I also hear much gossip and making fun of others. We all know bullying has become widespread. We also know social media can be used to shame people in vicious ways.

We all do it.

How is this shame?

We carry the attitude that others are wrong or stupid or worthless, and it is in the very air we breathe. We worry about the big wars. We get to worry about our own wars. Shame hurts.

I do not say this to point a finger. I have to watch myself all the time. I am most prone to judge those who are closest to me. Somehow, I guess I have presumed I have this right since we are close. I am wrong.

If we want a more peaceful world, we get to accept and love people for how they are. We get to honor peoples' rights to be unique and have their own beliefs. We get to make peace more important than being right. This is what intervenes on shame. This is what makes our world a more loving, safe, and peaceful place to be.

I feel sad tonight. I have just seen so much pain and hurt caused from shame. I work with the most amazing people who believe they are defective, unworthy, and unlovable. I want shame to stop. I want this for me and for you and for all of life.

Reflection: We can be conscious and choose peace above all else.

Day 255
Multidimensional

On Day 215, I mentioned needing to heal shame on many levels. Today I will talk about healing our wills.

When we are in shame, we experience feeling like we have no will. When shame is engaged, we feel powerlessness to stop it. We move into self-defeating thoughts or behavior and can't seem to stop.

How do we regain a sense of will in our healing? How do we get a sense of personal power back? We can't will it back. We have to acknowledge where we are, which is shame, and then begin to look at what is under the shame. Under the shame are our feelings and needs. Under the shame are our rights, choices, and boundaries. Under our shame is compassion and love.

Where do we start?

- Acknowledge we are in shame.
- Get the voice of shame outside of our heads by either sharing with a trustworthy person, or writing what it is telling us on paper.
- Turn to the voice of compassion and love and see what it has to say. It is important we write

this down or say it out loud to a trustworthy person.

- Name the feelings under the shame and let ourselves feel the feelings.

- Name the needs under the shame and see what we can do or what help we can get to get our needs met in a safe way.

- Begin to look at our rights, choices, and boundaries in the situation.

- Begin to notice that we now do not feel the powerlessness of shame, and lack of will. What we feel now is a sense of personal power.

Reflection: We did not try to arm wrestle shame away. We did not will our shame away. We turned in the direction of compassion and found the shame was changed into the ability to care for ourselves.

Day 256
One Thing Different

As this year moves on and we become more familiar with our shame, we can begin to say out loud when we are in shame. We may be noticing it more quickly and putting words to it before it takes off into a full-blown shame loop.

If we are in a relationship with someone, be it a friend or partner, it can be helpful to say, "I am feeling shame right now." We can say that as soon as we notice it. Some of us can then talk about the shame immediately. Some of us may need some time to internally process before we share more information. We can also take responsibility for our shame and not blame the other person.

In our shame-based world, we usually look for someone to blame or make responsible for our feelings. In truth, we are all responsible for our responses to others. Another person cannot "make" me feel shame. They may be uncaring, or unkind, or mean, but my response is my response. We will get on with our healing faster when we can say "I am feeling shame right now." I can then look for what my rights, choices, and boundaries are, and move into my personal power. I can own my own feelings, responses, needs, and take care of them.

If we say we are feeling shame we can then take care of our inner self that is feeling shame. Letting the others in our relationships know when we are triggered is vulnerable work. We can be very conscious of the people in our life that we are safe saying this to. We can look at our choices.

> *Reflection: Acknowledging our shame out loud can help us heal in our relationships with ourselves and others.*

Day 257

Voice of Shame

We can have a wide variety of experiences with shame. We can feel slightly embarrassed all the way to completely mortified. These range of experiences are all about shame. All of them have one thing is common.

In any of these experiences of shame we will believe that, "If you knew _____ about me, you would reject me in some way. Or, "now that you know _____ about me, you will reject me in some way." These beliefs are fundamental to all shame experiences. We feel exposed in some shameful way and certain of a response that is some form of rejection. We may not experience the rejection as coming from another. We may just reject ourselves.

Rejection can come in many forms. It may be fear of abandonment, ridicule, disgust, or rebuke. With the fear, we may find it extremely difficult and vulnerable to move into healing. We may not know how to have a different relationship with what we are experiencing or with what just happened. We may feel trapped in the embarrassment or mortification.

Whatever level we experience the shame on, the healing has a common process. We name the shame. We identify what triggered it (internal thoughts or external experience), identify and feel the underlying feelings, look at the needs we have and begin to develop healthy ways to get the needs met. We develop a safe support system to share and look at what love would say.

Reflection: The experience of shame may differ, and the process of healing has a common experience. We get to name the shame in order to move into healing.

Day 258
Maude

Barb (B)—Maude, I have a tool for intervening on shame, which I'd like to run by you. Is that okay?

Maude (M)—Anytime and anywhere is fine by me. I am with you always.

B—Oh, that feels so good. I want to remember that always. It brings me such peace. It will help for me to know you are with me always, and especially when I am feeling alone.

M—You are never alone. You are one with a vast ocean of love. Always. Nothing you can do or have ever done can change that. Now, what is this tool you want to ask me about?

B—Well, when I am in my shame and saying hard and harsh things to myself, like "nobody likes me because I am unlovable," I catch it and need to focus on a truth instead. So, a truth I say is "I am a good and lovable woman who is having a hard time believing I am lovable and loved." Is that true? Is that a good tool to use when my shame is engaged?

M—That is an excellent tool, Barb. It allows you to touch on the truth, even if you don't totally believe it or can't believe it at all.

B—Okay, I will keep working with this. I just wanted to run it by you first. Thank you.

Day 259

Poem

> What can possibly change Love?
>
> What could even remotely threaten a love so deep it is all there is?
>
> There is no place Love is not
>
> There is only constant Love
>
> So Be It
>
> Barb Tonn

Day 260

Healing Action

HAVE COMPASSION AND PATIENCE WITH YOURSELF!

Compassion and patience are critical actions we can take and practice for the rest of our lives. Consistently practicing compassion and patience with self and others will take us far in our healing process. However, many of us do not really know how to practice this.

We can start with a little willingness to learn how to be compassionate, kind, patient, sweet, and loving to ourselves. Willingness sends the message to love that we want to learn the language of love. It moves us in a new direction.

We can start by listening to people who are compassionate. We can pay attention to how we speak kindly to others, and our pets. We can then see how it would be to say these kind things to ourselves.

We can do some Flow of Consciousness Writing with the topic, "If I were being kind to myself right now, what would I say?" or, "if I were talking to a good friend who was struggling like I am, what would I say?" Then we can start writing without stopping and see what comes out. We can practice saying these same words to ourselves.

> *Reflection: We can set an intention to become willing to be compassionate with ourselves, at all times. We can learn how to forgive ourselves when we mess up. We can learn gentleness with ourselves.*

Day 261
Right

I have the right to say YES!

Just as we have the right to say no, we also have the right to say, "yes." When we pay attention to our personal truths we learn which answers fit for us.

It can be difficult to say, "yes," when others are not approving of our "yes." This can be especially true when it is someone close to us, or an authority figure.

As we step more and more into the truths of who we are, we may find we are saying, "yes," more often. The "yes" can make us feel very vulnerable. We may be stepping into arenas we never have before and may not be able to predict how it will turn out. We may be learning new skills and may spend time living in the poor or mediocre arena as we learn. That can be very hard when we have lived with the perfectionist in us telling us not to look silly.

"Yes" opens us to new possibilities and new experiences. When "yes" leads the way in our lives, we see doors opening that we may never have seen before.

We have the right to say "yes" even when we are not sure where it will take us. We always have choice and one powerful choice is to say, "yes."

Reflection: We don't need to defend our "yes." We get to speak it and move in the direction it takes us and accept the responsibility for the choice.

Day 262
Poem

Release Shame for All time

Is that possible?

At times, it rolls in quietly and ominously- like a thunderstorm that gathers and darkens and explodes-

With a great power and might and noise

Other times it skittles in- quick and fast- like a jackrabbit jumping out of your headlights

Release it for good?

Then I must be aware

No matter how it comes in

Ready to notice and

Quietly

Peacefully

Turn in the other direction

Allowing it NO MORE

If I want Peace more than anything

> Barb Tonn

Day 263
Rule

Shame-based systems are ruled by the extreme needs for predictability and safeness. Spontaneous interaction is seen as a threat. Therefore, responses are usually very repetitive and are characterized by manipulation. The shame-based system is "tight" and rigid. It is fear-based.

When shame rules a system, there is a deep need for people to keep control at all times. It, therefore, limits the responses of the people in the system. Safety is seen as the ability to manage all outside stimuli so that nobody is taken by surprise. This is why the system can get very disoriented when the unpredictable happens. It cannot be creatively spontaneous.

If we grew up in or live in a shame-based system we will live in fear and not safety. Deep down we feel the vulnerability of knowing we really can't control everything and that sooner or later things will happen that will not have been anticipated and will throw everyone into chaos. So the effort is to keep control at all times. To attempt to have everything rigid and predictable is a way to attempt control. It keeps our lives narrow.

As we step into our healing, we begin to expand and learn that we either have the skills to deal with the unexpected or we get to learn them. We begin to broaden our focus and allow "new" and "change" into our lives. We have freedom as we incorporate spontaneity and release the need to be in control at all times. We become more flexible. Our fears decrease as we learn that we are okay and safe in different and new situations, allowing in the longed for peace that fear and shame kept away.

Reflection: When we live in shame we live in fear and the need to control. As we move into healing, we open to spontaneity and the freedom of change and choice.

Day 264
Red Flag

A red flag that we are in shame is when we are in "self-defeating behaviors or thoughts" and either can't stop them or don't care. In the shame loop in the Appendix, this is the #4 position. The hallmark of this position in the shame loop is that we experience being powerless to stop the feelings, thoughts, or behaviors.

#4 in the shame loop is where addiction lives, and where our inner critics won't leave us alone. This inner critic is the voice of shame we hear in our head in the middle of the night. We keep replaying a situation where we think we made a fool of ourselves or made a mistake. We can't stop the thoughts that we are idiots or failures or frauds. This is when we eat the whole quart of ice cream or drink the whole quart of whiskey. We feel powerless to stop the "self-defeating" thoughts and behaviors.

When we are in this powerless position, we don't see any choices we believe we can make. We often feel trapped in "either/or," choices, and neither of those feels right.

It can be extremely helpful when we find self in self-defeating thoughts or behaviors to name the shame. We can say, "I must be in a shame loop." Then we can begin the process of following the steps in the Appendix. Once we name shame, we have a chance of moving out of the shame and getting ourselves back to the ability to identify our real feelings and needs. We can begin to look at our rights, choices, and boundaries. We can utilize the tools in this book to help us move out of self-defeating and into our personal powers.

> *Reflection: As soon as we notice that we are feeling powerless or out of control, we can begin the process of naming the shame and moving out of it.*

Day 265
Red Flag

I am going to expand on what we talked about yesterday. The concept of powerlessness is an indicator that we are in a shame loop. I used examples of being caught in negativity and not being able to stop the behaviors or thoughts. Today, I want to talk about the powerlessness we may experience when faced with moving into something positive.

Shame can keep us from moving forward into our greater good. We may want to get a degree and get close to graduation, but not be able to finish. We may want to end a certain relationship and move into something different, or make a commitment and be unable to. We may have an opportunity for a job more to our liking, or a pay increase, or the chance to do something we have always wanted to do and have been unable to follow through with. When we look honestly at what is getting in our way we often discover shame. We don't feel worthy of whatever it is. We feel terrified of being exposed as frauds or inadequate and unworthy of what is in front of us. This kind of powerlessness is shame.

When we feel powerless over stopping a negative or embracing a positive, we can be curious about the shame that is interfering. We can't intervene on the shame until we identify it as shame and look at the beliefs that are supporting the powerless experience. We can't identify underlying feelings and needs until we lift up the shame and see what is underneath it.

Reflection: Learning the shame loop and identifying when we are in "self-defeating" behaviors is a powerful move in the direction of healing.

Day 266

Tool

Being true to ourselves and living in integrity may not at first glance seem like they have much to do with healing shame. However, living in shame is the opposite of living in integrity. Shame has us identified with false selves. Those false selves feel true and real. However, they are false.

When we are in shame, we often are not living our truths. We identify with what we think we "should" do and are concerned with what "they will say" if we live in our truths. This takes us out of integrity with our true desires and true selves. It anchors us in shame.

Sometimes the pendulum swings to the opposite extreme. We may rebel against some authority or external construct and do the opposite of what is expected of us. However, when this is done out of rebellion and anger, we are often not acting in alliance with our true selves. We are "rebelling against," as opposed to "living in accordance with" our truths.

We can explore our truths by dreaming and doing Flow of Consciousness Writing with the prompt, "if I was living my life as my heart desires, I would..." or, "if I let go of all of my "have to" or "should beliefs," I would really want to..." This writing exercise helps us get an idea of what our truths are, and what our shame is interfering with.

Reflection: When shame is our identity we often are out of integrity with our true desires, our true self.

Day 267
Shame in Our World

If I told you that you were living in "victim consciousness," you would most likely feel shame. Nobody wants to be identified with being a victim. And yet, a major archetype in our culture is the victim archetype. What do I mean by that?

Many of us get locked into an either/or consciousness and many of us blame. When we are in either/or we are not living in choice. We limit ourselves and put responsibility for that outside of ourselves. "If it weren't for..." or "I'd be able to if..." are statements that we make when we are not in choice. Then, we often take it one step further and blame others because we aren't where we want to be. This is victim consciousness.

Moving out of this looks like always being aware we have choice. I do something because I choose to do it, not because someone made me. I have awareness that there are countless choices beyond either/or. I take responsibility for my choices and do not blame others that I am in the situations I am in, or have made the choices I have made.

Victim consciousness is part of our shame-based world, the "shame stew" that we live in. It is part of virtually every system we are in.

Reflection: When we find ourselves in positions where we don't know or won't own our choices, we are in victim consciousness, and that is part of shame. If we blame others for the situations in our lives, or our lack of peace, we reinforce shame.

Day 268
Voice of Shame

Impression management is a behavior that is driven by shame. If I feel shame about myself, and I don't feel good about myself, I will not want someone else to see that. So I spend time and energy in covering that up, and trying to say and do things that will keep others from discovering how shameful I feel about myself. This is impression management. I attempt to get others to see me in a certain way.

Impression management is exhausting, usually not successful, and reinforces our shame. It keeps us from having authentic, loving relationships based on truly loving each other for who we are. We can't build trust when we are impression managing because we always have a fear that we will be found out and that will cause the other person to go away. If can be very scary to NOT impression manage. It puts us in a more vulnerable position. We get to be, express, and honor ourselves without letting the fear of what others might think interfere. It is freedom.

We do not need to feel shame about impression management. It is a survival tool that many of us needed in our growing up environments. However, we can become aware of what it is costing us and if we want to continue to pay that price as an adult.

Reflection: The price we pay for impression management is the loss of ourselves. Is it worth it?

Day 269
Multidimensional

On Day 215, I mentioned needing to heal shame at all levels. The level I am looking at here is healing shame in our relationships.

Shame interferes with our ability to connect with ourselves, others, and a higher power. Shame does not allow us to truly feel connection with another. If we don't work on healing shame at the level of relationship, we are keeping ourselves in isolation.

The first thing we get to do is take a good look at our relationships. What drives them? How do we feel in them? Do we have them? Do we allow self to express as we truly desire while we are in our relationships? How is our relationship with self? Do we trust? Do we know how to take care of ourselves (boundaries) and yet allow others in? Do we allow ourselves to end relationships or do we just leave or walk away and not make closure? Do we get to say, "yes," and "no"? Are we happy in our relationships? Do we feel shame in our relationships?

As we look at ourselves in relationships we can become aware of where shame is leading the way. We may have trauma that needs to be resolved inside the safety of a therapeutic relationship. If so, my hope is that we each will find a therapist who is safe and can help us repair the damage from abuse or trauma, so that we can open to new and healthy relationships.

We get to name our relationship-shame just like all other shame. Then we can see what the shame is telling us and work with the tools in this book to find a different relationship with ourselves and others.

> *Reflection: Shame gets to be healed at all levels, including our relationship with ourselves, others, and our belief or lack of belief in a higher power.*

Day 270
Model for a Shame-Free World

Let me speak a bit more about ways shame makes its appearance in relationships.

One thing I notice when shame is present in a relationship is the tendency for one person to make the other person bad or wrong if there is not agreement. When shame is present, it is not possible to truly agree to disagree. **The fight to be right is the shame fight**.

If a relationship is done, over, or finished, there must be a bad guy or blame. It is not possible for people to move on simply because it is over.

If we truly live our lives "in process" then we get to pay attention to the energy in our relationships. Sometimes we just change and the relationship no longer fits our needs. Sometimes we change just because it is time to change. Our old way of being no longer fits. Sometimes we stop impression managing and what we thought was ourselves or other is not there. We don't need to make ourselves or other wrong for the change, but we often do.

We have learned that shame is about control. In our relationships, we often have tried to control in order for a relationship not to end. We can use shame in cruel and hurtful ways to keep the illusion of a relationship in place. We can also use shameful tactics once a relationship is over because we blame. This does not bring peace to ourselves or those we are around. Shame still dominates our lives and is nasty.

If love is leading the way in a relationship, and change has brought the relationship to an end, each person will be able to acknowledge the relationship, the gifts it has brought, and the need to move in a different direction. When relationships can be ended in kindness, respect, and love, there will be no need for a "bad" guy.

> *Reflection: It does not matter how old we get, we can always embrace change and honor our partners and friends. Sometimes that means releasing a relationship and moving in a different direction. We can do that peacefully if shame is not part of our consciousness.*

Days 271-300

Day 271
One Thing Different

Another presidential election is approaching and I have been listening carefully to how people are sharing. I am on Facebook and see the comments. How do we respond when someone is voting in a way we aren't? How do we respond to listening to the debates or reading something on the candidates?

In our shame-based culture, it is often very difficult to allow others the dignity and respect of their own opinion. We often think we are fine with differences, and then we hear how someone thinks differently than we do and it becomes our own little war.

If we truly want to live in a peaceful world, we get to look at our personal wars. We get to see how we shame others and by doing so how we make wars and move in directions away from peace.

We all have the right to our own opinions. We all grew up differently and have different experiences that support why we vote the way we vote and believe the way we believe.

We just get to look and decide how we want to be in the world. We really get a special opportunity during the elections to see where we are shaming and where we are peaceful.

Reflection: We get to notice when we are at war and where we can choose again and move in the direction of peace.

Day 272
Poem

Pauses

Shifts

Changes

They come if we let them

Turn a corner and a new view presents itself

I get lost and found again

Perhaps I never am lost

Home is in my Heart

Barb Tonn

Day 273
Red Flag

When we are in shame, it will be difficult to make eye contact and we may flinch away from touch. Our shame fears that if we were seen, we would be seen for what we believe is true about ourselves, that we are flawed or defective in some way. So we pull away and pull back, even from people we would normally feel comfortable being touched or seen by.

Being seen as defective in some way is profoundly painful. We would rather not be seen at all than seen in shame. This leaves us feeling very alone and isolated. To receive touch or be seen leaves us vulnerable to hurt and we have experienced so much hurt.

We may remember that a lot of shame originates when we thought we could trust someone and that trust was betrayed. We may not even be able to recall this betrayal, but we live our lives from these wounds. So, we have pulled back in order to not re-experience the original traumas.

When we see that we have pulled back, can't make eye contact, or be touched, we can be aware that we are in a shame loop. Once we have identified this, we can begin to utilize the steps in the shame loop in the Appendix, to find our way out of the shame.

> *Reflection: Much of our healing begins when we can identify when we are in a shame loop. Recognizing our red flags can help identify our shame more quickly.*

Day 274
Healing Action

One important action we can take to move out of our shame is to replace our self-critical and self-abusive inner dialogues with compassionate ones.

In order for us to replace the inner criticism we need to be aware of it. At times, it shows in our thoughts and at times it shows in our words and behaviors. We may become aware that we have very hurtful, negative, and at times, abusive, inner selves. We may notice that ourselves are very familiar and may be virtually the only inner voices we have ever heard.

I will state with absolute confidence and consciousness that the inner shame critic is NEVER telling the truth. It lies, demands perfection, does not allow mistakes, and uses shame to try to motivate us. It is essential to change that voice to one of compassion. We can begin to do this whether we believe the truth or not. The following is an example of how we can begin to change that critical voice.

- Inner critic: "You really are a failure. No matter what you do you make a mess of it."

- Inner compassion: "You are a worthy person who gets to learn, grow, change, and make mistakes. That is part of being human and you are human."

Reflection: Self-criticism and abuse will NEVER get us to truth or peace. We get to be willing to change it.

Day 275
Rule

Shame-based systems and people are ruled by competition and comparison. It can be with people within the system, outside of the system, and with one's self.

I did not realize how competitive I was until I had been in recovery for quite some time. I realized that I was constantly sizing myself up by comparing myself to others who were involved in whatever activity I was in. If I was running, or in a class, or involved in activities, I was always aware of how I was doing compared with others. I would compete and most often the other person did not even realize I was competing. I wanted to be the best, to win.

The part of ourselves that competes and compares is ruled by the shame that says we are never enough. That part has to prove ourselves in most every situation.

Once I realized I was competing and comparing, I was amazed at how constant that behavior was and how it had infiltrated most aspects of my life. I didn't get to just be. I always was feeling less than or better than. It was exhausting. With shame running the show, I never could just relax, enjoy, and be where I was.

Reflection: Competition and comparison are ruled by shame. We can change the competitive message to allow ourselves to just BE. We relax into a more peaceful way of being.

Day 276
Shame Indicator

SHAME IS LIKE A FIRE.

I recently heard someone describe their internal shame voice as "like a fire with a constant source of air feeding it."

Shame does go on and on and burns everything in its path. The fire builds instead of diminishes, and it rages on. Shame seems to be unstoppable and it is always destructive. In the middle of it, it seems like it has a life of its own and is not at all amenable to change. Like a big forest fire or house fire, it will eventually burn itself out. However, it can leave a lot of destruction before it does so, and it can take a very long time.

However, if a fire is caught soon enough, it can be diverted or stopped. It can be transmuted. The sooner we notice the shame, the sooner we can contain it and transmute it. It may appear uncontainable. That is not true.

Reflection: It may appear that shame will rage on, just as fire with a source of air. There are ways to intervene on fires just as there are ways to intervene on shame. However, it is important to use the correct tools. If we pour water on a grease fire it is not effective. If we pour more shame on shame it may appear to be endless.

Day 277

Red Flag

Feeling like, or believing that we deserve to be punished is an indicator, or red flag, that shame is present. It is different than feeling responsible for an action and taking the appropriate consequences. When we continue to feel like we deserve to be punished or won't be able to make amends, we are caught up in shame.

Some of us with a lot of shame feel a constant sense of deserving to be punished for just being. We may feel this and not allow self to make a decent income, or finish a degree, or be in a healthy and loving relationship. Our shame says we don't deserve those things.

Some of us will get ourselves in a situation where we will get caught and punished because we're out of control and can't stop. We are then utilizing outside resources to help us stop what we can't. Examples of such punishments are getting arrested, getting a DUI, being put in anger management classes for raging, or having a court order put on ourselves because we can't stop some out of control behavior. (I only wish that, along with the consequences, the court would order effective "shame reduction therapy" to intervene on the rage.)

We get to see when we are out of control and feel we deserve to be punished. We examine what is driving the behavior. We can look at the shame.

Reflection: Shame-based people often believe we deserve punishment. We don't have to wait to be punished to get help. Help can be kind and supportive.

Day 278

Specific Shame-Based Issues

Just as familial shame is passed on generationally, so is cultural and racial shame. I was reading a book about the shame the German people felt because Hitler was German. They carried and sometimes still carry the shame of what he did.

After the civil war, the southern people carried shame about the war and slavery. Because shame is carried and not named, it never leaves. Decades and generations later the shame is still felt. There is no release, no forgiveness, because the shame is not brought into the open.

When someone is raped, they often carry shame. They did not commit the crime, but because they were the victims of it and the perpetrator does not own their behavior, they feel the shame.

When responsibility is taken for a shameful behavior or when shame is named, the healing can begin. Without bringing the shame into the light, it can live on and be carried by people who had nothing to do with the original shameful behavior.

Reflection: We can feel shame even when it is not named. If we are carrying shame, we will feel uneasy and exposed as "less than." We can bring this into the light of truth.

Day 279

One Thing Different

LETTING JOY LEAD THE WAY

I am starting to not only see the wisdom in letting joy lead the way in my life, but am actually letting joy lead the way. I am letting joy be a part of everything I do. If I am not feeling joy doing whatever I am doing, then I stop doing it.

I recently closed my in-person counseling practice and moved to Albuquerque. I am resting and looking at what comes next. Sometimes I come up with an idea that comes from fear. It sounds something like, "I am fearful I won't have a good enough financial retirement, so I will do _____ because I can make more money." There is nothing wrong with the idea, but because fear motivates it, there is no joy. What I know for myself is that I deserve to live in joy and to enjoy my moments, work and all. So the question I ask myself is: If I am not operating from fear, and I just let myself do what I enjoy, what will it be?

When I live my life in joy, the shame is not there. When I live in fear and make choices from that fear, I live in shame.

> *Reflection: Whether we believe it or not, we deserve to live our lives in joy. What choices will we make if joy leads the way in our lives?*

Day 280
Model for a Shame-Free World

As we experience the constant sense of not doing enough or being enough, our shame mounts. As our shame grows, the sense of being out of control and powerless grows. As this happens, we end up feeling more and more rage. Some of us act it out by being hurtful to others, and some of us act it in by being hurtful to ourselves.

Our world is getting crazier and crazier. We get to question the original premise that there is something wrong with us. We get to go to the foundation and lay down a new one. If we don't, we will destroy ourselves.

Each of us gets to break down the shame and know that, whether we believe it, we are love. If we are love, then so are others.

Then, we get to begin to treat ourselves and others with love. When we are tempted to judge, make others wrong, hate, and fear, we get to notice and ask love for another way of looking at this situation or person.

We may not want to be content with doing this in a sloppy, haphazard way. We may want to make this the most important thing we do. We don't have to wait for others to change and lay blame outside of themselves. There are only ourselves to look at. We can only take responsibility for changing ourselves. We get to do the work and bring love, instead of judgment, into our thoughts and relationships. We get to be willing to forgive all. We get to make this our most important task. We don't need to do it perfectly. We just get to set intention and start to move in this new, loving direction. We get to extend peace to those we don't agree with, or understand, or hate and judge. We get to do the hard work.

Reflection: People are either extending love or asking for it. If others are asking, we get to extend love to them.

Day 281

Right

I have the right to determine and honor what my priorities are.

Knowing, believing, and living these words, helps us in truly claiming our lives. We take our lives back from shame and know we are worth a life that's fit for us.

What are our priorities? What is most important to each of us? The following are suggestions for helping us get in touch with our priorities.

- Label a paper "My Priorities," and begin at least three pages of Flow of Consciousness writing. (Do not pick up the pencil or stop writing until at least three pages have been written). Read what was written with curiosity and the intent to pay attention.

- We can recall what was important to us as we were growing up. We maybe had dreams we shared. Some were supported and some were not. Those dreams may be the keys to the doors of our priorities.

- We can make a list of things that are important to us. Then, we can see which ones are our truths and which are "shoulds" we have internalized, but aren't our truths.

- We can have someone sit with a pen and paper and write down whatever comes out of our mouths as we say the first things that pop into our minds that are priorities.

How do we honor the priorities? We get to note them and set intent to honor them. We get to be aware when we keep our priorities secret, or give them up for somebody else's dreams or priorities. We get to set goals, followed by baby steps that will move us in the direction of our priorities. We get to continue to tell our inner children, our inner selves, that we have the right to determine and honor our priorities.

When we honor our priorities, we step out of the shame. By doing so, we embrace our truth and live the joy filled life we deserve.

Reflection: Without shame guiding our way and convincing us otherwise, we get to know our truths and live in a way that supports us.

Day 282
Rule

I have talked about the "no talk" rule and how damaging it is. It is an integral part of any shame-based system, and a behavior of all shame-based people. I would like to expand on this rule by talking about a behavior that is profoundly shaming and takes not talking to a more hurtful and destructive level. When the "no talk" rule is carried to an extreme it can result in shunning.

The online Urban Dictionary defines "shun" as "to reject or banish someone or something."

If we have ever experienced being shunned, we know it is hurtful. We are left out with no way to return or understand why. We are not talked to about what happened, we are just banished.

Shunning is shaming. It reduces us to an object without feelings. It is rejection.

Some religions use shunning to publicly shame someone who has behaved in a way unsupported by their religions. It damages the people who have been shunned. The behavior may change, but the fear and damage the person experiences may never heal.

Shunning is something we get to look at and make conscious decisions about. It may be really hard to talk about some things. We may need support to talk, and we get to find a way. If we want peace, we learn how to talk and not shun.

Reflection: We get to learn the language of love and use it.

Day 283

Tool

The following is an exercise that can help us change shame beliefs about ourselves to truths. Many examples I have given in the book have talked about Flow of Consciousness writing where we write what our shame is telling us, and then at the end claim a truth. These are examples of truths we can claim, whether we believe them or not.

- When we believe we are unlovable we can say, "Whether I believe it or not the truth is that: I am a lovable woman (man) who is having a hard time believing I am lovable.

- When we believe we are stupid we can say, "Whether I believe it or not, the truth is I am an intelligent woman (man) who is having a hard time believing I am intelligent. When I don't know something or have made a mistake, it simply means I am human. I get to not know something, or make a mistake, and still know that I am an intelligent human being."

- When we believe we are not enough we can say, "Whether I believe it or not, I am always and forever enough. I do not have to prove myself to me or anyone else. I get to be enough and am enough, just as I am."

- When we are feeling unworthy we can say, "Whether I believe it or not, I am a worthy human being. I do not have to prove I am worthy, and it cannot be taken away from me. I was born worthy and it will never change."

Now, using these examples, we can write a list of what our shame says about us. Then, we can create statements that are the truths we are having a hard time believing. We get to sit with the truths and let the words sink in. If we get stuck, we can put it aside for a bit, ask a loving safe friend for help, ask our inner wisdom for help, and allow ourselves to write the truth.

Reflection: Shame is Never the truth. We deserve to hear the truth, whether we believe it or not.

Day 284
One Thing Different

Shame keeps us in an unconscious state. We get to notice how often we have gotten somewhere and can't remember how we got there. We get to notice how much of our lives we can't remember because shame was interfering with us being present to people and our environment. We get to notice without shaming ourselves. It is just more information to help us understand how much shame has interfered in our lives.

It is hard to go through life in an unconscious state and feel peaceful and fulfilled. It also can get us in real messes. It can look like we don't have a good memory. It can keep us off balance. We aren't really in the now. We are lost in the voice of our shame and our self-consciousness.

The process of healing from shame is a process of getting more and more conscious of when shame is leading the way and then turning in the direction of the truth. It allows us to be in the here and now in grounded ways, which help us take care of ourselves and helps, us feel peaceful.

We can set our intentions to be in the here and now and be mindful of when shame is in charge. We can then intend to turn in the direction of truth.

Reflection: Getting conscious in the present moment is a process that can greatly help us in the healing of shame.

Day 285
Healing Actions

When we are healing our shame, we are in the wonderful position of making closures in conscious ways. We learn not to blame. We learn to take responsibility for our choices. We live from our rights, and we set boundaries that fit for us.

If we are struggling in a bad work environment, we can make a choice for change without moving into the victim position and blaming. We may not be in a healthy environment. We may be working for less money than we deserve, or with people who are less than honoring. In the old shame system, we could become the victims, rage about injustice, feel despairing, and blame in order to move on.

In the new healing way of dealing with this situation, we can look at our rights, choices, and boundaries and make decisions for ourselves. We can note that we have the right to be with people who honor and value us. We can choose to move on without having to rage. We can move toward something new without wasting time on how horrible the situation was. When we get hooked into the victim roles, we get hooked into blame and can spin in the negative energy of shame forever. Or, we can say, "this is not working for me and I deserve a different work environment. I will choose something different."

This is the same dynamic we can use when intimate relationships and friendships are over. We can utilize this process when change is called for. We release the victim and blame dynamic and work with rights, choices, and boundaries as we make new choices. We step out of shame as we do this. We step into our power and peace.

> *Reflection: We can loop in shame forever or we can choose a new path of peace. Up until now, we might not have known how. We are learning a new way of living in the world.*

Day 286

Right

I had been training for a triathlon for months. It had been hard work and it had given me structure as I was getting used to my new city of Albuquerque and not having a work schedule. One day as I was doubling up on my activities because the day of the event was getting close I had a thought; I have the right to change my mind.

The thought came out of nowhere and it stopped me in my tracks. In the past, when I had worked hard for something, I would have viewed it as a failure if I had changed my mind. Instead, I felt exhilarated by the idea. Previously, my shame would have beaten me up if I had not finished something. However, I felt excited. I didn't let my shame get a word in. My inner self was really happy I had paid attention.

I checked in with myself by asking my inner self what she wanted. What I heard was, "I know I can finish the triathlon and I know it will exhaust me. I don't want to be exhausted and I don't want to do it."

I called my friend to tell her I did not want to do the triathlon. She yelled, "me either!" Together we decided to pass on the triathlon. It was so freeing. Shame didn't even get a little bit of a hold on me. My friend and I met in Taos instead of Denver. We listened to music, hiked, and soaked at a hot spring. It was delicious.

Reflection: We always have the right to change our mind, with NO shame.

Day 287
Multidimensional

On Day 215, I talked about healing our shame on all levels. I want to talk about healing shame on the level of our emotions.

Shame is like a blanket that covers our true emotions. We may look like we are having all sorts of emotions, especially rage, but we have buried our real emotions under the shame.

An example of this would be when we are about to do something we feel really scared of doing. However, we feel shame that we are scared. We tell ourselves that we "shouldn't" be scared and that there is something wrong with us for feeling this way. So now, we feel shame and the real emotion of fear gets buried.

Another example would be when we are feeling profound grief over the loss of a pet. However, we feel shame that we are so devastated over a pet when we really didn't respond with this much distress over the loss of a person. So, the grief gets pushed down because the shame convinces us there is something wrong with us for feeling so much over the loss of a pet.

Now, we have a backlog of fear and grief. Shame has blanketed both of them.

As we heal our emotions, we begin to name them and allow ourselves to feel the emotions. If shame enters, we name the shame and turn in the direction of a truth. We may say, "I have the right to all of my feelings."

We also heal our emotions as we begin to let ourselves feel the feelings we have buried in the past. We honor the feelings, even if they have been buried for a long time. We do not let shame stop us. We get support for our emotions. We honor them.

Reflection: We heal our emotions by letting ourselves have them and not allowing shame to put a blanket over them.

Day 288

Red Flag

What I have learned over the years is that many of the Red Flag indicators that we are in shame seem really elusive. Over time, I have developed my own personal Red Flag list. This list consists of Red Flags that I most frequently use, and has helped me move out of shame much more quickly. I identified which red flags are my favorites.

I want to expand on the red flag I spoke of on Day 284. Being "disconnected from what is going on around us" is usually a red flag that we have gone into shame.

What happens is that we get internally or externally triggered into shame and go into the shame loop. At that point, we are in a defensive posture, feeling a level of self-consciousness, are disconnected from our real feelings, and buzzing around in some sort of a powerless, self-defeating place. We are absolutely not in the moment. Instead, we are internally absorbed in some sort of a stream of thought concerning whatever triggered us or, we are involved in self-defeating behaviors. We are not connected to what is happening around us. We are checked out. When we come up for air and notice that we have been gone awhile, we have an opportunity to identify the shame and utilize the following steps to move out of it. These steps may be familiar by now. They are written in the Appendix.

1. Name that we must be in shame or a shame loop.
2. Possibly see what internal or external thought or action triggered us.
3. Begin to utilize the shame healing tools we are learning to help us move out of the shame. We can look at the underlying feelings and needs and begin to take care of them.

Reflection: When we become aware that we are not in the here and now, we can recognize that as a Red Flag that we are in shame. Some of us will notice that this particular red flag is a common one and can be added to our own personal red flag list.

Day 289
Poem

A Burst of Energy

A soft Extending

As Creation moves through me

Out into the world

An expression of Love

Spirit embracing Spirit

Creation expressing

Creation loving

Day 290

Red Flag

Another "red flag" that we are living in shame is when we don't feel deserving of our "good". We feel guilty if we experience good. We feel bad when we are in the presence of someone who is struggling when we are experiencing good and they aren't. It is lovely to have sensitivity when others are suffering and aren't experiencing good. However, we cross over into dysfunction when we don't allow ourselves our "good" when others don't have it.

When we live in shame, we live in some level of **not deserving**. Shame tells us we only deserve if we are perfect and since we never are, we don't deserve.

If we do not have awareness when we are carrying the belief that we do not deserve, we can unconsciously sabotage the good in our lives. It can look like our lives are getting in the way of our good. What is really happening is our shame gets in the way of our success by sabotaging it. It tells us we do not deserve the "good."

Sabotage happens consistently when we are getting close to something good happening. We take the opportunity to look at the shame that drives the sabotage behavior. As we see the pattern of sabotage and look for the shame, we uncover the inner voice that is shame. We then begin to change the shame voice that drives the sabotaging behaviors

An example of a shame sabotage behavior is:

We are close to getting a degree or certificate from a school. Something occurs that interferes with our schooling. It may be a car accident or an illness. We may need to stop our schooling for a while. It seems life is getting in the way of us completing our degree or certificate. However, if shame is involved, it is the shame that interferes with our returning to and completing school. If our shame identified self is threatened by our success we may permanently drop out of school. Not completing school reinforces the shame belief that I do not deserve successful completion. If we bring the shame into healing we can go back into school and finish the degree or certificate. We don't allow shame to permanently sabotage our goals.

We can release the inner message that says, "I don't deserve..." and replace it with, "I do deserve..." We can Google "Donna Eden teaching temporal tap." She teaches a simple technique for releasing old beliefs and replacing them with what we want.

> *Reflection: When we don't believe we deserve to experience the "good" in our lives, we often sabotage ourselves. It helps us to identify this pattern, name the shame, and consciously work on changing our belief systems.*

Day 291
Maude

Maude (M)—It is easy to get overwhelmed by the process of healing shame. Barb, you have been giving suggestions for months now. You are showing us how shame is anchored in our world. This can be exciting, and at the same time overwhelming.

> Barb (B))—I have noticed both responses. Sometimes people get mad at me because I mention it so often. I think it can seem like there is no point in even trying to change our shame core.

M—I appreciate how hard it can seem and equally appreciate your talking about doing one thing at a time and living in process. Our western culture struggles with process. We usually don't really know what that means. When an overwhelming feeling takes over, it is the shame talking. It is the voice in us that discourages us and convinces us to stop healing. Shame creeps in the back door and tries to stop our healing processes.

> B—What if we just notice the discouragement and create a truth to turn to when it appears?

M—Great idea. It might be something like "I am a lovable and worthy person who is working on changing a belief system that has been with me my whole life. The belief system I am changing is one that most people believe and yet it is not a system that is based on love and it doesn't bring peace. I want love and peace and am therefore going to keep moving in the direction of healing my shame, even when the shame tries to discourage me. I get to be in the process of healing for my whole life, and that is okay."

> B—I like that. I know it can be hard to keep going. We think we have made progress. Then a major shame loop occurs, and we begin to doubt our

progress. The truth is, we have made progress, and it is the nature of healing shame to keep seeing new places where we get hooked. We get to look at, notice, and know that the truth is that we are in a process of healing that is multidimensional and complex. We get to notice, get discouraged, and keep on moving in the direction of love, to the light. We "shine the light of truth on shame," and keep on going.

M—It is so important to know that there is hope. Although shame may snag us again and again, we can break the shame loop, and find more and more joy. The stories you have shared about your own healing have shown this. I encourage everyone to keep moving in the direction of healing. Instead of looking at shame loops as setbacks, we can view them as an opportunity to move more deeply into our healing. My goal in sharing today is to encourage others and reinforce the work that has already been done.

Day 292
Red Flag

I want to expand on what Maude said yesterday. Human beings have a very basic need to connect. We possess that need at birth. When we are isolated or abandoned emotionally, it causes great distress and often, severe emotional damage. The need to connect remains, but the ability to connect is damaged. Connection becomes shame-based. We are in a double bind. We may feel shame that we aren't connected and shame that we want to connect. As a result, we loop in shame.

When we live in shame, we often live in isolation. We can be surrounded by people but feel unable to connect. We can look like we belong, but deep down question our connections. We can doubt ourselves. We can end up feeling vulnerable, especially when we feel exposed. Therefore, we can live very defensively so that we don't risk exposing ourselves or risk rejection. In that defensiveness, we are very isolated.

In our day-to-day lives, we may act like everyone else, but when we close the door at the end of the day we doubt ourselves, doubt our connections, doubt our interactions, and feel very alone.

We move out of the isolation of shame by naming our shame. We identify and feel the underlying feelings, and care for our needs. At times, more professional help may be required to deal with the childhood trauma of emotional abandonment that leads to isolation. The fear of being re-traumatized as we attempt to break our isolation may be too great without professional help.

Reflection: The inability to connect to others is a red flag that shame, in all likelihood, is engaged.

Day 293
Red Flag

Where we feel the most vulnerable is where we are most easily triggered into a shame loop. Another way of saying this is, where we are the most self-conscious is where we are more easily triggered.

The following are examples of self-consciousness that can trigger shame.

- Our weights
- Our heights
- Our lack of finances
- Our ill-health
- Our races
- Our sexualities
- Our friends or lack there of
- Our recovery
- Our shame
- Our mistakes
- The status of our marriages
- Having something be important to me that is not at all important to someone else
- Feeling different

As I was making this list, I realized that it could go on for many pages. What is important in our healing processes is having the awareness of where we feel different and self-conscious. In that awareness, we can intercede more quickly if shame gets triggered, and/or possibly circumvent a shame loop altogether.

Reflection: Knowing where we are self-conscious helps us identify our red flags.

Day 294

Specific Shame-Based Issue

A shame I want to spend some specific time on is the shame of the unemployed. In the Western culture, we are often heavily identified with what we do for work, and how much money we make. The unemployed have often lost both of those identifiers, and struggle with profound shame.

A while back, I was watching a TV documentary on people who had lost their jobs. They had searched and searched, and they were unable to find new employment. They were dealing with profound losses, as well as a cultural bias that was shaming to them. The longer they were unemployed, the more they received the message that they were not employable. Often, they were told not to apply for a job unless they had a job. They were not even allowed into the interview process.

The shame they were experiencing along with the losses and fear is untenable. They were feeling hopeless and often suicidal.

As individuals, we can look at our own biases, how they might be shaming, and how we can change them. We can make changes in our own beliefs that make a difference in the mass consciousness. We can be aware of how we think of the unemployed and make a conscious effort to think loving and empowering thoughts to support them. There may be actions we can take that will help alleviate the biases or struggles of this part of the population.

I believe we don't always do this because there is a cultural shame about the way we have off-shored our labor force and judged our unemployed. Because we don't deal with the underlying belief systems, we can all get sucked into the shame and project it on the unemployed. We become part of the problem.

We each play a part when there is a cultural shame. The only place we have power is in changing our own beliefs. We are of one mind. When I change my mind, I make an impact. I may not see this, and we are making a difference.

We can treat our unemployed with dignity and respect. How would we want to be treated in a similar situation?

Reflection: Looking at our prejudices, biases, and how they send shame messages, and then consciously changing our beliefs is one way of creating a new paradigm. We move out of shame and into love.

Day 295
Red Flag

On Day 268, I spoke about the hesitation, or fear of embracing our good. My hope is that we can all claim the right and ability to embrace our good; therefore, I want to talk a bit more about this.

Avoiding good can plague us when we have shame core issues. It keeps us from truly enjoying and embracing the good in our lives. We can experience an underlying fear that we are undeserving of good and that good will be rationed out in life, leaving us in short supply. When the good feelings are happening, we can become anxious and experience fear that they will go away, perhaps never to return.

Many of us have a hard time celebrating because of this fear. If we sit and write about the anxiety we feel when things are going well, we will often unearth the underlying shame message. It may sound like, "I am not deserving of this _____. Sooner or later it will go away."

The red flags I write about can seem like everyday occurrences. We may relate to some or all of them. They may help us to see that we are in shame more than we ever realized. We may begin to learn the triggers that are most common for us in our lives and be able to circumvent the shame loop because of this information.

> *Reflection: We can begin to develop our own list of common places where our shame triggers us into a shame loop. A common shame trigger may be that we have a hard time accepting and embracing our good.*

Day 296
Forgiveness

A common question I am asked is "what is forgiveness?" I have mentioned that we cannot move into forgiveness when shame is the driving force in our lives.

As we begin to recognize shame, we begin to see the resentments, anger, and judgments we have held onto, sometimes for decades. They feel justified. Shame supports this. What shame does not do is allow us to look at is the price we pay for these judgments and justified resentments. As we begin to look honestly at these behaviors we notice how isolated and bitter we are becoming.

To move into forgiveness, we need to begin to move toward compassion. We get to see how things don't need to be personalized. We begin to let people (including ourselves) be human and make mistakes. We get to acknowledge that we all have bad days and unconscious moments. We get to give others the benefit of the doubt.

Forgiveness is about knowing that in our hearts we are all the same. We get to learn how to see beyond behavior and into the heart of a person. This does not mean we hang out with people behaving badly. It does mean that we take care of ourselves, and release the judgment. We learn to "be kind" because everyone is fighting the same battles.

> *Reflection: Forgiveness comes when we are compassionate. We can set intention to move into living our lives in kinder ways. We release judgments. We take care of ourselves without condemning.*

Day 297
Red Flag

KEEP MOVING FORWARD

We have a hard time stepping out of shame if we don't know we are in it. One of the ways we can know we are in shame is if we feel "stuck." The condemning voice of shame starts churning in our heads. We become stuck in self-defeating thoughts or behaviors. It is as if a sticky web is covering us. We just can't seem to move away from the condemning voice.

Someone once described being in her shame as feeling like "I am thumbtacked to the wall and I am just flailing there." I thought that was an excellent description of how we feel "stuck" when in shame. We often can know a direction we could move in that would be helpful, but just can't seem to move there.

So, if we are stuck, we see what our shame might be telling us about whatever it is we are attempting to figure out. For example, if we can't decide if we want to quit our job, then we can write out our thought processes. The writing might look like "If I quit my job my shame is telling me ____," "If I don't quit my job my shame is telling me ____," or "If I don't decide what to do my shame is telling me ____."

Then, we can respond to the shame and look at all of our choices.

It doesn't pay to argue with shame. We just look at shame and listen to what it is telling us. We then turn in the direction of choice and compassion and listen for what it might tell us. We claim a truth, whether we believe it or not. This would sound like: Whether I believe it or not, I am a worthy person who deserves _____. We fill in the blank and keep moving away from shame. We no longer are "stuck" in our shame

> *Reflection: Being stuck and unable to make a decision or move in a certain direction is a strong indicator one is in a shame bind. Once we identify the shame bind, we can begin to move again.*

Day 298

Healing Actions

When we feel we are bad, unlovable, or unworthy, it is hard to take care of ourselves. One of the hardest questions we can ask ourselves is, "what do I need?" We often have no idea what we need because we either feel shame about having needs, or have never been allowed to consider our needs.

When we grow up in an environment where our needs are not acknowledged, we often develop a belief that our needs are too much, not important, or wrong or bad. Many of us can be triggered into a shame loop just by being asked what we need.

However, in order to take care of ourselves and to heal shame, it is important to begin to identify our beliefs about our having needs, people who need, which needs are okay and which needs aren't okay. As we have learned throughout this book, we need to be able to lift the blanket of shame and see what our underlying feelings might need.

Many of us feel our needs are too much, and we feel "needy" and horrible about ourselves, if we have needs. Even basic human needs can trigger shame. Many of us have no idea what we need much of the time. Shame has shut our needs down.

As we learn about our shame beliefs around having needs, we can begin to consciously change our beliefs to support our healing processes. We learn to identify our needs without experiencing shame, and how to take care of our needs.

> *Reflection: Honoring our needs is an important part of healing our shame.*

Day 299
Specific Shame-Based Issue

Financial status can trigger shame more than most issues. If we are financially sound, shame says it is never enough. If we are struggling financially, we can feel like we are failures. If we are retiring, we may feel shame that we did not prepare enough. If we are underemployed, we may live in fear and a sense of failure.

Often, shame has a set of beliefs around what we think we "should" earn, how we "should" look if we are financially set, and how our life styles will look if we are financially sound. When our lives do not match these "should" beliefs, we can feel shame.

When we are in our shame, we look outside of ourselves to determine our self-worth. How others see us can be a huge factor in triggering our shame. Our beliefs about our self-worth can be very intertwined with our finances.

I challenge all of us to honestly examine our beliefs about our finances, and our worth as it relates to our finances. We may say that our worth is not determined by our finances because we feel shame that it is. If we can't really, honestly, without shame, look at our beliefs, we can't name the shame and change the beliefs. We will loop in the shame because we are unconscious of our belief systems. (This is the case in all areas of our lives, not just with finances.)

> *Reflection: We get to be enough, just as we are. Our worth is not defined by how much money we have. **We do not have to prove ourselves**. By examining and changing our beliefs we begin to live in the peace that we deserve.*

Day 300
Healing Actions

We have grown up learning the language of shame. As I have been showing with my examples, it has made its way into all aspects of our lives. We learn how to judge, compare, blame, project, hate, not forgive, and live in the fear of shame. It is part of our culture. Different subcultures may have different experiences of shame, or different shame triggers, and it is in all subcultures. There is shame that we have shame.

There is no way we wouldn't have shame. To pretend we don't, or deny it is there, is an exercise in futility. It just is.

After we begin to identify the shame in ourselves, and the messages in the world around us, we get to choose to begin to unlearn the language of shame. We get to begin to internally reference, take responsibility, release judgment, and forgive. We get to learn compassion, and see the love and oneness behind the behaviors. We get to learn how to be human instead of insisting we need to be perfect. We get to stop comparing and learn we are enough just as we are. We get to learn and make mistakes and grow. We get to accept ourselves as we are. We get to each count equally. We get to learn a completely different way of being in this goofy old world. This new way has a chance of bringing us peace and harmony.

The shame of shame keeps many of us from really acknowledging how much shame we have lived with. It keeps us from surrendering and moving into a way of being with each other that fosters connection, and self-esteem, and love.

Reflection: We get to "unlearn" shame and "learn" love.

Days 301-330

Day 301
Multidimensional

There are two levels in which we are healing our shame.

Level one: We are healing in the here and now. We are intervening on the shame loop. The steps for intervening are in the Appendix. Many of the tools in this book are designed to intervene on our shame as soon as we become aware of it, in the here and now.

Level two: This is where we do our work on what anchored the shame in place. It is the "there and then" work. We do our trauma, family of origin, and inner child work. We are releasing the trauma in our system so that we do not trigger into shame. This is often the work we do with a professional therapist.

We can make great progress in intervening on our shame and utilizing the strategies we have been talking about. Often, however, we need help releasing our shame in the body, which is the trauma work. Once this work is done, we are less likely to trigger into shame. If we do trigger, it is less intense, and more easily intervened on.

We can go into shame because we have worked so hard on our shame, and our healing, and still trigger into a shame loop. We can feel like we have not done enough or worked hard enough. What is more accurate is that we may just be reaching a deeper place, a deeper wound that is holding the shame in place. As we get help and do this work, we will find that the tools we are using will feel more effective.

Reflection: We get to learn about what holds our shame in place and create our own healing process. Each of us has a different healing path. We learn how to honor our path.

Day 302
Multi-dimensional

On Day 255, I talked about healing shame on all levels. I now want to focus on healing shame on the intellectual level. I have made reference to healing on this level throughout the book. This level of healing is where we address the belief system that supports the shame.

This is where we identify what the shame is telling us, and what the belief is that it supports. An example of what shame is telling is when we notice that our shame trying to convince us that we are too old to make a change in our career. We will look stupid if we go back to school and attempt to get a new degree. We know the voice is the voice of shame because it puts us down, limits us, and keep us from moving forward in our life. The belief it supports is a limited belief about what we can do and become after age _____.

Once we identify the underlying belief we can begin to consciously change our belief system. We can utilize the previously mentioned "Temporal Tap by Donna

Eden." We can create affirmations. We can create a mantra to work with. "I am never too old to go for my dreams and create a new life" is an example of a new belief.

We may be unearthing our belief system for the rest of our lives. We may be amazed to discover what our belief systems say and become aware that it is often the voice of shame. We get to change our belief systems.

> *Reflection: Healing intellectually is about healing our belief systems. It is never too late to do that!*

Day 303
One Thing Different

We can make a choice for ourselves without making someone else wrong for thinking or believing differently than we do. The "norm" in our culture primarily supports the behavior of making others wrong if they think or believe differently than we do. Making others "wrong" so we can be "right" is part of the shame that is anchored in our culture.

It is time for a new presidential election so I will use it to illustrate my point. "If I want this candidate then you are wrong if you want the other. If I am a Republican, then you are stupid to be a Democrat, and vice versa."

Another example that is common is what happens when a relationship is over. It is hard for us to be able to say, "this relationship served me, and I loved this person I have been with, and we are going different directions because it no longer serves the highest good of each person." We tend to want to blame, shame, and make wrong in order to change directions.

The culture we live in is a shame-based culture. Shame is supported by blame. Shame does not honor differences. Shame does not support change.

We have an opportunity to picture what it would be like if we make changes, vote the way we want, move in our own direction, without having to defend ourselves or make others wrong for being different. There is no shame in being how we are, and for others to be as they are.

> *Reflection: It is really hard to take ourselves out of "being right" and just allow ourselves and others to "be."*

Day 304
Shame in Our World

Healing shame is a spiritual path. It helps us connect with our true selves, and live in love as opposed to hate and fear.

The primary identification on this planet is with shame. Original sin is the belief that we are born flawed and need to amend for this the rest of our lives. Whether one is raised in a religion that supports this, or not, shame is in the foundation of our world.

Learning the truth, that we are love, is a process of unlearning the old shame-based paradigm. First, we get to question the belief that we are flawed and therefore need to sacrifice and prove ourselves. We get to turn in the direction of love, even when we truly don't believe that it is our essence. Many of us will deny our shame. We will say, "I know" I am lovable. However, the voice in our heads would say otherwise. Shame hates and judges and punishes us with suffering. Shame keeps us jumping through the hoops of having to prove ourselves our entire lives. We keep busy so we don't have to see this vicious loop we are in.

Denial is a defense against our identification with shame. Projection is what we do with our inner belief. I won't look at my identification with shame so I project it out. You become my focus. You become the bad guy." How I see the world is an outside picture of an inner condition.

Reflection: Denying our shame and projecting it onto others keeps us stuck in shame.

Day 305
Voice of Shame

Shame-bound people are motivated by a drive for predictability and safety. They view spontaneity as a threat. They tend to be manipulative in order to keep things under control, and have a narrow range of responses.

Just reading that could trigger shame. Triggering you is not my intention. We get to do our own inventories in order to look at what shame has done to our lives, and determine if we really want to continue down the path we have been on.

We feel inadequate and it scares us. So we try to keep things under control so that we feel more in control. We do this by limiting our choices and responses. The more predictable events are the more we believe we will be able to manage. We are anxious.

There may be nothing wrong with this if it gets us what we want. However, we may be paying a big price for this tight control we keep on ourselves and those around us. We may lack spontaneity and miss many fun and interesting opportunities. We may deal with a lot of anxiety. We may be living in denial of how truly out of control we are of many things in our world. Then when something happens which we couldn't control and which causes us pain, we have fewer coping strategies.

As we heal our shame, we open to the world and to experiences. We get to expand our lives in ways that fit for us and don't confine us to "tried and true." We create more life experiences from this spontaneous place because we are not so fearful of messing up, or as concerned with how we appear to the world.

Reflection: We have paid a painful price with shame as our teacher. By trying to keep everything predictable, we have limited our choices and experiences.

Day 306
Shame Defined

There is a quote by a man who has been my mentor in understanding and healing shame.

His name is: Gershen Kaufman. In his book, *Shame— The Power of Caring*, he makes a powerful statement. He says, "Shame is the affect which is the source of many complex and disturbing inner states: depression, alienation, self-doubt, isolating loneliness, paranoid and schizoid phenomena, compulsive disorders, splitting of the self, perfectionism, a deep sense of inferiority, inadequacy or failure, the so-called borderline conditions and disorders of narcissism." (P. viii)

I have seen shame underlying psychiatric diagnoses over and over in my 30 years as a therapist. And yet, how often is shame directly addressed in the therapy room? June Tagney, co-author of, *Shame in the Therapy Hour* in an interview is quoted as saying, "although people rarely mention shame during the therapy hour, it's ubiquitous in the therapy room."

I believe it is profoundly important and essential in anyone's healing process, whether in formal therapy or in one's individual work outside of therapy, to learn the language of shame and bring his or her shame into healing. If we do not, we will be missing the foundational work in our healing processes.

Reflection: Whether we are in formal therapy, or working on our own, shame is the foundational work in our healing processes.

Day 307

Voice of Shame

The other day, I was speaking with someone who said, "My body is my own business." She established a personal, and important boundary for herself with that statement.

In our shame-based world, we often hear comments by others, about peoples' bodies. The comments are usually unkind, but occasionally kind. They involve comparing ourselves to others, and judgment. Whether the person is receiving negative or positive attention, it is not for us to judge someone else's body. Shame is about judgment.

Because we can't hide our bodies, they become a perfect target for shame. We all show up in them. Do we have the right to walk around commenting on the fat, skinny, or ugly? We all have the right to live without criticism or judgment from others. We get to release our criticisms and judgments of others.

As I have shared, I grew up in a home where the god of thin was worshipped. If one got fat, then that was a big shame. There were always comments about how fat people were. It was not said to the person, unless they were one of the family, and it was a judgment. I hated it. I hated hearing it. It felt hurtful. My family was like so many families who voiced their shame and directed it to others for how they looked. We were very much a product of our culture. It has taken me my whole life to get comfortable with my body, just as I am.

Reflection: Our bodies are our own business.
We get to learn how to leave the body
comments out of our conversations.

Day 308
Voice of Shame

We have learned that attacking others reinforces shame and if we really want peace, attacking is not okay. That is, we don't think it is okay, most the time. It depends on our subculture and belief systems if it is okay sometimes.

However, do we hear much about attacking ourselves? Do we learn how damaging it is when we attack ourselves? Do we hear the voice of shame that attacks ourselves for the smallest of errors, and won't settle for anything less than perfection?

Healing shame is about listening to a voice of compassion. It is about learning to turn to love. Would compassion or love say the kinds of things to us that we say to ourselves? Would we say the things we say to ourselves to our friends? Are we friends to ourselves?

Attacking ourselves is our right. However, once again, we get to look at the consequences of self-attack. We get to see if we really want those consequences. We get to get conscious of the damage it does to our self-esteem and to our relationships.

We get to learn to listen to our inner voice (and sometimes outer voices) and notice what they are saying to us, and about us. We get to change and listen to different voices. The choice is ours, and we get to make it consciously.

Reflection: How we talk to ourselves about ourselves makes a difference.

Day 309
Red Flag

As a therapist, I have worked with a lot of people who carry a great deal of anxiety. I have been to countless workshops on healing anxiety. I have techniques galore to help people intervene on anxiety. Many of them are quite useful. However, except in a workshop that I took from Dr. Kaufman (mentioned on day 306), anxiety was never linked to shame.

If we carry a high level of anxiety or a thread of anxiety runs through our days, there is a good chance that we have shame core issues. We can learn techniques to diminish anxiety, but if we don't deal with the shame that holds the anxiety in place, we are not healing at our core. Instead, we are just dealing with the symptoms. Shame tells us we are not enough. There is something wrong with us and sooner or later people will find out and negative consequences will occur. We work very hard to hold things together, to prove ourselves, and to conquer our fears. However, deep down, we believe we aren't enough. Why wouldn't we feel anxious? Life is like walking through a minefield where we can trip up on our shame at any moment. Of course, we are anxious.

We get to heal our shame. We get to bring our traumas to light. We get to unlearn the language and beliefs of shame and learn the language of self-love and compassion. As we bring our shame into healing, our anxiety diminishes. As we learn our rights, choices, and boundaries, and live from them, our anxiety diminishes.

> *Reflection: Anxiety is a red flag that shame is anchored in our core. Healing our anxiety requires addressing our shame.*

Day 310
Shame in Our World

One of the reasons I have focused on resolving shame in our world is because I so want to find a way to live more peacefully. When shame is leading the way, we have no chance of living in peace. One of the dynamics in a shame-based world is the constancy of war.

The dynamic that I am focusing on here is our fighting against things we don't like. If we listen to our speech we will find we use fighting analogies a lot. "I am fighting against this cold" and "I am fighting against the way animals are treated," and "I am fighting against old age." I could write pages of examples. It may not seem important, and it is another way we constantly support war.

What if we simply stood "For" things we want in our lives?

Examples of standing "for" would be:

I am building a strong immune system

- I support the humane treatment of animals
- I am learning to live vivaciously in each moment
- I embrace myself whatever my age

These statements create a dynamic for peacefully stepping into something we want to support.

As we create a world that is peaceful and loving, we get to be deeply aware of all the places we aren't peaceful and loving, and change those places. If we use half-measures, we will get half-results.

We can't wait for others to change before we do, or change will not happen. We get to find all the places in our lives where we continue to create shame and war and pain, and bring them into healing.

Reflection: We will be amazed at how many wars we participate in each day. We get to change that.

Day 311
Model for a Shame-Free World

A wonderful energy worker and friend of mine named Tia said, "Life is a process, not an event. We will not arrive, but we will move higher and higher into our divine light and deeper and deeper into our own loving authenticity."

This quote clearly describes the process of healing shame. We move into the light of our true essence. We are in a process that is alive and creative and full of movement. We are learning to leave the dark, painful dynamics of shame behind, and move into the love that is our true essence.

I have talked about healing as a process. In our western culture, we have little, if any, experience of process. We usually want to just be done, and the faster the better. That is not how shame heals. We grow in our awareness of how shame has infiltrated every thought form in our world. We begin to see all the subtle and not so subtle ways shame is supported and passed on. We get to learn how to intervene on shame in our personal life, and how to bring that healing into our world. It is a process that gets to take the rest of our lives.

So often in this world, we feel powerless over things that really impact us. In our process of healing shame we have personal power. We can change how we see ourselves and the world. We determine how our seeing influences our feelings and our choices. We empower ourselves by changing our personal beliefs, and how we view the world. We make choices that support peace in our minds and in our actions.

Reflection: We empower ourselves to make choices and changes that move us toward peace.

Day 312

Voice of Shame

There is disagreement about the word "shame" and what it means. Many use the word "guilt" when talking about shame. Many also use the word "ego." We have begun to hear the word "shame" more frequently. However, the lack of agreement as to what it means can bring confusion.

Eckhart Tolle uses the word "ego" in much the same way as I use "shame." Miguel Ruiz talks about the domestication process in much the same way as I have talked about the origins of shame. Ruiz says, "We surrender to the beliefs of our parents, and the world, with our agreements. When we agree to something we say, "Yes" to it. This is what Ruiz calls the Domestication of Humans. There is much research on shame and many tools to help us move through and beyond it. (Thank you to the dedicated souls who did the research on shame.)

At this point, I think what is most important is that we address shame. The agreement in our language would make that easier, and the disagreement in our language does not need to get in the way. The "shame" or "ego" construct in our world is destructive. If we wait for agreement in our language regarding shame before we begin healing, it will be the same as waiting for others to change before we do. Instead of waiting for agreement, we can begin to move in the direction of healing. When we stumble on a term, or writing that sounds like it is talking about healing shame, we can be open to what it has to say. We then avoid getting sidetracked by the different words used for shame.

With shame as our core belief, we live our life in a completely opposite way than we would live if we truly believed we were loveable and perfect just the way we are.

Reflection: Whether we call it ego or shame, it is a lie.

Day 313
Tool

CHOOSE AGAIN

In the 12 Step community, there is a slogan called KISS- Keep It Simple Sweetheart.

In healing shame, we are dealing with a multidimensional, false belief about ourselves, which can feel anything but simple to heal. However, there is a necessary step we can take when we are healing shame, which is "simple."

Whenever we hear the "voice of shame" in our heads, we are listening to the "voice of shame" as our teacher. That teacher is familiar, mean, teaches a curriculum that is not true, and will never change. We get to notice, to stop, and to choose another teacher.

The other teacher is the teacher of kindness and love. This teacher is much quieter. This teacher shows us how to love. This teacher knows our essences are innocent and pure. This teacher will never change. This teacher is forgiveness.

Personally, I want to learn from the teacher of love. I want to learn how to be kind to myself and to others. I want to learn how to live in peace. What I know is that it is one or the other. I either listen to the teacher of "Shame" or the teacher of "Love."

I may have to choose between these teachers a million times a day. However, it is a step in the direction I want to go.

Reflection: We get to decide if we want a new teacher.

Day 314
Healing Actions

Healing shame is about claiming our true selves. We move out from under the piles of "should" and "have to." We begin to listen to the teacher of love who will show us how to find peace and live in the true essence of who we are.

Many of us, when first in recovery from shame and addiction are fearful of getting lost. We have identified with our false selves for so long, that it is scary to imagine being without them. I can remember when I first sobered up. I had no idea how to live life as anything but the party girl. I did not know how to dance, have sex, converse at gatherings, or live my life without alcohol. As I began to consciously heal from shame, I became aware of how identified I was with myself as a woman who felt like a failure and was unlovable. I couldn't begin to imagine feeling differently about myself, or how to live without shame.

I have been in recovery from alcohol and pot for over 38 years as of the first printing of this book. I have been actively working on healing my shame for over 30 years. I am here to witness to the fact that change is possible. I now view myself completely opposite to the way I viewed myself when I started my healing process. I now love myself, and the way I show up in the world. I have more peace than I ever thought was possible. Change happens in this process of healing.

> *Reflection: It is scary to change. As dysfunctional as the old may be, it is familiar. The fear I am addressing here is the fear of losing ourselves. My 30 years of healing shame work is proof this won't happen. We don't lose ourselves, we find ourselves.*

Day 315
Shame Indicator

I have talked about the "shame of our shame." It is important to understand this dynamic. "Shame of our shame" can interfere in our recovery if we do not understand it.

We may be ashamed of the things we have done that we feel shame about. We may feel shame about the way we feel about ourselves. We may fear bringing our shame out and sharing it because of how others will view, or judge, us if they know how much shame we have. We may not want to risk the rejection we are sure will follow after we share our shame in the presence of others. This is what I mean by the shame of our shame.

Our original sharing when we were young often resulted in shame. We experienced betrayal at the hands if those we thought we could trust. Our new sharing is an opportunity to rebuild the trust that was originally ruptured. The new sharing may feel frightening. We have choices beyond sharing or not. We get to learn how to share in safe ways so as to not frighten ourselves.

Let's look at the lie of shame. Let's look at sharing with those we have begun to build trust with in healthy ways in our relationships. No, we don't share our shame when we first get to know people. No, we don't share our shame where the shaming occurred (at least until we are truly ready). We begin to build relationships where people are there for us, and have become trusted friends in our lives. As we develop trust, we begin to share at deeper levels than we have before. Then, we can begin to risk sharing our shame. We don't share it all at once so that we feel terrified and overwhelmed. We share a bit and let people be there for us in loving ways. As time goes on we learn how to share shame in safe ways. It is a process. It is an important process because "shame of our shame" can stop our healing.

Reflection: We are good people who deserve to have our shame heard by loving ears and seen by loving eyes.

Day 316
Shame Loop

I am going to make a bold statement and say that whenever we are dealing with addiction we will find shame. There may be shame of the addiction, shame at having been out of control, shame about our behavior when we are acting out in our addiction, and shame core issues we already carry. When we look at the shame loop in the Appendix, we will see addiction in #4 of the shame loop. It is our self-defeating, out of control behaviors that we can get stuck in. To effectively move out of the active addiction we need to deal with shame.

I wrote a drug and alcohol program for a psychiatric facility in Colorado Springs in 1988. It had a strong shame reduction component in it. I was convinced that we had to address the shame to help our clients step into a solid recovery. I still believe that.

We can also look at our addiction to our shame. We can't seem to stop being hard on ourselves, or believing there is something defective or unlovable about us. We feel powerless to heal the shame that we identify with.

The 12-step communities work the steps to begin to bring their addictions into healing. We can do the same with shame. If we have the language of the 12–steps, we can utilize what we know and how we work the steps as we bring our shame into healing.

Reflection: If we have addictions, we have shame. As we move into healing we get to address the shame underlying our addictions.

Day 317
Tool

It can be very helpful to find some words to use as a mantra that consistently remind us of truth. A mantra that helped me a lot was, "I don't have to prove myself to anyone." I found that repeating the words to myself in many different types of situations really helped me shift out of my patterns of looking to others for approval, and living my life in constant competition. The mantra reminded me that I am good enough just the way I am.

I came up with those words for myself during one of my Flow of Consciousness Writing times. Other words that can be very helpful are:

- I am good enough just the way I am.
- I get to just be.
- Whether I believe it or not, I am lovable, just the way I am.
- I get to show up in the world in the way that fits for me.
- I do not need to compare myself to anyone. I am okay just the way I am.
- I am a good and worthy woman/man.
- I am a lovable woman/man.
- I get to learn how to trust life and my process.

- I am in the process of healing and it gets to take as long as it takes.

As we get to know our shame and how it tends to show up, we can find words that we can consistently use to remind self of what we either never knew, or forgot.

Reflection: The broken record or mantra technique of repeating words helps keep us on track.

Day 318
Shame Originator

A humbling fact of healing is that we often have developmental delays to make up for. When we are caught up in addictions, or trauma, or shame-based and addictive systems, we are living in survival. We are focused on getting our basic needs met. While this is going on, we miss many of the developmental tasks we would be completing if we were not in survival.

There is an old book called, *Passages*. It is about the developmental stages we go through as we grow. I remember reading that book while I was still caught up in alcoholism. I remember thinking that the descriptions the author used would have put me in the adolescent category. I was in my late 20's at the time. It confused me. What I know now is that I started drinking as a teen. At that point, I stopped developing in some areas. When I stopped drinking, I had some missing pages in my developmental book that I had to go back and fill. I didn't have good relationship skills. I wasn't good at setting life tasks and following through. I had not learned how to leave people and situations in a functional way, and conflict was difficult. Those are just some of my examples. Those are all things I would have learned as a teen, if I had not been in my addiction.

There is no shame in discovering that we have some developmental delays. Those delays just are a part of our healing processes. We learn to identify the skills we are missing. We then set some goals to learn the skills we are missing.

> *Reflection: We get to look at what is true for us and deal with the facts. Without shame, we can address our developmental delays.*

Day 319
Right

In Charles Whitfield's book, *Healing the Child Within: Discovery and Recovery for Adult Children of Dysfunctional Families*, we are given a list of rights we all have. It is titled, "Personal Bill of Rights," and it is found on p. 116-117. One of the rights I love on the list is:

"I have the right to change and grow."

As I previously mentioned, in shame-based systems, we often get put in a certain role. No matter how hard we try to get out of that role and change, we are still seen in the same role. If we were the screw up, we are always seen as the screw up. If we were the one who kept all the communication going, it became our task in the system to continue to do that. If we were the heroes, we could do no wrong. When we try to discuss having a problem or a struggle, we are often dismissed.

We have the right to change and grow. We have the right to look at our old roles and change them. We have the right to learn and make changes based on what we are learning.

What we can't control is how other people view us. We may have the right to change and we might change, but it does not mean others will acknowledge or honor the changes.

Reflection: Whether others ever acknowledge our changes, we get to make them and feel good about them.

Day 320
Tool

Have you identified shame at the core of what you believe about yourself?

As a therapist who has specialized in healing shame for the past 30 years, I can tell you that I have sat in the presence of countless people who clearly have shame at the core of their being. Yet, they are unable to identify with the shame. I often will ask, "Do you feel shame is a word that would describe how you identify with yourself?" Often I will hear, "no." Part of that is because there is not common language about what that question means. Part of it is because of the shame of the shame that I have talked about. Part of it is because we just don't know the shame is there. I have developed some questions to help us explore any shame we might not have previously identified. I invite you to just look at the questions with openness and curiosity.

Shame Indicators:

1. Do you find yourself thinking, "if they knew the truth about me, they would not think much of me, or they would not want me in their lives?"

2. Do you find yourself often comparing yourself to others and coming up less than?

3. Do you frequently use the words, "should" or "shouldn't" to determine how to behave in the world?

4. Do you have a strong inner critic (of yourself and/or others)?

5. Do you rage? (This is different from anger. If you are either thinking or acting destructively toward self, other, or property, it is rage. Rage is shame.)

6. Do you consistently doubt yourself?

7. Despite proof that you are smart, accomplished, loved, and adequate, etc., do you truly believe you are not?

8. Do you have to prove yourself to others over and over, or do others have to prove themselves to you over and over?

9. Do you have painful events and memories that stick in your mind with vivid detail and cause profound embarrassment when remembered?

Although this list is not all-inclusive, if we have answered yes to any or all of these questions, we may want to be curious about the shame that we carry. These questions are indicators that may point to the fact that we have shame in our cores.

> *Reflection: As we learn more about shame we often learn that our life experiences have been anchored in shame. Once we realize this, we get to use the tools in this book to move into our healing.*

Day 321
One Thing Different

We get to choose what works as opposed to what we think we should do. This choosing can be very helpful in our intimate relationships. If we come into our relationships with a pile of unconscious beliefs and expectations about what a relationship "should" be, we can struggle.

We think the other person should _____, and if they don't, they don't love us, or the relationship is bad. We have a list of things that we take for granted, and then when they don't happen, we feel like failures. We then often act in self-defeating ways. These self-defeating ways indicate we are in a shame loop.

Shame navigates relationships by letting "should" lead the way. Unvoiced expectations destroy the relationship.

What if we just get to create a relationship that truly is about the two people involved, and not about the experiences we learned from our families, or a fantasy of romantic love? What if we talked about what we wanted and needed and what works for each of us? What if we then put together lives and relationships that really fit for us?

One thing I know is that what I need now, as a 60+-year-old is very different from what I needed as a 20-year-old. My relationships look very different now than they did in my 20's, because I am very different.

> *Reflection: We get to learn how to be in relationship in ways that honor how we show up now in our lives, and in ways that meet our needs. No "should."*

Day 322
Maude

Barb (B)—Maude, I am close to the end of my writing. I finally see the light at the end of the tunnel. What I see now is how strongly the voice of shame wanted to sabotage my writing and make sure that I never finished this book. Understanding the shame sabotage helps me make sense as to why it took me so long to write this book.

> Maude (M)—Barb, shame can be so sneaky. It can get in your head and sound like the voice of reason and truth, and all the time it is lying. What did it tell you?

B—The voice of shame went between telling me I knew nothing about shame to telling me I was a failure because other people had written about shame and I had nothing new to say. Shame wanted to convince me that just writing a book of practical examples of how shame interferes in our lives, and day-to-day interventions was not enough. It said that because I can still have shame knock me on my butt, I "should" not be writing. My shame told me that it had taken me too long to write my book and I "should" just give up.

> M—It almost worked, didn't it? You have almost stopped writing the book countless times. Shame told you that your book is different than what other famous shame authors have written. So, yours must be wrong and not worthy being completed or published.

B—Yup! You have the main picture of what I have been grappling with.

M—What kept you going?

B—I have been using my own tools. I have been writing out what shame has been telling me and then claiming a truth. I have done my own trauma work. I have talked to people about what my shame is telling me. I listened to their kind words. I have been really vulnerable and let others read my work and then listened to their words tell me that this is helpful and practical. When my shame gets triggered, I have been intervening on the shame loop. I have allowed myself to put this book together in the way that fits for me. I have been refraining from comparing it to other authors. I have had fun putting you (Maude) in the book and including my poems. I have let myself write this in the way I have talked to clients for over 30 years. My clients have been helped, so, I think this will help others.

M—So, you have practiced what you have written about. You have let your creative process lead the way and you have not let shame shut you down. You are risking showing up in just the way you want. You are releasing your shame in order to put this book out there. I applaud you, Barb.

B—Yes, and it is scary. I feel vulnerable. I am doing something that works for me, and facing the fear of what others think of my work. When I publish this book, I am done. What the Universe does with it is none of my business. I am responsible for following my inner guidance by writing this book. That is all I need to do.

M—Thank you for sharing your process so honestly. When we bring our shame into healing, it can try to shut us down. You didn't listen. Nice work.

Day 323
Healing Action

I have spent over 30 years listening to people share their shame. I have witnessed profound pain and the shame of feeling alone and unique. I have heard people say that no one would truly understand them if they knew their stories. What they didn't know is how alike we all are. I learned, by listening to them, how common we all are. Shame crosses all boundaries and impacts all people.

When we share in safe groups, we have an opportunity to experience a level of commonality. It is sometimes hard to transfer this learning outside the group. It feels important for me to share that, in our shame, we feel unique and bad. We are sure we are alone, that others would not understand, and that we would be rejected in some way if we shared. Everyone in shame feels that way. There are very few people who have not experienced shame. Shame is something we all are healing from. Shame is a broken construct and a universal experience in our culture. We learn the commonality of shame by hearing others in our safe groups.

I am not advising that we shout our shame from the rooftops. I am advising that we find safe people and begin to share. It is in that sharing that great healing happens. It is where we get to learn that we aren't alone and that our shame is lying. When I share and you not only continue to care for me, but you also relate to me, healing is happening.

> *Reflection: We all have shame. Healing*
> *happens when we begin to break the isolation*
> *by sharing our shame with safe people.*

Day 324
One Thing Different

Change "One" Thought

Sometimes it can seem like so much or too much to change, as we learn the process of healing. It helps to pick just one thought we want to change, and focus on that. Changing just one thought won't be the total process of healing shame, but it is part of the process.

Sometimes when I am writing my "morning pages— a term from Julia Cameron's Book, *The Artist's Way*—I will write a thought that totally amazes me. I realize it is my thought and I become very aware it is a thought I do not want to carry around anymore.

For instance, a thought I realized I did not want was how I subtly (or not so subtly) want my husband to do certain things to show he loves me. The new thought I want to focus on is: "What if, the way he is and shows he loves me is absolutely perfect, now and always." It completely shifts the energy. Now, I can notice all the ways he shows his care and love for me, as opposed to looking for only the designated ways I have invented.

Changing thoughts can help me feel so good and peaceful. I look for ways to create more peace in my life. Changing my thoughts is one way.

> *Reflection: We move forward by loving ourselves as we are, and allowing change to occur when we are not getting what we want from our lives.*

Day 325
Forgiveness

Forgiveness is a process, not an event!

In our culture, we either have something or we don't have something. I believe, because of this, it is hard to picture the processes we often need to go through to reach forgiveness.

The following are steps we can utilize to facilitate for

1. Identify if we are holding a grudge, resentment, or judgment toward a person, or a group.

2. Identify what holding that grudge, resentment, or judgment is costing us. (Time, peace of mind, ruins relationships, leads to avoidance and isolation, turns into bitterness, etc.)

3. Become more willing to forgive than be right.

4. We get to notice when we are living in judgment and become willing to turn in the direction of love. We get to know that people are either expressing love or asking for love. We can ask ourselves what "love" would do or say to this person, group, or in this situation.

5. We can now choose to begin to move in the direction that love/compassion is showing us.

6. Forgiveness is a process of reaching compassionate acceptance of ourselves and others. It allows one to be human. It is a way of extending love.

When we reach a place where we realize what our unforgiving mindset is costing us, we may become more willing to do something different.

Reflection: Forgiveness is a process, not an event.

Day 326

Healing Action

When we are being codependent, there is a loss of "self" in relation to others. The codependent person looks to others for information about what they need. If we are codependent, it is difficult for us to identify our own needs.

A clue about what one "needs" may come from looking at what one "gives." If we need support, we often are wonderful at supporting. If we need a back rub, we may be great at giving backrubs. If we need unconditional acceptance, we may see that we give unconditional love.

One of the factors that may contribute to the challenge of identifying what we need is the shame we feel for having needs. It is okay for us to give to others, but not to ourselves. We think that makes us selfish. To a codependent, being selfish is not a good thing. We get to learn that the flip side to selfish is taking care of ourselves in positive, loving ways.

If we are unable to identify our needs or take the responsibility for caring for them, we will most likely struggle in our relationships. We will be unable to take care of ourselves.

Early in my recovery, I was on vacation with my boyfriend. He asked me what I needed on that particular day. I immediately started listing all the things we could do. They were all things I knew he would enjoy. He got frustrated with me because I wouldn't say what "I" needed. It was the first time I realized that my not claiming my needs and wants could put unwanted pressure on the other person. Until that point in time, I thought I was just being nice by putting my wants and needs aside. What I was being was codependent, and it was not helping my relationship or myself. It was a real eye-opener for me to realize that I needed to take responsibility for myself and claim my own needs and wants. It was not healthy to give that responsibility to someone else.

Reflection: It is important in our relationships to claim our needs and wants, take responsibility for communicating our needs, and getting our needs met.

Day 327
Healing Action

One of the things I have talked a lot about is identifying our rights, choices, and boundaries. I will expand on what I mean when we are claiming our choices.

Frequently when asking clients to identify choices, they claim two. Those choices sound like either/or. Most likely when we are identifying choices this way, we are still in the shame loop. We are often in a double bind.

"If I do _____, I will feel terrible, and if I do _____ I will feel terrible."

Choice is important because it is meant to move us out of victim consciousness and into our personal power. Shame is where we live when we are in the victim role.

When looking at choice, the minimum that will help us move out of the victim role and into our power are three choices. The more choices we can come up with, the more empowered we will be. When we list choices, we can write down the absurd. They can be things we most likely would never choose, but are still options. We can have fun with this list of choices, and we can ask others for help so that we get help in thinking outside of the box. Once we have compiled a good list of choices, we can scratch out the ones we truly won't consider. We then can make a conscious list from the ones that remain.

Claiming when we have made a choice is helpful in living in our power. Even if we choose not to make a choice, change our minds about something, or are doing something we know isn't for our highest good, we can say, "I am choosing to ___." In that way, we give ourselves the responsibility for what we are or are not doing. Taking responsibility is important in healing our shame.

Shame does not let us see we have choices, let alone support us in consciously choosing. Making lists of choices for important decisions, as well as day-to-day ones begins to move us powerfully in the direction of health and away from shame.

Reflection: We "always" have choices.
Sometimes we don't like any of them, and we
get to choose. We then begin to see our life in a
different and empowering way.

Day 328
Poem

> If Fear comes in and latches on
>
> A Fearful thought won't let go
>
> I notice and turn my face to Love
>
> It seems to make a difference
>
> I learn the language of compassion
>
> I learn to look through Loving eyes
>
> At what I had only judged before
>
> I pause
>
> I rest
>
> I find Peace
>
> Barb Tonn

Day 329
Multidimensional

We heal our shame on many levels. On previous days we have looked at healing our shame physically, emotionally, cognitively, socially, returning our will to the care of "love," and spiritually. As we have been working with our shame on all these levels, we begin to step into the wholeness of ourselves, and out of the fragmentation of shame.

What we are getting to see, and getting to learn, is that the lies of shame have dominated our lives on all levels. We are seeing that they creep in when we least expect it, and into places we thought we had healed. We also are getting to know what our own personal red flags are, and where and when we are most vulnerable to being tripped up and falling into our shame.

Healing shame is similar to someone who has been walking up and down the same path in a canyon for a very long time. We know where the path is tricky, where the dangers are, and when we need to be the most cautious. However, as aware as we are, we don't always know when something new has entered our canyon. We can be walking along and out of the blue get bit in the back of the leg by a rattlesnake. It strikes us and fills us with venom. We are alone, and the venom is flooding our systems. We can't get it out because of where it struck. So, what do we do? We sit quietly, and wait for help. Hopefully we have a signal on our phone. We may tourniquet the venom off and slowly and carefully make our way to help. Most likely, sooner or later, the venom will leave our systems. We will heal from the bite.

No matter how long we have been healing, how much we know about our triggers, or have healed the traumas where our shame is anchored, we can still get "triggered (bit by the rattlesnake.) We don't need to take "being bit" as a sign that we have not done our work, or that we haven't made progress. It is just the nature of shame to attack us when and where we least expect it.

Reflection: Shame is part of our world. Shame can show up when we least expect it. We have the tools, and we will be able to intervene more quickly than we previously were able to, before we did our work.

Day 330
Tool

Another "codependent voice" I have grappled with over the years is the voice that wants me to take responsibility for fixing other peoples' problems. Recently, I had that voice surface when one of my friends was really struggling. He was struggling financially, and that was an area I was feeling successful. My shame was telling me I was a bad friend if I didn't fix his problem, and especially bad because I "should" give him money because I had it and he didn't.

It brought up the old question of: "what am I responsible for in relationships?" Shame puts us in a bind by saying we "should" fix things that in reality we can't fix. Instead of us being responsible "to" others in relationships, shame says we are responsible "for" others. If there is something I can do, then I "should" do it. In this case, I had money, so I "should" give it to him.

What I know is that I can't take on the responsibility of fixing others. There may be a time where I can lend a helping hand, or lend money. However, the problem is in the sense of responsibility shame puts on me to fix someone else's issues. I may say, "I can't," but the more empowering statement is, "I won't."

I have learned that it is not possible for me to fix others, and it will exhaust me if I try. My worry, my trying to find solutions, and my putting a Band-Aid on a long-standing issue of someone else's is not healthy or useful.

I am responsible "to" people I am in relationship with, but not "for" them

What does that mean? I am honest, I am present when we are together, I do not blame, I take responsibility for my needs, and I get to choose, without shame or guilt, if I want to lend a hand or not. Shame would not give me a choice. I get to have choices.

I wrote out what my shame was telling me the night I was talking to my friend. Then, I claimed a truth. The truth was: I am a good person who has a friend who is struggling financially. I have the right to choose how to support my friend. There are no "shoulds" that are telling me the truth. I am not responsible for fixing my friend. We are both good people doing the best we can.

Reflection: Shame constantly puts us in dilemmas. We get to be responsible for taking care of our own needs. We are not responsible for fixing others.

Days 331-365

Day 331
Model for a Shame-Free World

I recently had an experience reinforcing the truth:

We get to make mistakes without feeling shame.

I sing in a choir. We work hard on our songs and enjoy our live performances. The other day we were singing in a live performance and in our second song we missed our cue. The band kept playing and the director kept directing, but the choir froze. It was a surreal moment. We all just stood there. A couple of times people attempted to enter in, but then stopped. Then, as if it had never happened, we found our place and ended the song together.

That could have been a shaming experience. However, it wasn't. The director was amazing. After the performance, we got together and she stressed that we had found our places and come back together. Never a word of recrimination or anything about what went wrong. We laughed and went on to perform the next performance flawlessly.

This experience is a perfect example of being human, making a mistake, loving ourselves, and moving on.

Reflection: Mistakes don't have to be shameful.

Day 332

Model for a Shame-Free World

One of the biggest gifts of having been a therapist for so long is that I have learned about so many subcultures. I have witnessed a rich diversity of thoughts, belief systems, life experiences, and life values. Some of these views and values are very different from what I have been exposed to.

There is a subculture, or various interest groups, for just about any activity or interest. What draws us to these different groups? Who do we want to hang around with? Who can say that one subculture's way of looking at the world is right and the other is wrong?

I have been humbled when listening to others who think differently than I do. There have been times someone shared an experience or talked about an interest, and my first internal response was negative. However, as I learned to listen, walk a mile in their shoes, and to replace judgment with curiosity, I could be open to why they were drawn to what they were, and thought the way they thought.

Shame offers a very narrow way of looking at the world and a very small sense of what is "right and acceptable." As we learn to respect ourselves and our right to express as we do, we learn to respect how others express. We may not want to live the way someone else lives. Without shame leading the way, we can grant ourselves and others the dignity and respect of possessing belief systems and choosing to live in ways that are different from our own.

Reflection: We all have the right to believe as we do without criticism or judgment from others.

Day 333
Shame Indicator

The word "shame" is showing up more frequently in general conversation. I take this as a good sign that we are making progress in putting language around a subject that we previously could not identify.

The other day on TV, a very respected and popular broadcaster was talking about the shame people experience when they are not part of a group. He was specifically talking about some of the social media groups, like Facebook. He was describing the shame people feel when they are left out.

It surprised me that shame was used to describe their experiences. I was surprised that the concept of shame had become such a household term. It felt so accurate. Part of what we have talked about is how shame isolates us and how we end up feeling on the outside looking in. Social media reinforces this sense of isolation so many feel. Of course, we can be a part of social media groups and still feel apart from. However, to be unable to find friends, or be included in these groups is particularly painful for many.

Maybe we are finding ways to talk about the experience of shame, and by doing this we will ease people's sense of isolation. We see we are not alone in our experiences of different things and of being different. We begin to get a sense of connection from our similarities instead of looking at our differences.

Reflection: As we begin to talk about shame, we begin to release the isolation of it.

Day 334
Shame Loop

I was really close to being done with the daily writings. I saw about seven more hours of work as I put them in a final form. That was not much; compared to the 100's and 100's of hours it had taken me to get that far. However, in my last week of writing I could not sit down to write to save my soul. I was talking with my husband about this and he said, "It is probably because you are so close."

Bingo.

I talked about this earlier in the book. The chemicalization process is where the negative, or shame, gains momentum as we get closer to an accomplishment. Whether it is finishing a book, graduating from college, completing an exercise goal, or some other goal that is important to us, shame can happen. Shame is not supportive of us feeling good about ourselves. It does not want us to feel success, in whatever way we define it. So, the closer we get to our goals, the more likely we are to experience a "shame attack or shame loop." Once we know that, we can begin to see it when it happens. As we see it, we are less likely to have shame pull us off our goal.

My husband helped me realize that the closer I got to the completion of my book, the more the shame and avoidance attempted to step in and stop me. As a result, I started writing with determination to finish. Shame was not going to keep me from finishing something I had worked so hard on and believed so deeply in.

Reflection: We get to notice that when we get close to finishing something important to us, shame will most likely try to interfere. We get to choose if we will let it stop us.

Day 335
Healing Action

If we try to force shame to go away, it seems to dig in harder and not budge. I have learned that we can't talk ourselves out of shame. We can't arm wrestle with it or force it to leave.

One thing we can do is look at it, hear it, and then turn in the direction of compassion and love. We ask, "What would compassion and love say?"

What I have noticed is that shame comes in on one side of us, in one ear. Just notice. Once we identify on which side shame enters, we can turn our heads in the other direction. My shame always enters on the right side. When I want to listen to love, I turn to my left. It may be the opposite side for others.

We are often intimately aware of our inner critics. Our inner critics are harsh, judgmental, and unkind to ourselves and others. The loving voice has always been there, but shame is loud and familiar, so we tend to hear that first. Our inner compassion is a still, soft voice. It is kind.

It may take a while for us to hear the voices of love and compassion, and we get to persist. We can get quiet and turn in the direction of love. If it takes us some time to begin to hear the voice of love, we can "act as if" we hear it until we actually do hear it. We can also speak to ourselves like we would speak to someone we love, or a child. We listen to how loving parents speak to their children. We know that within each of us is a similar voice that is always there and always ready to speak to us with kindness.

Reflection: When we notice shame on one side, we can turn in the direction of love on the other.

Day 336
Voice of Shame

I know people have truly begun to understand shame when they say, "it is everywhere." I was reading the novel, *The Devil Wins* by Robert Parker and there was the quote, "You look hard enough at anything and you'll find shame in it."

When we truly begin to listen to what people are saying, the inferred judgments, overt judgments, and general conversations, we will hear shame. We all speak this way unless we become very conscious of what we are really saying and inferring. Even when we become aware of it, we can still unintentionally send shaming messages to others with our looks and unspoken judgments. It is in the fabric of our world.

Once we begin to become aware of the insidiousness of shame, we have a better chance of not getting hooked by it, or sending shaming messages to others. We can even stand back and smile and realize that we could not possibly live our lives in a way that others would not judge. The only way non-judgment will ever happen is if there is a mass consciousness paradigm shift in our world. Until then, we can do our best to be aware of shame, not let it hook us, and send love and acceptance to others.

We learn to live by our conscious, internal beliefs and values, and look away from the external expectations and judgments of others. So, we notice how frequently we receive critical, judgmental, and shaming messages. We notice and then claim our internal truth. This is a life-long process.

Reflection: We get to learn to lovingly smile at the absurdity of shame.

Day 337

Shame Defined

I was speaking with someone today who was deeply triggered in her shame. She is a brilliant therapist, author, recovering person of approximately 30 years, and an amazing woman. All she could say was, "I am useless."

The part of her that has done a profound amount of healing work on her shame knows, intellectually, that her "being useless" isn't true. However, in her shame, she felt completely useless.

When our shame is triggered, it quickly can take us from feeling like a contributing member of our society, to a place where we don't feel at all like we belong or contribute at all.

She was in #4 on the shame loop that is found in the Appendix. Her inner critic was in charge, and her inner dialogue was one of self-contempt. She was unable to get the inner shame voice to stop. She felt powerless and out of control.

I listened to her and reassured her that I was present and hearing her. After a while I told her that I didn't expect her to believe me, However, I would tell her anyway that her shame was lying to her.

She was able to see what had triggered her. She had re-experienced something that she has worked hard on healing and the old shame kicked in. Because she had worked on it, she really felt like a failure that shame had engaged again. Once we knew what had triggered her, she was able to name her feelings, and express her emotions. What she needed was to have someone safe hear her.

I share this story because I have talked about how shame can sneak in and trigger us, even after we think we are complete with an issue. At times, when we are triggered by something old, we can get discouraged. Due to my friends' previous hard work she utilized her healing tools and was able to release from the shame loop quite quickly.

She utilized the following healing steps:

- She reached out to someone she trusted.
- She knew she was in shame and named it.
- She was able to identify what triggered her. It was not an external trigger, but an internal trigger that came from her thoughts about herself.
- She identified and felt the underlying feelings.
- She took care of her need to be heard.

(The above healing steps are listed in the Appendix.)

She was still slightly triggered at the end of our call, but she was on her way out of the shame loop. She needed to take time to take care of herself, and she was going to do some writing to see if there was anything else the part of her that was feeling shame needed.

This story demonstrates how shame works, and how much help we have when we use the tools we are learning in this book.

> *Reflection: The work we do on healing our shame really can make a positive difference when we are triggered into a shame loop.*

Day 338
Red Flag

It is important to notice and name shame so that we can consciously begin to use our tools for healing. One of the things I have frequently talked about is noticing the voices in our heads. I repeat and repeat some of the very important points in healing. I do this because, although simple, we often forget to utilize these steps.

If we pay attention, we will find that there are fairly constant background voices in our heads. They are either the voices of shame or the voices of love. Knowing they are one or the other makes them simple to identify.

If the voices in our heads bring peace, they are the voices of love. If they bring upset of any kind, they are the voices of shame. We get to notice, and if they are the voices of shame, we get to choose again. I am not saying that is easy, but it is simple.

We may need to choose again hundreds of times a day. The voices of shame have often gone unchecked for our entire lives. They sound familiar and true and we have not questioned them. Or, if we have questioned them, we haven't known how to change.

We can set an intention to only listen to the voices of love, which bring us peace. The voices of shame may still go on and on, but we get to choose not to listen.

Reflection: We can keep it simple. If we hear the voice of shame, we can choose again. We get to choose the voice of love.

Day 339
Healing Action

It is through our relationships that profound healing happens. In watching our relationships, we learn how we project our pain outward, how we blame others and ourselves, how we mistrust, how we allow shame to keep us from resolving conflict. We make being right more important than peace. We refuse to forgive.

It is in relationship that we can learn how to share in a vulnerable way, be accepted and loved, learn how to forgive, heal our inability to trust, and see love reflected in another's' eyes.

It may take a lot of healing to get to the point where we truly begin to let others into our vulnerable thoughts. Our fear of rejection and pain can run very deep. We get to go through whatever vulnerable process is necessary to open to deeper relationships. It is through this vulnerable risk taking that we begin to feel like a part of something and connect.

Our shame has kept us isolated. Even when we are with other people we can feel completely alone. We have set up internal barriers that are hard to let down. We get to determine when to let our boundaries down. We get to establish our boundaries in the way that most honors us.

We connect in our relationships with ourselves, others, and something greater than ourselves. We get to learn how to stop letting shame keep us from feeling the love of others. We are lovable. That is the truth. We get to see love reflected in the eyes of others.

Reflection: Our relationships may be in therapy groups, 12-step groups, individual therapy, friendships, families, partners, and with our own eyes as we look at ourselves in the mirror. We get to feel connected and part of something.

Day 340
Tool

Many of us do not know how to be compassionate with ourselves. We don't like how we look when we show up in the world, or how others see us. Because of this, we aren't able to tell when someone sees us with the eyes of compassion. Yet, learning compassion is a critical step in healing shame. We may treat ourselves as we were treated in our formative years, and for many of us that was not kindly. So, how do we learn this skill? How do we honestly treat ourselves with compassion and kindness?

We start with setting an intention to be kind to ourselves. We begin to notice when we aren't kind toward ourselves and how that feels, and when we are kind to ourselves and how that feels. We begin to become less tolerant of when our shame beats us up and criticizes us. We get curious about how kindness would sound by watching others who are kind, and listening to how they treat themselves and others. We may even "act as if "as we learn how to be compassionate with ourselves.

A tool I love for learning how to be compassionate with ourselves is, "mirror work." "Mirror work" involves looking deep into our own eyes in the mirror. We look beyond the surface of our appearance and deeply into our own soul. We notice.

We don't tolerate any criticism or meanness. We just look. I remember when I first started really looking into my own eyes. I saw deep sadness and exhaustion. I felt tenderness toward that me that was so sad and so tired. I wanted to help that me that I saw reflected in that mirror. I know now that what I was feeling was great compassion toward myself.

Many of us don't like how we look. We may learn to like how we look, but this exercise isn't about how we look. This "mirror work" exercise is about what we are feeling as we look deep into our souls, and what our souls need. We then have an opportunity to respond to those feelings and needs with kindness.

> Reflection: Mirror work is a tool that can assist
> us in learning about kindness and compassion.

Day 341
Specific Shame-Based Issue

The further I travel in my own healing process, the more I step out of living in survival and into living in joy. Shame keeps us struggling. We don't feel good about ourselves. We are in the exhaustion of trying to prove ourselves, and measuring ourselves by what we think others want. There is not much room for true joy in that struggle. Even when we do something that could be truly enjoyable, our shame can interfere.

This shame work is not easy. Changing our perception of ourselves from one of being shameful to one of being worthy is a life long process. However, there is light at the end of the tunnel.

Earlier in the book I shared my Pyromaniac singing experience. (This experience was when I took a challenge. I rehearsed with 11 other women for 5 rehearsals. At the end we sang 2 solos in front of 125 people. We had a live band back up.) I was terrified because I had always been told I could not sing. I was sure I would make a fool of myself. I walked through the fire of the experience, and amazing things happened. The shame of my voice that I had felt my entire life is gone now. I reclaimed my voice and the right to enjoy it. It is now slightly over a year since that experience, and I am now singing in three choirs.

This is just an example of what happens with shame leading the way. We put limits on ourselves. We believe the worst, and won't test the waters. We limit our joy. We may not wish to sing, but there are things that we know we would love if only...

Maybe we haven't even let ourselves dream because the shame has kept us in survival. The first step may be to dream. We get to have our dreams and we just may find that we can actually do the things we dream.

Reflection: Shame keeps us from truly stepping into joy. I love singing in three very different choirs. Shame shut down my voice for a long time. I am so grateful to have reclaimed it.

Day 342
Right

I have the right to be playful, relaxed, and frivolous.

In theory, we may agree with this right. However, we may not truly act as if it is true. Or, we may only allow it when all the work and duties are done. It comes at the end of the "to do" list, to do the fun things.

Life has been very serious if we are doing the work of healing shame. We maybe did a lot of partying or acting out in our addictions, but most likely this type of behavior had a frantic and hurtful quality to it. Shame limits pure joy. Shame limits us by insisting that we are only worthy if we are working at something. We can have fun and be playful only when the work is done. However, is our work ever really done?

We can do our work, and keep our responsibilities, and make being playful a priority. We get to learn that it is as important to relax and play, as it is to work hard. It helps us live in compassion and to bring joy to our world.

If someone (often ourselves) tries to stop us from being playful, or doing what helps us relax, or calls us frivolous, we can kindly turn in the direction of our inner wisdom and claim the right to do what brings us joy. We don't need to defend the right, or prove others wrong. We just get to step into what brings us joy.

Reflection: Balance is what we are moving into. We get to balance the work and the play. We get to enjoy our lives. Yes!!!

Day 343
One Thing Different

IT REALLY IS NEVER TOO LATE

As a life-coach, one of the things I hear frequently is "I think it is too late ___." I have a card in my office that reads, "It is never too late to be what you might have been." I have run across that saying many times in the last few years, and for good reason. Our shame, false selves, and/or ego selves, would have us believe that we are too busy, old, worthless, stupid, lazy, to really claim our dreams or desires.

In truth, until we take our last breaths, it isn't too late. As a coach, I help people change the false beliefs that keep them from truly creating the lives that they want. Our shame-based self doesn't want us to feel content and happy and peaceful. It wants us feeling inadequate, confused, and in turmoil. We work on releasing the shame so that we can claim our dreams.

Part of creating what we want is to become willing to look in a direction other than the direction shame is pointing us in. Many of us have gotten stuck in looking in the direction shame dictates, and we miss the rainbow. I help people hear a different voice, look in a different direction, and step into their lives in a different way. We get to be willing to believe that it is never too late to _____. (We get to fill in the blank.)

> *Reflection: We get to be willing to challenge any belief that limits our happiness.*

Day 344
Shame Loop

I want to write one more time about breaking a shame loop. Learning when we are in a shame loop and how to step out of it are two of the most important healing tools we have at our disposal.

Once we identify that we are in a shame loop, we can refer to these steps. (The loop and steps are in the Appendix.) We can utilize these steps to move out of the shame loop.

I am listing the steps here, with a few comments to help us move through the steps.

1. We must identify we are in a shame loop.
2. We identify if something external triggered our shame (something someone said or did), or if our internal voice triggered our shame.
3. We identify the core shame belief about ourselves that was triggered. It will be something like: "I am stupid," "I am a failure," "I am not good enough," "I am a fraud," "I am unlovable."
4. We say to ourselves, "If I had not gone into shame when _____ triggered me, I may have

felt _____, and that feeling part of me may need _____."

5. Begin to allow ourselves to feel the feelings that were under the shame, and advocate for our needs. This helps us intervene on shame in the "here and now."

6. We also continue to do the work that locked the shame in place. This may be family of origin work, identifying and changing the belief system that is anchoring the shame, or doing trauma work. This work intervenes on shame in the "there and then."

Reflection: We can take steps in the here and now, to assist us in releasing from a shame loop

Day 345
Model for a Shame-Free World

Healing shame is a process. The concept of "living in process" is not one that is very familiar in our world. We tend to be moving quickly, focusing on the goal instead of each moment. "Living in process" is the art and grace of living fully in each moment. We focus on living mindfully in the moment and make that enough. We may be moving toward something, and whether we get there or how fast we get there is not the focus. We come to enjoy the trip and the moments and the integrity of each moment.

If we take time to notice, we will often find that we are focused on something in the future and feel anxiety about it. Or, we are focused on something in the past and feel depressed. Only when our focus is on the here and now, can we find true peace.

We can find peace while we are in the process of healing shame by focusing on where we are right now. We can set our intentions to live fully in each moment. In doing this, we can embrace our healing processes.

If we are feeling impatient, chances are we are not living in our process of healing. We want to be healed now, and are jumping the gun. As we embrace our moments, we begin to appreciate each step we take as important to our overall healing.

> *Reflection: We are developing a completely different thought system as we heal shame. Healing shame is a life-long process, during which we learn how to find peace within each moment.*

Day 346
One Thing Different

Many of us live our lives doing what we think we "should" do. Many of us are good at believing we know what others "should" do. Many of us ask others what they think we "should" do. The trouble with all of these "shoulds" is that they come from beliefs that are outside of us and may not fit our own inner truths at all.

If we live according to what others think we should do, then if things don't go well, we can end up blaming others. We may not take responsibility for having chosen to take someone else's "shoulds" as our truths. We bypass looking inside to determine our own truth,

When we make a conscious choice from our internal truth, instead of defaulting to what others think we "should" do, we empower our self. We may make mistakes, and that is okay. Mistakes are part of learning, growing, and being human.

It is important not to let ourselves get trapped into telling others what they "should" do. If they take our advice, it can lead to them blaming us if it doesn't go well. It is still the other persons' responsibility for following our advice, but giving advice gets messy and can easily lead to blame. In truth, we don't know what is best for others. It can be hard enough to determine what is best for ourselves. We get to pass on giving advice.

Reflection: We can change the word "should" to "could." We can set a boundary for ourselves to not let others "should" on us, and not to "should" on others. This puts us on a pathway toward loving kindness and peace.

Day 347
Healing Action

"What if each of us believed that we are as powerful and strong as we allow ourselves to be? What if we quit trying to be accepted by everyone and gave up trying to not alienate anyone and let ourselves be as strong and powerful as we are? The most difficult part of any endeavor is taking the first step, making that first decision."-Robyn Davidson

This quote is a lovely reminder of how we live when shame does not lead the way. It leads us directly to our truths, and to the love and peace at the core of ourselves. We can't, no matter how hard we try, be accepted or liked by everyone. In trying not to alienate others, we end up being alienated from our true selves. We live small instead of living in our power and strength.

If we make the first decision and take the first step from strength, we will find that our shame takes more of a back seat. Sometimes we have to act as if we are strong and powerful until we actually believe it. This moves us out of the victim mentality and into choice. We get to choose. We get to be who we came here to be and accomplish what we came here to accomplish.

We get to learn how to accept ourselves, just as we are. It can be a huge relief to get off the "impression management" bandwagon, and just let ourselves live.

Reflection: I get to learn how to live in my power and strength.

Day 348
Model for a Shame-Free World

There is a lesson in "*A Course in Miracles*" which says:

"I want the Peace of God

The Peace of God is everything I want."

(A Course in Miracles, page 390, Workbook for Students)

I am one of those people who say I want peace, more than anything. Yet, when I make others wrong, fight for my opinion, grump my way through a day, think horrible things about another person, etc., I am not truly living my intention.

I am striving to think peaceful, loving thoughts about others and myself. It doesn't make me a bad person when I fall short of this goal, but it gives a direction to my life that I want to move in.

If the word God is not what you want, then take it out and say, "I want peace." To live in this way is different than living in shame. It makes our world less about shame and more about love. We can only do what we can do, and we are responsible for what we think and how we behave. Do we really want peace?

> *Reflection: We get to learn and act as we choose. Are we choosing peace or shame?*

Day 349
Model for a Shame-Free World

We all have read or heard stories about people who do unfathomable things to themselves and/or others. These are things like murder, self-abuse, or crowd rage. We can sit and believe we would never do such things. We can believe we can control ourselves so that would never happen.

We live in a shame-based world. We all have the potential to rage if the circumstances were just right. We all have the potential to be horribly destructive. Granted, most of us would be able to stop short of doing the "unthinkable." However, if we talked to many who have murdered while in a rage, we would most likely find that they never thought they would do such a thing.

To point the finger at those "horrible" people or to try to control externals, like guns, misses the mark. If we do not deal with the underlying shame that is out of control in our world, we will forever be witness to the people who do the unfathomable. Rage originates in an environment of shame. Our world is getting crazier and crazier because we feel so out of control. We try to get control back by raging.

Shame lives in hierarchy, blame, and justification. We get to look at the roots of the rage/shame and heal from the inside/out, instead of trying to control externals. We are out of control, as a world. It is not about gaining "control," it is about each of us taking responsibility for ourselves, our choices, and healing our shame.

Reflection: Pointing the finger, or denying our own rage does not stop shame. Shame is in each of us, and it can be brought into healing.

Day 350

Tool

There are countless ways to notice the voice of shame and turn in the direction of the voice of compassion. I have witnessed healing in a variety of creative and unique ways. I encourage us all to utilize the skill sets that we already have when bringing our shame into healing. Some examples are:

- If I am an artist, I can paint or draw or color the voice of shame and compassion. I can depict them in ways that will help me identify them in my day-to-day life.

- If I am a musician, I can sing or play an instrument to represent the sound of shame and the sound of compassion.

- If I am a dancer, I can feel shame in my body and dance it, and then feel compassion and express it in movement.

- If I am a writer, I can depict shame and compassion in stories, myths, fiction, plays, and dialogue.

- If I am a sculptor, I can create images of shame and compassion.

We can all express and create in ways that use our talents and skills to depict the voices of shame, compassion, and love.

In truth, although shame is the voice that we have always heard first and is the loudest, the voices of compassion and love are always present. Once we begin to pay attention to the differences in the voices, it becomes easier and more natural to listen to compassion and love.

We get to find countless ways to help us discern the voices of shame and compassion. Healing from shame is about finding love in our essence. Our loving essence is where we get to live our lives. "Light and love" is the creative essence at the core of our being.

> *Reflection: We get to creatively find ways to help us discern the voice of shame and hear the voice of compassion and love.*

Day 351
Healing Actions

We have worked with these tools for almost a year. We have read concepts repeated over and over. We may be frustrated at the repetition. We may be excited and we may be overwhelmed.

This book helps us:

1. To recognize shame in our world, and when it is triggered inside us.
2. To have tools to intervene on shame so that we can find our way to peace.

My hope is that, through the repeated use of our tools, we will more effectively intervene on shame when we are externally or internally triggered. There are simple and reliable tools we can utilize to intervene, and we get to be vigilant.

Important Intervention Tools:

Our personal "Red Flag" list.

- Tools and healing actions that we have tried that we are most likely to use and have found the most effective.

- A list of new rules to live by that support our peace.

- Strategies that help us identify and hear the voice of kindness.

- Reminders that we are in a process of healing.

- A support system for healing.

- Our own template for living that supports our dreams, rights, choices, and personal boundaries.

- An awareness of what is most likely to trigger us in our world, and a way to respond in kindness.

- A daily reminder of the loveable, worthy person we are and always will be.

Our "take-aways" from this book get to accompany us in our ongoing adventures of healing.

Reflection: Repetition is a tool. Repetition helps us all develop a new paradigm of healing as we unlearn the old, and step into the new.

Day 352

One Thing Different

As this book gets close to completion, I want to spend time sharing my personal change and how it created "hope" in my life.

As I have gotten older and have truly stepped into a different relationship with shame, I have discovered how much easier it is for me to be human and have limits. I am more relaxed because I am not fixated on how others perceive me.

The old constant self-consciousness has changed to a kindness toward others and myself.

A significant thing I have owned is my right to "claim my humanness and have limits and boundaries." I used to feel shame about having limits and I feared exposing them because I would appear weak or less than. I always wanted to prove myself as superhuman, and I was exhausted.

Healing shame has allowed me to be human and this has brought great peace to my heart and soul. From that space, I can allow the people in my life to be human. I can extend kindness to others because I feel it toward myself.

I worked hard on my healing. It took me a long time to name and acknowledge how much shame I carried and how hard my life was because of shame. As I have released my core shame and replaced it with self-love and inner peace, I have learned that I just get to "be." What a relief!

Reflection: There is hope that the self-conscious feeling we carry with shame will lessen and leave as we continue our healing. We get to have peace.

Day 353
Forgiveness

There was a story in the news this winter that I felt in my core. It felt like a powerful depiction of the inner child that is alone in his/her shame.

A woman had her child in her car and stepped out to fill some water bottles at an outside water filling station. A man jumped in her car and drove off with her daughter still in the car. An Amber alert went out and the car was found, but the little girl was not in it. The city went on high alert and the police were searching everywhere. One policeman was turning around in a dark and empty parking lot and his lights swept over something. He stopped to see what it was and it was the little girl. He had a camera on his body, so the image of the little girl as he ran up to her was captured. He said, "Honey, are you okay?" She looked up and said, "I am cold."

It struck me that our inner child who has been caught up in shame, also feels alone and cold, like the little girl in the dark, abandoned parking lot. She/he needs our help to get into the warmth, and the light of healing. Our inner child needs our help to connect with others.

Reflection: We are helping our inner child as we do our shame healing work. We are shining light into the darkness and isolation of our inner child's shame, and bringing them out so they can live again.

Day 354
One Thing Different

Shame can interfere with the important skill of asking for help. We all need help from time to time. At times, it is critical that we get help. Shame can convince us that it is shameful to need help. It convinces us that it is important to not look needy, and if we ask for help we will be showing we are needy. We can also be fearful of rejection if we ask for help.

Shame can also interfere with our trusting help when we get it. Shame interferes with the very human need we all have of being in relationships and being interdependent on each other.

There are some steps we can utilize if isolating behavior is something we are familiar with:

- Notice when we need help.
- Notice what the shame is telling us when we need help.
- Begin to be willing to identify what a loving voice might say to us about this need.
- Begin to be willing to move in the direction of compassion toward self by asking for help with our needs.
- Become willing to be vulnerable.

- "Act as if" it is okay to have needs and ask for help.

- (Because it is okay to have needs and ask for help.)

- Make a list of several things we may need help with and start by asking for help with the smallest need we have. (It may feel huge.)

After a while, we may find that we are not "acting as if" any longer. We may realize that we have made great progress in taking care of our needs and not feeling shame that we have them.

Reflection: Needing help is universal need. It is OKAY!

Day 355
Sitting with Maude

As Christmas gets closer, I decided to sit with Maude and ask her how shame can get in the way of our celebrating the holiday season, no matter what religious orientation we have or don't have.

Barb (B)—There was a recent shooting in our country and it is the Christmas season. I was thinking of our world and shame and how this shooting could be a result of all the shame and powerlessness people seem to live in. Could you give me some insight into this? Could you give me some hope?

Maude (M)—It saddens me to see the state of consciousness in the world, and how it is impacting us. The shooting is a representation of how deeply wounded people are. Many people feel alone and powerless, like they don't quite measure up. Some cross the line and act out the powerlessness. That is what happened to the young man who went on the shooting frenzy.

B—I see the pain this has caused and worry about the reactions of people to the sorrow. I also know that when people feel powerless they try to control the uncontrollable and move deeper into fear.

M—This is true. People feel powerless when something like this happens and the response is a deep sense of needing control. It keeps us from facing what is really going on and doesn't allow for the deep healing process. Many people just get busy and do something so they don't have to be conscious of the fact that our model for living is flawed from the ground up. We don't recognize the importance of looking at our personal contribution to the consciousness that produces such rage and shame.

B—I think most of us would balk at the idea that our consciousness could contribute to anything so heinous.

M—Yes, I know. However, if we believe in our oneness, then we also get to look at how each of us contributes to this. We all have fear, judgment, shame, and rage. We don't work on healing and forgiveness, or if we do, we hold certain things back. Whatever we do, we contribute to the whole. We maybe didn't pull the trigger, but we have our own triggers that we pull on a daily basis. We get to clean up our side of the street. We see the rage on the outside. We get to see the rage on the inside. Of course, we don't take responsibility for what someone else did, but we look at how our consciousness contributes to a rage- and shame-filled world. In this way, we look at the tragedies and see them as a sign that the mass consciousness needs an overhaul and that we each have our part in that.

B—Is that the hope?

M—Yes. As the holy season or "season of light" is upon us, we have a chance to see what our inner holy beliefs are, and how to give birth to them in our world. We can respond in fear or super control or anger. It is important to recognize those. And then we can go beyond those to cleaning up the places in ourselves which contribute to the overall consciousness of hate and fear. We can work toward forgiveness and releasing judgments. We can extend love and find acceptance instead of resentment. We can truly look at what this season represents and use it to heal from these types of tragedies. That would be a great step in the healing process. Here is a prayer:

All that is, is Holy.

To holiness I offer my prayer.

Let all that has blocked the awareness of love- be removed.

Let all the hate, shame, judgments, and fear be released into the blinding light of Love.

May we know that all that is true is "Love."

May the quiet and peace of Grace be our only wish.

May we only know "Oneness."

May we all have "Peace."

Maude

Day 356
Shame in Our World

I am going to expand on yesterday (Day 355).

When people experience the constant sense of not doing enough or being enough, shame mounts. As shame builds, the sense of being out of control and powerless increases. When we rage (as the shooter did in the previous daily), we are in shame. When we act shame out we end up feeling more and more rage. Some of us "act shame/rage out". The shooter is an extreme example of "acting rage out." Most of us do not "act our rage out" in such an outrageous way. We may rant and rave at others, or cut people off on the highway, etc. Some of us "act rage in." When we "act in" rage we get judgmental and critical in our thoughts. We can't stop the thoughts.

Our world is getting crazier and crazier. Instead of trying to change the world, we first get to question the original premise that there is something wrong with us. We get to change the destructive false belief that says something is wrong with us, and insert a new belief that says we are lovable and worthy. If we fail to change our false belief system, we will destroy ourselves, each other, all of life, and the planet. Each of us gets to break down the shame and know that, whether we believe it or not, we are love and we are enough. Then we begin to treat everyone and everything with love.

When we are tempted to judge, make others wrong, hate, and live in fear, we get to notice and seek another way of looking at our lives. We can no longer be content to do this in a half-hearted way. This gets to be the most important thing we do. We can't wait for others to change and lay blame outside of ourselves. We do everything we can to change each judgment into love. We become willing to forgive "all." This forgiveness becomes our most important task. We don't need to do it perfectly. We just get to move in the direction of love and forgiveness. We extend peace to those we do not agree with, understand, hate, or judge. We do the hard work. Moving in the direction of loving -kindness empowers us to make the changes that impact all of life in a positive and loving way.

Reflection: People are either extending love or asking for it. If they are asking for love, we get to extend love to them.

Day 357
One Thing Different

When we do not take responsibility for our choices and when we blame others, we often end up giving others the power to "unzip" us. We leave our zipper on the outside where others can open us up, "unzip" us, any time they want. When we don't take charge of our energy, don't bring our shame triggers into healing, and leave ourselves unzipped by not setting boundaries, we are giving others the power to determine how we feel.

When we become "unzipped" we will find we are saying things like:

- You made me mad.
- You upset me.
- You made me sad.
- It is your fault I feel _____.
- If you hadn't _____, I wouldn't feel so _____.

In truth, we are responsible for whatever we feel. We may want to blame others, and our feelings are our own. We also can't take responsibility for how others feel. Each of us has our own belief systems and our own set of filters, which all our thoughts filter through. For example, what upsets one person may bring a sense of sadness to another. If we take responsibility for what someone else feels, we will feel crazy, because we aren't living in truth.

If we find that someone else has said or done something which we responded emotionally to, and we don't take responsibility for ourselves, then we have given someone else dominion over us. We have let them unzip us.

Reflection: We can learn to have our zipper on the inside. We get to decide what we feel and need. We get to be in charge of our selves, our feelings and what we let upset us.

Day 358
Poem

Peace

It comes in silently

Never is it strident or rough

Never is it unkind

It sounds soft and sweet

It is compassion

It ushers in Peace

It is always present

It is my holiday prayer for all of humankind, all of life

To know Peace

Barb Tonn

Day 359
Model for a Shame-Free World

I am choosing Christmas to talk about the shame we can feel when we do not believe in a god. We may hide the fact that we don't believe because we don't want to be judged.

I am choosing Christmas to talk about how we can shame others for not believing as we do. We may do it overtly by our words and actions, or covertly by our inner judgments.

I am choosing Christmas as a time we each can own our spiritual belief systems, without shame, and honor others for believing as they do. We get to consciously choose to do this. We get to make this be our season of honoring ourselves and others, just as we are.

I am choosing Christmas as a time to bring the shame of how humanity has used religion, to war, and judge, and harm each other out into the light of healing.

I am choosing Christmas as a time when we can choose acceptance, forgiveness for how we have judged and been at war with each other, and bring peace to each heart we meet.

I am choosing Christmas as a time to release shame and bring love into "all" of our relationships. We include our relationships with "all" of life, with ourselves, and with whatever god we may or may not have.

Reflection: I am choosing Christmas to ask us all to stop our warring and turn in the direction of love.

Day 360

Forgiveness

To demonstrate forgiveness, I want to share a personal story.

My Dad died around the holidays. He was coming to visit me, but was found unconscious at home. He had been there three days. He never regained consciousness. I flew to where he was and was with him as he died. I had a few days with him in ICU. I tell this because it was a time of profound healing.

My dad had always been difficult for me. My family, like most families had its dysfunction and shame. My heart had not forgiven my dad.

On top of that, I was dealing with the caregivers my dad had put in place who let him down. They were supposed to have sent help if he could not be reached by phone each day. They failed to send help when they could not reach him.

It was Christmas and I felt so much pain. I wanted to reach a place of forgiveness with my dad, and all the caregivers who had not sent help.

What was I to do?

I wanted peace. In the moment of some of my deepest sorrow, I needed to use all the tools I have mentioned in this book to reach that peace. I wanted peace more than anger and being unforgiving.

When we have shame, we cannot reach forgiveness. I let myself write what my shame was telling me, and then claimed my truth. My truth I claimed was: I am a good person, and my dad and all the people who let my dad down are are good people. Some of them made mistakes, and I know that everyone did what they thought was right, and the best they could at the time. I know that my dad had always done the best he could with the background he had, and the skillsets he had acquired. I wanted peace more than I wanted to be right. I wanted to be peaceful with my dad as he died.

I chose to release the judgments I carried and accept my Dad and the caretakers who made mistakes, as part of the oneness of love. We all make mistakes. We all get to be human. We all get to be forgiven.

As I worked with my shame and anger and released it into forgiveness, I finally felt peace. I was with my dad as he died, and I had a big smile on my face. I was his cheerleader as he let go of this life and moved on to wherever we go. I loved him and forgave him. I just got to be his daughter. It was lovely and peaceful.

I know, with all my heart, that if I had not done the shame work and healing work that I had done, that I could never have reached the peace I did with my dad's dying, the circumstance surrounding his death, and my life with my dad. I am eternally grateful for the work I have done that has brought me peace in the most difficult of situations.

I just wanted to share this personal story because it is my hope that it will inspire others to do their own shame work and find the peace they never believed they could have.

Namaste

Day 361
Tool

We have recently talked about looking in the mirror and making contact with our own souls. I repeatedly focus on mirror work because it is such a powerful tool in our healing toolbox. We look and respond to the feelings and needs we see mirrored back. We use the mirror to help us see what is really going on inside of us in the here and now.

Another way we can work with a mirror is by looking at ourselves in the mirror and not apologizing for who we are, how we look, the choices we have made, or how we show up in the world. Instead of apologizing, we give messages of acceptance.

We use a mirror to practice self-acceptance and forgiveness. For the mistakes we have made, we look in the mirror and speak kindly to ourselves. We say, "You are a good and lovable woman/man who has made a mistake, and you are still a good and lovable woman/man." Many of us who have had shame in our cores have avoided mirrors. We have been very critical of how we look and what we see reflected back. Our work is to begin to appreciate our unique selves. Mirror work helps us see the progress we are making. Where before we couldn't look at ourselves with kindness, we learn to look at ourselves with appreciation and kindness.

The mirror work is not about how we look, although as we do mirror work we become less critical of how we look. The mirror work is a way to make contact with ourselves, and see ourselves with eyes of love. We care for and do not apologize for ourselves.

Reflection: When I can look at myself in the mirror, without apology, I know my shame is healing.

Day 362

Healing Action

As this year draws to a close, let us look toward next year to be different. Let us set intention to release shame on a daily basis.

We get to release shame for ourselves, and set intentions to send loving messages to our fellow travelers. We get to release judgment of our selves and others. We get to intend to be kind. When we mess up, and we all will, we get to extend forgiveness and start again. Shaming our selves and beating our selves up never gets us anywhere but mired in more shame.

We get to do what we can to make this world a less shaming, more loving place to live. We certainly cannot change others, but we can change ourselves. Just like people going into recovery from addictions, we have to really be sick and tired of the old way of shame to do the hard work of healing our shame. We get to be motivated by our deep desires for a more loving, kind world.

Our world is shame-based. We get hit with shame every time we step into the world. We can know that and refuse to accept shame from others. We all use shame when we feel out of control and when shame is all we know. When we are on the receiving end of shame or when we shame ourselves, we can notice and choose forgiveness of our selves and other. It takes dedication, and we can all move in that direction.

Reflection: We all have the ability to release shame in our selves and our world. We can learn to do that on a daily basis.

Day 363
Right

I Have the Right to be Happy,

I want to end the year with one more right. "The right to be happy" is what this book has been about. It is the exact opposite of how we feel when we live in shame. We all have the right to be happy and to create a happier world.

When shame leads the way in our lives, we will never find happiness because shame is the voice of judgment, hatred, non-acceptance, rage, comparison, blame, and unkindness. The shame voice has been in the background our whole lives, and it has not led to happiness. We get to change that.

In the book, *The Four Agreements* by Don Miguel Ruiz, he presents four agreements to live by that can create a new earth. He also talks about it taking the rest of our lives to practice these changes. Such is the case with healing shame.

When we choose to heal our shame, we are committing to a completely different way of living, thinking, and expressing in the world. We are talking about changing the paradigm on our earth from one of shame to one of love and compassion. We will stumble many times, and we will often not feel supported or understood by others. We can, however, continue, forgive, and move into a new way of living with ourselves and our world.

> *Reflection: I know, for myself, that there is a way of living, other than shame. Love is the way.*

Day 364
Healing Action

It is in our relationships that we learn the most about shame and the most about healing. We get to see how unkind we are before we learn how to be kind. We judge and learn forgiveness. We project our stuff onto others and get to see in them what we don't see in ourselves. We get to acknowledge our mistakes and learn about forgiveness in our relationships.

My husband and I have worked really hard to create a marriage that is about loving and not about shame. We have learned to speak our truths and honor what works verses how we think we "should" be. We have learned how to set boundaries, honor each other's space, take time for ourselves, have different interests, and mutual interests. At times, it has been extremely hard. We both grew up in the "shame stew" and in truth knew nothing of true love. We carried so many "should" and "shouldn't" beliefs. At times, we both wanted to give up. We didn't know how to navigate the hard times, step into a more loving and kind way of being with each other, or forgive and move past our judgments. My husband has mirrored my pain and rage. He has seen me. Being "seen" hasn't been easy. However, we have learned a different way to be in relationship, and it is not about shame.

Reflection: We heal in our relationships. Our original "shame injury" is in relationship, and it is in learning to trust and love in relationship that we bring our pain into healing. It does not have to be a marriage where we heal. Our friendships and family relationships also hold the potential for bringing our shame into the light of love and learning to trust again.

Day 365
Model for a Shame-Free World

We have done it. We have given a year to looking more deeply at our shame and the shame in the world. We have looked at all the levels shame has impacted us, and begun the process of bringing that shame into the light of healing. Are we done?

I surely wish I could clap my hands together and say we were done, and that we would never have to deal with shame again. However, that is not true. Shame is woven into the fabric of our lives and the world.

What we have gained from spending this year together is awareness of shame, tools for healing, and hopefully determination, to move away from shame and towards love.

At times, we may be tempted to throw up our hands in despair and give up. We may think we have healed something only to have it bite us in the rear end where it seems impossible to heal. That frustration is all part of the healing process. We all will have those days when we just don't think change is possible. We get to look into our eyes in the mirror and extend compassion toward ourselves and move forward anyway.

The process of writing this book has mirrored my own healing process. My shame brought me close to deleting this book many times. I would not have been able to finish this book if I had not been:

- Using my own tools
- Writing out my shame and then the truth
- Reaching out to friends
- Letting myself have my despair and then moving forward again
- Forgiving
- Being vulnerable in my sharing
- Working with my inner wisdom—Maude

It is with great humility and profound gratitude that I say good-bye. I have learned more about healing shame by writing this book than I would ever have thought possible. My hope is that those who **shine the light of truth on shame** will feel the same determination that I did for bringing their own shame into healing. To **shine the light of truth on shame** begins to bring global healing and hope to souls who have been burdened with the pain of shame.

Thank you for walking in this light with me. Thank you for witnessing my story and participating in this healing path. Each one of us who does this work impacts the whole. We work together. I believe learning to shine our own loving light is worth all our hard work. We have the right to happiness and living in the light of peace.

Thank you and peace to all of your hearts,

Barb and Maude

Appendix

Shame/Rage Loop

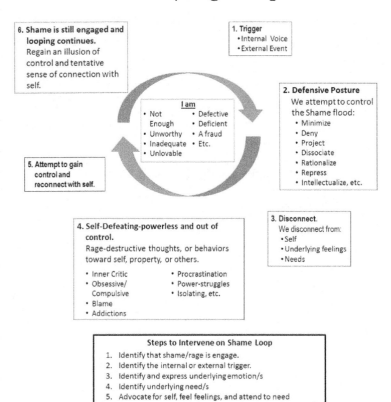

6. Shame is still engaged and looping continues.
Regain an illusion of control and tentative sense of connection with self.

1. Trigger
• Internal Voice
• External Event

I am
• Not Enough
• Unworthy
• Inadequate
• Unlovable
• Defective
• Deficient
• A fraud
• Etc.

2. Defensive Posture
We attempt to control the Shame flood:
• Minimize
• Deny
• Project
• Dissociate
• Rationalize
• Repress
• Intellectualize, etc.

5. Attempt to gain control and reconnect with self.

4. Self-Defeating-powerless and out of control.
Rage-destructive thoughts, or behaviors toward self, property, or others.

• Inner Critic
• Obsessive/ Compulsive
• Blame
• Addictions
• Procrastination
• Power-struggles
• Isolating, etc.

3. Disconnect.
We disconnect from:
• Self
• Underlying feelings
• Needs

Steps to Intervene on Shame Loop
1. Identify that shame/rage is engage.
2. Identify the internal or external trigger.
3. Identify and express underlying emotion/s
4. Identify underlying need/s
5. Advocate for self, feel feelings, and attend to need

© 2017 Barb Tonn

About the Author

Barb Tonn, MA is a psychotherapist and life-coach who has specialized in "healing shame" for over 30 years. She has compiled tools that were most successful in working with her clients and healing her own destructive shame core. She lives with her husband and sweet animals in Albuquerque, New Mexico.

You can find out more about Barb and communicate with her by visiting www.life-coaching-online.net

Sunflowers were used on the cover of this book because they symbolize reconstruction and hope. Sunflower seeds were planted after both the Chernobyl disaster and the Japanese tsunami for radioactive cleanup. They extracted the lethal cesium-137 and strontium-90 from the groundwater and returned the environment to normal. For this book, the "Sunflower" is used to represent the healing of toxic shame.